Table of contents

How to Grow Just About Everything

1,001 Ways to Get Abundant, Beautiful Flowers and Delicious, Mouth-Watering Vegetables From Your Garden or Window Sill

Publisher's Note

This book is intended for general information only. It does not constitute medical, legal, or financial advice or practice. The editors of FC&A have taken careful measures to ensure the accuracy and usefulness of the information in this book. While every attempt has been made to ensure accuracy, errors may occur. Some websites, addresses, and telephone numbers may have changed since printing. We cannot guarantee the safety or effectiveness of any advice or treatments mentioned. Readers are urged to consult with their professional financial advisors, lawyers, and health care professionals before making any changes.

Any health information in this book is for information only and is not intended to be a medical guide for self-treatment. It does not constitute medical advice and should not be construed as such or used in place of your doctor's medical advice. Readers are urged to consult with their health care professionals before undertaking therapies suggested by the information in this book, keeping in mind that errors in the text may occur as in all publications and that new findings may supersede older information.

The publisher and editors disclaim all liability (including any injuries, damages, or losses) resulting from the use of the information in this book.

Upkeep to keep your garden looking its best 286

Vertical designs for spectacular upward interest . . .300

Water features that make a splash 313

Age-friendly designs keep you gardening for life

Make your garden work for you as you age

Gardening should not be a chore or something that leaves you feeling exhausted. Gardening is an activity that should make you joyful, energized, and successful throughout your life.

But what if you have physical problems or limitations that make it difficult to get around? When your garden space is working against — not with — you, it can quickly turn something you once loved into something you avoid. The answer is adaptability.

In this case, being adaptable means making tweaks and changes to gardening practices so you can have a successful experience no matter what your age, ability, or needs.

Any garden space can be adapted to meet the needs and desires of those using it. With a little creativity on the front end, you can make your garden work for you. Here's how to get started.

Assess your abilities. Take a look at any physical limitations you may presently have. What kind of financial resources do you have? Do you have anyone able and willing to help you tend to your garden space?

Take a look at your garden. Think about your current garden setup, including everything from size and organization to water systems and how you wish to use your garden space. Ask yourself what needs to change to allow you to have more freedom and success in your current garden.

Count your resources. You'll find many online resources, adaptability experts, and people at your local Cooperative Extension office who can help you meet your needs. Make a list of all that are available to you.

Come up with a plan. Get your notebook and pencil and begin designing and adapting your garden space so that your garden can work for you. Think about creative and cost-effective ways to address what is currently challenging to make it easier.

Construct a plan to fit your budget and other resources available. If you cannot do everything you desire to make your garden meet your needs, consider downsizing your garden space to make it work.

8 smart design elements to create an accessible backyard

Even if you don't have anyone living in your home who uses a wheelchair, make a warm welcome statement by designing garden areas accessible to everyone. Here are some top design elements to keep in mind when planning your space.

Level ground. Before you even begin your garden design, take the time to level the ground. While gentle slopes approaching the backyard area are OK, steep grades are definitely out of the question.

Clear and flat pathways. Wheelchairs need quite a bit of room to turn around. Keep this in mind when designing pathways. All paths should be at least 4 feet wide and constructed of a smooth material such as concrete. Provide wider, smooth-surface sections for turning around. Edge the path with a slightly raised border as a guide to keep wheelchairs from rolling off the sides.

Custom seating. Tables are a great feature to add to any well-designed backyard. Ensure that there is plenty of room for wheelchairs to pull up under tables. For casual seating, make room for wheelchairs with an appropriate height beverage or snack table.

Lightweight gates and easy-to-open latches. Modifying gates and fasteners so that those in a wheelchair can easily operate them is essential. If possible, consider electronic gates that open and close on their own.

Mindful irrigation. If you are including an irrigation system in your backyard, consider the direction that the sprinkler heads are pointing. If possible, keep all spray off of pathways that may become slippery when wet.

Flat and open spaces. Wide-open spaces are very welcoming to persons in a wheelchair. Tight and crowded spaces may create navigational distress and frustrate wheelchair users.

Perimeter planting. Framing open spaces with attractive perimeter plantings such as shrubs and shade trees make your backyard beautiful and private while providing ample protection from the hot sun.

Flowers at the right height. Any flowers that you plant along pathways or in open spaces should be between 24 and 30 inches tall so that persons in a wheelchair can enjoy them.

What tricks can I use to enjoy my favorite hobby without pain and stiffness?

If you find it more challenging to work in your garden now that you're older, you are not alone. Here are just a few ways to make gardening more manageable as you age.

Lift it up. Raised beds are excellent for controlling weeds, soil, and moisture, but they can easily be adapted to cultivate a less physically taxing form of gardening.

Buy or construct raised beds with legs to lift your garden to table height to sit to work. Don't make your beds any larger than 2 feet wide so you can reach across the whole bed from one side.

Use the right tools. Padded, adjustable, and ergonomic tools will be your new best friends in the garden, particularly if you have arthritis in your hands or have a weak grip. You will also want lighter tools that you can actually carry and use effectively.

Garden in spurts. Break up your garden tasks into manageable 20 to 30 minute chunks or sprints instead of a whole day marathon that leaves you worn out and unable to do any other activities for the next few days.

These small bursts of gardening will allow you to accomplish everything you need to get done. Plus you can plan your time in the evening or morning to avoid the heat of the day.

Keep the joy in gardening — even with back pain

Millions of Americans suffer from back pain, making some things, like gardening, difficult. If you're one of those who experiences mild to moderate or occasional back pain or stiffness, good news. You don't have to give up your love of plants when you take the time to do a few things before, during, and after each gardening session.

Of course, if you have severe back pain, be sure to check with your doctor before working in the garden.

Warm up your body. Gardening is a form of exercise. That means you have to take the time to stretch and get your blood flowing before you tend to your plants. Marching in place for a few minutes and doing some gentle stretches are a good idea.

For an excellent pre-gardening stretch, lay on your back, pull your knees into your chest, and bring your head forward. Hold this stretch for 30 seconds, then repeat.

Don't overdo it. Once you are out in the garden, be sure to take frequent breaks and don't do too much. Avoid performing the same activity for too long at one time. Switching it up will engage different muscles and keep you from getting stiff.

Watch what and how you lift. Always lift ergonomically by bending at the knees and not folding at the waist. Hold objects close to your waist, and slowly straighten your legs as you stand up.

Use a wagon or a dolly when you can, and minimize the loads you carry. For example, a small watering can will put less strain on your back than a large, heavy one. Wearing back support may also help protect you from injury.

Enjoy the help of a wheeled assistant. A garden scooter is one of the best tools you can use to avoid aggravating your back. Stretching and twisting put a lot of pressure on your spine and can encourage inflammation. Wheeled scooters provide support while you prune and plant and can help reduce your stretching and twisting.

One ancient spice may be just what you need to reduce inflammation and pain. Turmeric contains curcumin, which gives the spice its signature yellow color. Researchers have found that curcumin can ease symptoms of osteoarthritis and rheumatoid arthritis, including pain and inflammation. Add turmeric to your favorite egg dishes, soups, stews, and even smoothies to reap its benefits.

Use long-handled tools. Tools with long handles can make gardening with back pain easier. For example, extended-handled trowels and cultivators can help reduce bending, which may aggravate back pain.

Go vertical. Vertical gardens above your waist that don't require any over-the-head reaching are easy on the back and allow you to enjoy a beautiful and productive garden space.

You have many options for vertical plantings, such as hanging baskets, windowsill planters, wall gardens, and more.

Create your own all-natural muscle balm

After spending time in the garden, you may find your muscles are a little stiff and sore. Over-the-counter rubs and creams may offer temporary relief, but these can be expensive and contain unwanted additives.

You can easily make your own homemade muscle balm using just a few natural ingredients. Keep a jar handy for any time you experience minor aches and pains.

What you need:

- glass measuring cup
- 2 ounces unrefined coconut oil
- 8-ounce glass jar with lid
- 1 teaspoon ground ginger
- 1/2 teaspoon ground cayenne
- 1/2 ounce yellow beeswax, chopped
- 5-10 drops each of peppermint, camphor, clove, and eucalyptus essential oil
- cheesecloth
- fine mesh strainer
- 1 ounce almond oil
- 2 ounces shea butter

How to make it:

1. Heat the coconut and almond oils in a glass measuring cup in the microwave.

2. Add the ground ginger and cayenne and let the mixture stand in a warm location for 30 minutes.

3. Put the beeswax in a glass measuring cup and into a pan of simmering water. Be careful as the wax melts as it will be quite hot. Add in the shea butter, stir until melted, and keep warm.

4. Strain the oil infused with cayenne and ginger through a cheesecloth over a mesh strainer into the measuring cup with the shea butter.

5. Stir well and remove from the heat and let cool before adding the essential oils. Stir gently to combine.

6. Pour mixture into a clean jar with a tight-fitting lid. Let cool before using it. The balm will store well for several months.

7. Rub onto sore areas and massage in a circular motion. Your skin will feel warm.

Make this easy-to-reach herb garden in 7 simple steps

For just a few dollars and about 30 minutes of effort, you can have this attractive, functional hanging herb garden on display in your kitchen.

What you need:

- soil
- pea gravel
- herbs
- pipe clamps
- 3 wide-mouth mason jars
- hammer, nails, screwdriver
- 1 wooden board (big enough to fit 3 or more wide-mouth mason jars)
- spray paint for clamps, if desired
- heavy-duty picture-hanging hardware

How to make it:

1. Sand down your board and paint it if desired. It will be hanging on your wall, so you'll want to make sure it

matches your kitchen decor. You can also use a reclaimed board or piece of Barnwood and leave it unfinished for a rustic feel.

2. Attach the picture-hanging hardware to the back. Once the herbs and jars are in place, it will be fairly heavy. Keep this in mind as you choose your hardware. A wire strung across two triangle ring hangers would be an excellent option.

3. Spray-paint the pipe clamps gold or brown if desired. If you prefer silver, leave them unpainted.

4. Secure the pipe clamps to the board using small nails and a hammer. Place them an equal distance apart.

5. Place pea gravel in the bottom of the jars to help with drainage, and plant your herbs. Decorate the jars with a fun label or tag indicating the herb growing inside.

6. Slide jars into clamps and tighten with a screwdriver.

7. Drill a screw into a stud in your wall to ensure you have a sturdy place to hang your decorative kitchen herb garden.

Design a garden all your senses will love

A sensory garden is a unique, accessible space created with the specific intention of evoking the senses — sight, smell, touch, taste, and sound. Both adults and children with sensory processing issues, including hearing and sight impairment and autism, can benefit from this type of garden.

Plants are the superstars of any sensory garden, but you can add other stimulating elements such as wind chimes, water, and textured touch pads. No matter what your objective is, you'll need these types of plants to accomplish your goals.

- brightly colored, large-flowered plants with a pleasing shape to look at

- plants that have an interesting feel to stimulate touch

- highly aromatic plants and those whose aroma is enhanced by manipulating foliage or flowers

- plants that make an interesting sound when their foliage or seed rustles in the wind or is shaken

- plants that are sweet, spicy, and earthy to awaken the taste buds

Not sure where to start? The plants below will give you a wide variety of options for a beautiful, sense-stimulating garden you'll be proud to share.

Touch	Sight	Smell	Sound	Taste
lambs ear	poppy	thyme	rattlesnake grass	nasturtiums
silver mound	sunflower	basil	bamboo	spearmint
feather grass	zinnia	lavender	quaking grass	tomatoes
geranium	Swiss chard	mints	animated oats	rhubarb
parsley	marigold	rosemary	false indigo	carrots
pussy willow	chameleon plant	lilac	sweet corn	wild strawberry
gayfeather	butterfly weed	roses	money plant	chives
borage	hollyhock	bee balm	pearl grass	chocolate mint

Terrific terrarium project keeps you off your feet

If standing for long periods is difficult or painful, try your hand at tabletop projects that are fun and add beauty to your home. Invite a few of your garden lover friends over, and give this easy terrarium project a try.

What is a terrarium? It's a combination of rock, soil, plants, and attractive decor pieces in a beautiful glass container — kind of like an aquarium for plants. This cute, tabletop project is easy and makes a lovely gift or decor item for your home.

What you need:

- clean glass container such as a fishbowl, glass jar, or a vase with a broad bottom

- rocks, marble-size or bigger depending on the size of your container

- activated charcoal. It helps to filter the water and keep fungi away

- sterilized, lightweight potting soil

- variety of small plants. Choose plants with texture, color, and ones that won't overcrowd or outgrow your container. Some good choices include Friendship plant, Starfish flower cactus, Nerve plant, Baby tears plant, African violet, and Spiderwort.

- optional fun decor items like tiny pine cones, moss, shells, ceramic animals, miniature garden gnomes, and decorative rocks

How to make it:

1. Clean your glass container with mild dish soap and water. Rinse thoroughly and dry completely before beginning your project.

2. Gather your supplies and cover your table with a piece of newspaper or craft cloth.

3. Add about 1 inch of rocks on the bottom of your container.

4. Add a 1/2-inch layer of activated charcoal on top of the rocks.

5. Fill the container halfway with lightweight and steril potting soil.

6. Remove your plants from their containers. Be sure to remove most of the old soil, and gently spread out the roots.

7. Arrange your plants inside the terrarium. Leave space in between plants and gently pat down the soil around them.

8. Add in your decorative items such as pebbles or pine cones.

9. Water the plants. Be careful not to over water. Spritz daily to keep plants moist.

How can I encourage my grandchildren to develop a love for gardening?

Research shows that the more time you spend with your grandkids, the less stress you have. That's right — grandchildren are the ultimate de-stressing medicine and can bring so much joy to your life.

Creating a children's accessible garden allows you to spend time with your favorite little people doing what you genuinely love to do. Here are a few essential tips and elements to consider when creating a child-friendly garden space.

Create pathways to accommodate wagons, bikes, and scooters. Kids will enjoy whizzing through the garden on wheels or if young, being pulled along in a wagon. Kids like and need to be in motion. Meet this need by making sure your pathways are level, wide, and made from a solid material.

Have kid-friendly tools on hand. Children have small hands and sometimes not the best coordination. Help your grandkids feel successful when they help in the garden by having kid-sized tools available.

Plant a child-sized theme garden together. Kids will love a little lemonade garden, a butterfly garden, or a magical fairy garden that they can plant and tend to all season long. This gives them a sense of ownership and provides the perfect platform to impart your gardening wisdom.

2 tricks to adapt tools for arthritis

Arthritis is one of the most common conditions to develop as you age. In fact, over 50 million adults experience swelling, pain, reduced range of motion, and stiffness in their joints, prohibiting them from accomplishing a number of garden tasks.

If you are one of these people, don't let your arthritis keep you from doing what you love. These simple tricks will help you make the most of the tools you have and will help you keep gardening, despite your sore hands and aching knees.

Grab the gloves. It isn't necessarily a way to adapt your tools, but wearing a pair of padded garden gloves while you use your shovel, rake, or clippers may be just what your hands need. Gloves can relieve a lot of the stress on your hands, strengthen your grip, and allow you to use less pressure to accomplish the same goal.

Pad your handles. While the best option would be to buy new, lightweight, padded tools, you may not have room in your budget for a brand new set of garden tools, especially if the ones you already have can get the job done.

In that case, pick up some inexpensive foam pipe insulator wrap, and duct tape it around the handles of your tools.

This will comfortably pad them and reduce the strain that comes from grasping the handles.

Top 3 ways to plant smarter, not harder

No matter what you do in life, it is always good to know how to work smarter, not harder. Gardening is no exception, and with the smart planting tips found below, you can enjoy a beautiful garden without the pain of overworking.

Choose native plants. A native plant is one that occurs naturally in a particular region or habitat without human introduction. Growing native plants means less work because they have adapted to the area in which they grow.

Look for low-maintenance perennials. Next to native plants, low-maintenance perennials are one of the smartest additions to your garden. Growing the classics is a great way to plant smarter, not harder.

Beauties like black-eyed Susan, sedum, purple coneflower, daylily, hosta, and peonies are among the top easy-care perennials for any garden.

Plant bulbs in the fall for no-work spring color. Welcome spring with color pops throughout your garden using bulbs. The best bulbs are those that are perennial, bringing you beautiful color year after year.

Once you have planted your bulbs in the fall, you need only sit back and await their showcase of color come spring. Choose from a wide variety of fall bulbs, including tulips, hyacinths, crocus, daffodils, and more.

> Growing tomatoes in a hanging basket makes them easier to reach. Many varieties do well that way, especially Cherry Cascade and Tumbling. Choose a pot that is 12 to 14 inches in diameter, preferably one with a reservoir for water, and use high-quality, lightweight potting soil. Feed tomatoes during the growing season with an organic feed, and enjoy delicious tomatoes at your fingertips.

Transform old hose into energy-saving soaker

Lugging a heavy hose around your garden can leave you feeling exhausted and ready for a nap. A neat way to save your energy is to install soaker hoses. Also known as drip hoses, soaker hoses make watering a large area a breeze.

Not only are soaker hoses easy on your back, they will also save you money in water bills because they are so efficient. Once you set up your drip system, it is as easy as turning it on to run for a little bit each day. Or better yet, put it on a timer so you can set it and forget it.

You can transform that old garden hose you have lying around into a practical soaker hose in just a few steps.

1. Drill evenly spaced holes (through one side of the hose only) down the entire length of the hose using a 1/4-inch drill bit.

2. Screw a hose cap onto one end.

3. Place it in your garden and turn it on to gently soak your plants.

Take your strawberry patch to new heights with recycled barrel planter

Conventional strawberry gardening methods require quite a bit of kneeling, bending, twisting, and reaching. All of these activities can leave you feeling quite stiff and sore.

But good news — you don't have to give up your love of growing strawberries. By creating a barrel strawberry garden, you can avoid those aggravating movements that have left you sore in the past.

What you need:

- drill and drill bits
- jigsaw
- tape measure
- strawberry plants

- marker
- gravel
- potting soil/compost
- 55-gallon plastic food-safe barrel
- 3/4-inch diameter, 30-inch tall PVC pipe
- straight-edge
- coarse sand
- organic fertilizer

How to make it:

1. Put on eye protection and always work on a level surface.

2. Drill a 1/2-inch starter hole in the barrel side, 1 inch down from the top edge.

3. Cut off the top of the barrel by inserting a jigsaw blade into the hole.

4. Sand the edge you just cut with medium-grit sand paper until smooth.

5. Turn the barrel upside down.

6. Drill 1/2-inch drainage holes in the bottom of the barrel about 3 inches apart with rows 3 inches apart.

7. Use a straight-edge and a felt-tip marker to draw a 3 - inch line 5 inches from the barrel's bottom, parallel to the barrel bottom.

8. Draw more lines, 8 inches above the 5-inch line up the barrel until you get to the last line, which will be 5 inches below the barrel's rim.

9. Measure 10 inches up from the bottom of the barrel, 8 inches from your first row of lines. Space lines 8 inches apart.

10. Repeat this around the barrel, offsetting the lines by alternating the starting point between 5 and 10 inches.

11. Drill a hole at both ends of each line. Place your jigsaw blade into one hole and cut along the line to create a

planting slit. Repeat this for each line. Create a planting cup by pushing the plastic above the slit while pulling it out on the bottom.

12. Drill 1/4-inch holes in the sides of the PVC pipe. Space the holes 2 inches apart and in rows that are 1 inch apart.

13. Move your barrel to its permanent location. You can set it up on cinder blocks to elevate it to the desired height. Remember, strawberries love sunshine.

Now that you have built your strawberry barrel and put it in the perfect place, it's time to fill it up and plant.

1. Fill the bottom of the barrel with 2 inches of gravel.

2. Place the PVC pipe upright inside the barrel, resting on top of the gravel.

3. Fill the pipe with coarse builder's sand.

4. Mix the potting soil with the compost, and fill the barrel up to the first row of planting slits.

5. Set a strawberry plant in the slit, with the crown level with the rim of the slit. Fill the slit around the strawberry roots with soil. Water the soil in the barrel until moist and add soil and plants in each slit to the top of the barrel. Plant more strawberries on top, spacing them 8 inches apart.

To make sure your strawberries flourish, water the barrel twice a week by pouring water into the PVC pipe and soaking the soil. Check the soil around the plants in the planting pockets, and water if it feels dry.

Add compost tea or other organic fertilizer to the water once every two weeks when the plants are producing fruit.

Bees, birds, butterflies, and other beneficial pollinators

5 tips to create the perfect pollinator paradise

The next time you sit down to enjoy a salad or even your morning cup of coffee, you might want to thank the hard-working pollinators who made it possible.

About 1 out of every 3 bites of food you eat is possible only because tiny creatures like butterflies, moths, bees, birds, bats, beetles, and other insects carry pollen from one plant to another. This fertilizes the plants and allows them to produce seeds.

If you'd like to attract more of these helpful travelers to your yard, you may think you need to focus on bright colors and fragrances. While these are important, there are other things you can and should do to welcome birds, bees, and butterflies. Here are five tips to transform your yard and garden into a pollinator oasis.

Keep things messy. You may love your garden to be neat and tidy, but this is not always the most attractive to the creatures who carry pollen from plant to plant. Keeping at least one part of your yard a little untidy with some overgrowth provides a great place for them to rest and hide.

Aim for diversity. A wide range of garden plantings draws a diverse collection of pollinators. Aim for a variety of colors, fragrances, textures, and sizes that bloom all season long, from spring through fall. A great way to achieve this is to plant native flowers that pollinators love.

Grow a pollinator-friendly lawn. In the early 1800s open grass lawns were a symbol of status and were used for entertaining. By the late 19th century, with the birth of the first lawnmower, more and more people adopted the practice of planting a well-manicured lawn.

Most grass lawns are wind-pollinated and do not contain additional low-growing plants. Turn your yard into a pollinator magnet by including plants like white clover, creeping thyme, violets, and dianthus.

Provide water sources for bathing, drinking, and playing. Nothing is more fun than watching a group of birds taking an afternoon bath in your garden. Provide diverse water options such as shallow birdbaths, butterfly puddling areas, ponds, streams, and hanging water drip systems. Or just place small dishes of water throughout your garden.

Let your culinary herbs bloom. Harvesting your herbs regularly keeps them from blooming. But once you have gathered plenty of herbs from your garden, let them blossom and they will draw a wide range of pollinators. Bees love mint, basil, oregano, rosemary, and fennel flowers.

Easy-to-grow flowers attract a kaleidoscope of butterflies

Butterflies are a beautiful addition to any garden. Not only are they fun to watch, but they also help with pollination. Here are six low-maintenance plants that can transform your yard into a stunning butterfly magnet.

Cosmos. Start this striking flower quickly from seed. Perfect for adding some height to the garden, cosmos plants can reach heights up to 8 feet. Pink, rose, lavender, crimson and purple flowers reach 3 to 4 inches in diameter and are perfect for cutting.

Lantana. A fantastic flower for a hot and dry climate. Butterflies flock to its intoxicating aroma and a bright rainbow of red, orange, yellow, and pink blooms. It thrives in dry conditions and heat and will bloom heavily from spring until fall.

Zinnias. Scatter these annual seeds evenly over warm soil and rake to barely cover. In no time, you will see sprouts and soon long stems topped by multi-colored, butterfly-attracting flowers. If you can get the butterflies to share, snip a few stems for a beautiful bouquet.

> Butterflies cannot drink from open water sources. Dig a hole in the ground for a small pail and fill it with sand or mud. Keep the bucket contents wet, and provide a few sticks for butterflies to perch on when they drink.

Dragon wing begonia. This beautiful plant boasts shiny green leaves and brilliant red or pink mounding flowers up to 12 inches wide. With plenty of sun in the morning and light shade in the afternoon, this beauty will beckon butterflies from afar.

Butterfly weed. The name says it all. If you want butterflies, you need to include this plant in your garden. Flat clusters of orange blooms perch upon 1- to 2-foot stalks with glossy leaves that form a spiral pattern up the entire length of the stem. Grow butterfly weed in clay, dry or rocky soil, and in an area that receives full sun or a little afternoon shade.

Purple coneflower. If you are searching for a flash of late summer color that will keep butterflies coming back for more, this is your plant. Sturdy and tall stalks reach up to 5 feet in height, and daisy-like flowers up to 6 inches across wave in the wind.

A hardy perennial, coneflower will consistently come back year after year throughout the entire United States. Once established, coneflowers are drought hardy and very low maintenance.

Do my vegetables need the help of pollinators?

Some veggies do require their assistance to produce fruit. These include squashes, watermelons, pumpkins, okra, muskmelons, and cucumbers. Without adequate pollination, veggie fruit may be misshapen and small.

To draw insect and hummingbird pollinators to your veggie patch, consider companion planting using flowers and herbs.

- Basil not only improves the taste of lettuce but also attracts loads of bees.
- Dill, sage, thyme, and oregano left to flower will attract pollinators to your vegetable garden.
- Calendula is like a welcome sign for pollinators and pairs well with sweet peas, runner beans, and summer squash.
- Combine beautiful cosmos with cucumbers to ensure big and healthy fruit.
- Other great choices for a pollinator-friendly vegetable garden include bee balm, rosemary, bachelor's button, and rosemary.

Plant as many flowers as you can in and around your veggie garden to encourage a diverse population of pollinators. If you have space, consider a flower border around your entire veggie patch.

Design your garden to tempt hummingbirds to stay

Birds are essential wildflower pollinators throughout the world. Plants that rely on birds for the distribution of pollen share some common characteristics. They have lightly scented flowers that are bright red, yellow, or orange. Sticky and sweet nectar within these plants draws birds for a snack and helps the pollen hitch a ride on bird feathers.

In the continental United States, hummingbirds are the primary pollinators for wildflowers. Wildflowers in Hawaii depend on the expert nectar-feeding bird known as the honeycreeper, and in Australia, it's the honeyeater.

Here are some garden design tips that will not only draw hummingbirds to your garden but also keep them around longer.

- Native plants are best as they are familiar to hummingbirds.

- Plant for diversity to draw different species of hummingbirds.

- Focus on flowers that are open during the day.

- Include plants that remain colorful all season or all year long.

8 gorgeous flowers that hummingbirds will love

Knowing how to plant gorgeous flowers that attract hummingbirds is one of the first steps toward bringing more of these beautiful birds to your backyard naturally.

Here are some of their favorite plants that will provide loads of beauty for your yard as well as plenty of sweet nectar for the hummers.

Plant name	Features	Sun	Soil	USDA zone
bee balm	perennial; 2-4 feet; red, purple, and orange cultivars	full sun, part shade	rich, medium moisture to wet	4-9
cardinal flower	perennial; 4 feet; scarlet red, rose, and white cultivars; will self seed	full sun, part shade	rich, medium moisture to wet	3-9
salvia	common variety is a perennial; 18-36 inches; very easy to grow; mauve, pink, purple, and blue cultivars	full sun	dry to medium moist, well-drained	4-11
bleeding heart	perennial, hanging heart-shaped flowers in white and pink	part to full shade	rich, moist, well-drained	2-9
trumpet creeper	prolific vine with stunning red, yellow, and orange tubular-shaped blooms that quickly cover walls, fences, and other structures	full sun, part shade	average, well-drained	4-10
lupine	dwarf and taller varieties in purple, blue, white, pink, and yellow grow 2-4 feet	full sun	evenly moist, well-drained	4-8
butterfly bush	brightly colored shrub in pink, purple, and blue; taller and dwarf varieties	full sun	medium moist, well-drained, tolerates drought	5-10
petunia	easy to grow; good for container gardens; pink, white, red, blue, and mixed colors	full sun	medium moist, well-drained	10-11 or annual

2 things you should never do if you want pollinators

You can do many things to create a pollinator-friendly habitat. But you can also do some things that will harm these beneficial birds and bugs or chase them away. Here are two essential things that you should never do.

Don't use pesticides containing neonicotinoids. The widespread use of these harmful chemicals is responsible for the death of bees, butterflies, and ladybugs. This pesticide remains in plants for its entire life and poisons nectar, pollen, and soil and surface water.

It is possible to buy bee-friendly plants containing dangerous chemicals without knowing it. Commercial greenhouses often treat potting soil with products containing neonicotinoids, especially ornamental plants.

Before buying plants, do your best to determine if they have been exposed to pesticides containing neonicotinoids. You should also use only organic pest control measures in your yard and garden.

Be careful about over-weeding. Are you an overzealous weeder? If so, this may be decreasing the number and type of pollinators that visit your yard and gardens. When you create a new garden bed, be sure to leave a little of it wild, and you will be amazed at how many more pollinators you attract.

Think of your garden as less of a showpiece and more like a wildlife habitat. Sure, you may not win the yard of the month, but you will have beautiful flowers, huge veggies, and constant entertainment from birds, bees, butterflies, and other pollinating pros.

Super simple recipes attract an abundance of birds

Whip up these yummy homemade treats to make your garden even more appealing to your friendly neighborhood pollinators. You can make these goodies in just a few minutes with ingredients that you probably already have in your kitchen.

Natural stovetop hummingbird nectar. Instead of buying packaged hummingbird feed from the store, fill a large stockpot with water and grab some white sugar from your pantry. Set the water to boil over medium-high heat and remove it from the stove once it is simmering.

Stir in 1 cup of sugar for every 4 cups of water until it dissolves. Store leftover sugar water in the refrigerator for up to two weeks. Remember to change the water and rinse out the feeder at least once a week.

You don't need to add red food coloring to your sugar water — it can be toxic to hummingbirds. The vibrant red color of the feeder should be enough to catch the eye of these tiny winged creatures.

> Want to attract more hummingbirds? Hang long strands of orange polyester yarn from trees and shrubs throughout your garden and near hummingbird feeders. Shrubs and trees that have bright orange and red berries and flowers also work.

No-melt summer suet. The birds in your yard work hard and deserve a little treat. If you already feed them seed, consider adding a suet feeder and filling it with this easy-to-make suet that won't melt in the summer heat.

What you need:

- 2 cups quick-cooking oats
- 2 cups cornmeal
- 1 cup flour
- 1/2 cup sugar
- 1 cup crunchy peanut butter
- 1 cup of leftover bacon grease. Save your bacon grease in a bowl on the counter to use it in this suet.

How to make it:

1. Add bacon grease and peanut butter to a microwave-safe bowl and cover loosely with a plate or lid to prevent splatter. Microwave 30 seconds at a time, stirring in between until well combined.

2. Mix remaining ingredients in a bowl and add in the peanut butter, bacon grease mixture.

3. Stir well to combine, and press into old recycled suet molds. Cover with plastic wrap and freeze until hard.

Time-tested tricks draw bees to your garden

When it comes to pollinators, bees are at the top of the class. They dine and feed their young on pollen and nectar. In doing so, bees constantly carry pollen from flower to flower.

Here are some tips to attract more bee pollinator pros to your garden.

Consider single flower-topped flowers. Single-headed flowers contain an abundance of bee-attracting nectar that is easily accessible to bees. Popular varieties that bees love include daisies, calendula, and crocus. Focus on yellow, blue, and purple as these are bees' favorite colors.

Create a dedicated wildflower patch. Wildflowers are easy to grow, pest resistant, and provide a fantastic place for bees to forage. Clear out some ground, scatter some seeds, and watch the bees appear.

Plant fruit trees. Bees love to gather pollen and nectar from fruit trees. Including a good variety of trees such as apple, cherry, pear, peach, and plum in your yard and garden area is very welcoming.

Other flowering species such as magnolia, redbud, locust, serviceberry, locust, American basswood, and tulip trees beckon the bees to visit.

Clear some ground. Native "ground nesting" bees form small, non-aggressive colonies. These bees need access to bare soil to make their underground abode.

To encourage nesting, leave some areas in your yard uncovered. To suppress weeds and prevent erosion, consider shredded leaves or compost, which is easier for bees to penetrate.

Build an impressive brush pile. It may seem counterproductive to winning the yard of the month, but a brush pile is one thing that pollinators, including bees, love. Dry grasses, wood, reeds, and logs are particularly attractive to bees.

If you wish to hide your brush pile, plant a few tall ornamental kinds of grass, and tuck your brush collection in behind them.

Should I provide water for bees? If so, what is the best way?

Bees, like all living things, need water to survive. Providing some water sources that are accessible to bees will help to keep these valuable pollinators around your yard and gardens. Here are some creative and effective ways to make sure your bees stay well-hydrated and healthy.

- Float some corks. Fill a pail with water and set a handful of corks on top of the water for bees to land on. Keep the water fresh and the bees will thank you.

- Marbles in a clay saucer. Load a shallow clay saucer with marbles and add some water. The marbles make a perfect place for bees to land and hydrate.

- Downspout waterer. Place small pebbles in your downspout. When it rains and water fills it up, bees will happily sit on the rocks and drink.

Butterfly and bee projects on a dime

Attract loads of bees and butterflies to your yard without breaking the bank with these fun and easy projects.

Jar butterfly feeder. Although butterflies will happily feast on your flowers once they bloom, setting out a butterfly feeder in early spring will draw them to your property earlier.

What you need:

- pint-sized mason jar with a lid. Paint the cap red or yellow, if desired.
- hammer and one nail
- natural sea sponge (a regular, unused kitchen sponge will work as well)
- twine

How to make it:

1. Punch a small hole with the nail in the lid of the jar.

2. Cut a strip of sponge (about 1- to 2-inches wide) and use the nail to push it through the hole. It should be a tight fit to keep the water from leaking out when the feeder is upside down. A small piece of sponge should be on either side of the lid.

3. Flip the jar upside down, and tie a piece of string around the jar at the mouth.

4. Tie a long piece of string to the string you just tied, perpendicular to the jar.

5. Tie the other end to the opposite side, making a loop and then repeat with another piece of string.

6. Tie the two loops together and hang. Add more loops if needed for stability.

7. Fill with sugar water and replace the lid. If the sugar water leaks, you may need to thread a new, larger piece of sponge through the hole.

8. Embellish, if desired, with fun fabric flowers or other items.

Stay-a-while bee hotel. Solitary bees will love having a place to call home with this easy, inexpensive bee hotel.

What you need:

- 2-liter plastic bottle
- craft knife
- garden clippers
- bamboo canes or other hollow tubes
- sandpaper
- strong twine, such as jute
- modeling clay

How to make it:

1. Cut off both ends of the bottle to create a hollow plastic tube.

2. Use sandpaper to smooth away any rough edges.

3. Gather enough bamboo canes to fill the bottle, and cut them with garden clippers to make them about 2 inches shorter than the bottle.

4. Tie the bundle together tightly with twine.

5. Instead of adding a back to your bee hotel, attach modeling clay to one end of the hollow canes.

6. Tie a piece of string through the bottle to hang it, and fill it with the canes. Be sure to stuff it well to keep them from falling out.

7. Hang the hotel in full sun facing south or east.

" Early lessons produce great rewards

Marilyn's parents loved birds of all kinds, and this love was instilled in her from a very early age. By the time she was 12, she could identify dozens of local bird species. She knew their calls, their colors, their favorite habitat, and their food preferences.

Marilyn's job was to fill up all the bird feeders every week. The feed was just one way her parents lured beautiful birds to their yard. They also had unique watering stations, nesting materials, and various piles of brush and native plantings.

All of these naturally attracted birds because they provided shelter and areas where they could feel safe to raise a family. In short, her parents created a bird paradise right in their backyard.

When Marilyn asked her parents why they did so much for the birds, her mother would remind her that they were an essential part of spreading pollen from one plant to another, which helped make flowers beautiful and vegetables big and tasty.

Today, Marilyn has created a bird oasis in her own backyard similar to what she helped tend as a child. She says she is grateful to her parents for instilling a love for her feathered friends and for teaching her how to create a natural environment that welcomes them to her yard for her own family to enjoy. "

How to easily entice nighttime pollinators

Although nocturnal pollinators aren't as showy as their daylight counterparts, bats, moths, and certain beetles play a significant role in helping your garden bloom and produce a bountiful harvest. Follow these easy steps to help create a pollinator paradise after dark.

Plant night-blooming flowers. It stands to reason that flowers that close as the sun goes down aren't the best option for these friendly nighttime visitors. Along with daytime blooming flowers, include white or light-colored flowers open to the moon. Here are some beautiful choices.

- moonflower
- evening primrose
- tuberose
- 'Casa Blanca' lily
- gardenia augusta

Include fragrant flowers. Some flowers that bloom during the daytime will remain accessible at night, which means that moths will always be able to access hidden reserves of nectar with their long, searching tongues. Be sure to plant heavily perfumed flowers with plenty of nectar, such as:

- morning glory
- tobacco
- yucca
- gardenia

Add a bat house. Taking steps to attract moths and beetles to your garden will automatically help lure in bats since they feast on these nocturnal insects. However, you can go the extra mile by hanging a bat house in your yard or garden.

Since a bat house is a little more complicated than a birdhouse, it may be best to buy rather than build, but if you feel confident in your carpentry abilities and understand the requirements, this can be a great weekend project.

> Never hang a bat house on a tree, as this can make it easier for predators to access the bats. Also, shade can make it too cold. Bats prefer a warmer, more open environment, so hang the box on a pole or a building like a garden shed.

Special plant does double duty in your garden

What mysterious plant attracts beautiful butterflies to your garden and helps repel pests? It's fennel, a flowering plant in the carrot and parsley family.

This short-lived perennial herb has beautiful feather-like leaves and yellow flowers that beckon butterflies. Also, fennel foliage is a favorite treat of the swallowtail butterfly caterpillar.

Even more significant is that many pests are repelled by it, including slugs, aphids, and snails, all of which can do severe damage to garden plants.

Sow fennel seed in your garden as soon as the soil warms. To improve germination, soak seeds overnight before planting. Fennel likes well-drained soil and a sunny location and will happily reseed and grow up to 6 feet tall.

Design a small-space nectar-rich container garden

Whether you have a small patio, balcony, or rooftop space, you can still plant a wide variety of pollinator-pleasing native plants in containers.

The best options are perennials or small woody plants that don't require a ton of space. Keep in mind that native plants are best, and the key to success is to consider all-season attraction.

Be as diverse as possible so that lots of different pollinators will visit. And always pick your containers based on mature plant size. When possible, choose dwarf cultivars.

Here are some plants you'll want to consider.

Spring bloomers	Summer bloomers	Fall bloomers
wild bleeding heart	anise hyssop	New England asters
wild geranium	butterfly weed	tall fall sedum
moss phlox	purple coneflower	Russian sage
prairie smoke	downy skullcap	fountain grass
golden alexanders	narrow-leaved mountain mint	dwarf sunflower

3 things to remember for the perfect shady pollen-rich oasis

A common misconception is that pollinators only visit sunny spots loaded with light-loving flowers. The truth is, pollinators love hanging out in the shade where they recharge their batteries and are likely to visit plants while they are there.

Some, like carpenter bees, actually prefer to nest in shady areas. Hummingbirds seek out insects in the shade and will sip on nectar-producing plants at the same time. Here are some tips for creating a spectacular shady garden.

Assess the shade. Spend some time watching your yard and garden area to determine what kind of shade you have. Doing so will help you choose the right plants for your pollinator paradise garden.

Plants that require partial sun need at least four to six hours. Partial-shade plants need protection from the afternoon sun. Full-shade plants require less than three hours of full sun each day.

Don't ignore the soil. The amount of light your garden gets is significant, but following close behind is what kind of soil it has. If your soil is dry, it is more difficult (but not impossible) to find plants that will thrive, as most shade-loving plants prefer moist soil.

Struggles can also arise if your soil is too wet or loaded with clay. It may be necessary to amend your soil and experiment a bit with different plants until you find the right fit.

Pick a diverse collection of shade-loving plants. Load your shady pollinator paradise with a wide variety of plants that bloom throughout the season. Bees, butterflies, and elegant moths will grace your shade garden when you choose these plants and other shade-loving pollinator enticers.

- bleeding heart
- Jacob's ladder
- viola
- jasmine
- bell flowers
- verbena

- honeysuckle
- trillium
- yarrow
- hosta
- astilbe

Protect the monarch butterfly with a backyard habitat

Sometimes the best thing you can do in your garden is to narrow your focus and pick something specific you want to accomplish. When it comes to pollinators, this is especially true.

For example, creating a butterfly garden is fantastic, but setting up a monarch butterfly garden will help you specifically target this incredibly populous species and aid its long, yearly southern migration.

Thankfully, monarch butterflies aren't too picky and will flock to your yard if you add just a few simple elements.

Plant milkweed. Milkweed and monarchs are tied so tightly together in the life cycle that it is rare for one to exist without the other. Monarch caterpillars only eat the leaves of the milkweed plants, making it an essential contribution to any butterfly garden.

Be sure to choose a milkweed variety that is native to your local area, as there are dozens of species of this flowering plant.

Always plant milkweed in groups of at least six plants. Any less than this and the caterpillars may not have enough milkweed to sustain them through adulthood.

Add rocks. Adding large, flat stones to your monarch habitat, especially around your milkweed, will give the butterflies a safe, warm place to rest their wings and prepare for another round of pollinating.

Consider adding a spot with small gravel or sand, or a rock with a small divot that can be filled with water to let the butterflies "puddle" and take up water and nutrients. Replenish the water in this area daily.

Register your way station. Once you've added more plants for nectar, a bench for butterfly watching, a few decorative elements, or anything else your butterfly garden seems to be lacking, consider registering your garden through the monarch way station program.

This act usually costs under $20 and is a great way to contribute to protecting these beautiful, essential, delicate pollinators.

Make butterflies happy with a fruit feeder

This simple butterfly feeder will attract monarchs and other butterflies who will happily visit your garden. This easy project will bring hours of enjoyment as you watch all the different types of butterflies snack.

What you need:

- ripe fruit
- orange juice
- drill and drill bit
- plastic 12-inch pot drain plate
- heavy string cut into four, 12-inch pieces

How to make it:

1. Put four holes, evenly spaced, around the edge of your plate.
2. Pull a piece of string through each hole, tie a knot to hold each piece at the bottom of the tray. Tie all pieces together at the top.
3. Hang the plate from a tree or other semi-shaded location at least 3 feet off the ground.
4. Fill the plate with overripe fruit such as bananas, watermelon, and oranges. Add some orange juice to keep the fruit from drying out.
5. Clean the plate weekly and change the fruit.

Container gardens: think outside the window box

Time-tested tips for beautiful outdoor containers

A container garden can be as simple as one pot planted with your favorite plant or as substantial as a wide variety of containers gathered together for a dramatic impact.

Container planting is popular because you can make a big splash with minimum effort. Plus it's perfect for those with limited mobility or persons living in apartments with restricted space.

Although container gardening is similar to conventional gardening, potted plants require some specific things to be healthy and look their best. Here are some time-tested tips to keep your outdoor container garden thriving all season long.

Containers. The biggest mistake people make when planting container gardens is to choose pots that are too small. They must be big enough to accommodate mature plants. Make sure there are plenty of drainage holes so the potting mix does not get soggy.

Planting medium. Always use a lightweight potting mix that drains well. If you plant cacti or succulents, use a cacti blend. Because pathogens can overwinter in the soil, it is essential to use new soil each season with annual plants.

Plants. Healthy plants do best in containers, so choose wisely. Know the mature size of plants, water, and light requirements to make the best choices for vibrant growth.

Allow a few days for plants to acclimate after you buy them before planting them in pots. Always spread the roots before planting to allow for healthy growth.

Watering. Potted plants have high water needs because they have limited soil from which to draw moisture. Check daily and know the specific water needs of your plants. Top plants with a light layer of mulch to help retain moisture.

Feeding. Container plants do best when fed regularly throughout the growing season. Consider an all-purpose organic feed and pour directly on the soil, not on the foliage or flowers.

Pruning. Pinch or snip off spent blooms to encourage healthy growth and prolific blooming. Remove any dead or decaying debris from the container to keep pests and disease at bay.

Off-season care. Overwinter perennial container plants that are cold hardy to two growing zones below your zone. Mulch the plant well, and place it in an unheated garage or shed. Water the plant deeply a few weeks before the first hard frost and again a few weeks before the spring.

DIY potting mixes for happy potted plants

Container garden plants require a lightweight potting blend that allows for excellent drainage. It is important to note that potting soil, also called potting mix, does not contain any soil. It is a soilless blend of ingredients that allow for healthy growth.

You can buy specialized mixes at your local garden store or save money by whipping up a batch of your own. Here are three recipes for container potting mix that will keep season after season in an airtight container in your garden shed.

Cactus and succulent mix. This mix is great for cacti and succulents. Combine the following.

- 3 gallons coconut coir fiber
- 1 gallon perlite
- 1 gallon vermiculite
- 2 gallons coarse sand

Potted trees and shrub mix. For healthy potted shrubs and trees, combine the following.

- 3 gallons organic compost

- 2.5 gallons coarse, clean sand

- 3 gallons coconut coir fiber

- 2.5 gallons composted pine bark

- 3 gallons perlite

- 1 cup worm castings

- 1/4 cup organic cottonseed meal (for acid-loving trees and shrubs)

All-purpose container mix. For vegetables, flowers, and tropical plants, combine the following.

- 6 gallons coconut coir fiber

- 4.5 gallons perlite

- 6 gallons organic compost

- 1 cup worm castings

Does the type of pot I use really matter?

For healthier, prettier plants, it is vital to learn when to use terra cotta, wood, and plastic pots. They are not the same.

Here are some simple tips you can follow to select the best container for your plants. Each has its benefits, so consider which pot is best for your intended purpose.

Terra cotta or clay. These pots dry out quickly and are best for plants that are drought-resistant or require minimal water. Because they are porous and prone to cracking, terra cotta containers should not be left out over winter.

Wood. Planting directly in wood can result in moisture problems. Use a liner or seal the wood to avoid rotting and cracking issues. Wood containers are best for annual plants.

Plastic. Be sure that any herbs, veggies, or fruits are grown in food-safe plastic. Provide plenty of drainage holes to prevent soil from becoming too wet. Plastic containers can crack in cold weather, so store indoors over winter.

Concrete. These can be quite heavy to move around and are best for larger, statement gardens. Insulate concrete planters in cold regions to keep them from cracking.

Ceramic and metal. Choose ceramic and metal containers for indoor plants, and ensure they have proper drainage.

How to create a hypertufa trough planter

If you love the way old stone looks but hate the weight, a hypertufa planter is just the thing for you. Hypertufa planters have all the appealing characteristics of rustic stone with half the weight. Perfect for any container project and easy to make, once you start, you won't stop making them.

What you need:

- plastic wrap
- wire brush
- rubber gloves
- portland cement, 1 part

- peat moss, 1 1/2 parts
- perlie, 1 1/2 parts
- water, 1 part
- 1/4-inch hardware cloth
- old containers to mix ingredients
- face mask to cover your nose and mouth
- 1-inch diameter dowel rods cut to 6-inch lengths to make drainage holes
- large plastic dishpan to use as a mold (under 18 inches is best)

How to make it:

1. Put on your gloves and face mask.

2. Prepare the mold by wrapping it in plastic. Be sure that all parts are well covered.

3. Place the hardware cloth over the mixing container. Screen out any more substantial pieces, including sticks.

4. Add all dry ingredients together and add one part water. Do not make the mixture too soggy. Aim for a texture that is like thick oatmeal. If you add too much water, add more dry ingredients until you get the desired consistency. The mixture should not drip water when squeezed.

5. Pack the mixture into the mold. Make sure the walls are at least 2 inches thick on the bottom and sides. Pack it firmly and remember that the trough rim will be visible, so you will want it to be smooth.

6. Insert two to three dowel rods in the bottom for drainage.

7. Cover the trough with plastic, and place it in a dry place for about 48 hours before unmolding. Keep in mind that slow curing will make your finished trough strong.

8. Carefully remove the trough from the mold and take off the plastic.

9. Use a wire brush to smooth the edges and attain the desired texture.

10. Leave the trough outdoors for two weeks to cure before planting. The rain and elements will give your trough character.

Creative — and cheap — way to make a potting stick

One of the best ways to work the soil around plants as you place them in containers is to hold the plant in your left hand, put a little potting mix around the roots, and gently work the plant up and down. Then pat the soil lightly using a potting stick.

Don't have a potting stick? Quickly turn the handle of an old broom into one by cutting it to about 12 inches long and sanding the rough end.

Use the stick to tamp down the potting mix around container plants as you pot them. The stick allows you to get in under the plants and gently push the soil down.

Plant a lasagna spring bulb garden for 'molto bello' color

Like the famous Italian dish, a lasagna bulb garden is put together using a layering technique. It will give you lasting color for several months starting in early spring.

What you need:

- lightweight potting mix
- large and deep container
- early, mid, and late spring-blooming bulbs including tulips, narcissus, and crocus
- bonemeal

How to make it:

1. Fill one-third of the container with some potting mix. Sprinkle some bonemeal on top.

2. First layer. Plant your largest bulbs like mid-spring-blooming daffodils about 4 inches apart with the pointed side up. Cover with soil.

3. Second layer. Make sure that you have about 5 inches of potting mix, and sprinkle in with some bone meal. Plant tulips about 2 inches apart.

4. Third layer. Plant your smallest bulbs, like crocuses, on this layer. Add enough soil so that you can plant bulbs 3 inches deep. Sprinkle bone meal on the soil and plant bulbs. Ensure that they are almost touching each other, with the pointed side up. No worries if you plant them the wrong way — they will find their way up and out.

5. Cover bulbs with potting mix, and top your container off with some small, sharp gravel to deter pests.

6. Water your container well, and set the container out somewhere behind a shed or other inconspicuous location where it will get plenty of natural light and water.

7. In early spring, move your lasagna bulb garden to a place where you can enjoy it.

8. After the last bulbs have bloomed, give them a healthy amount of fertilizer, and move it back to its inconspicuous location until next spring.

> Never combine shade-loving plants in a container with those that need full sun. This is a recipe for disaster. Similarly, never combine plants that love water with those that prefer soil on the dry side. Always group plants with similar light and water needs together for the best results.

Love your container roses and they'll love you back

Container roses make a great accent to any hardscape area. Here is how you can love your roses so that they stay happy and healthy.

Watering. Roses prefer moist soil that drains well. Consistent watering is essential. Daily watering is necessary during hot and dry weather. Insert your finger into the soil mixture. If it feels dry, water. The best time to water is in the morning — just be careful not to splash the foliage.

Feeding. Roses are quite heavy feeders. In containers, roses need even more attention. Each spring, fertilize plants using a slow-release organic rose food. During the growing season, apply fish emulsion monthly to keep flowers bright and happy.

Deadheading. To encourage lots of blooms, remove spent flowers and clip the stems back to a new set of leaves.

Pruning. Use clean and sharp pruners at the beginning of the season to clip out any dead wood back to a set of healthy and outward-facing buds.

Repotting. To keep your container rose happy, repot it every two or three years. If a new pot is needed, pick one at least two sizes bigger than the original container.

Fill the new container with fresh potting mix and some organic compost. Allow the top of the rootball to sit just below the top of the container, and add more potting mix and compost around the rootball.

Firm the mixture down so that no air pockets remain close to the roots. Water well once you have the rose planted in its new home.

Overwintering. Stop feeding roses in late July to prepare them for winter. Stop deadheading in September to encourage durable wood and cold tolerance.

The best way to overwinter a container rose is to bury it in the ground. A vegetable garden with loose soil makes the perfect winter home. Dig deep enough to bury the pot, and cover with several inches of straw or shredded leaves to insulate the plant.

If burying your rose is not an option, move it to an unheated shed or garage, and water once a month if the soil seems dry to the touch.

Repurpose a ladder to hold your containers

Breathe new life into an old stepladder with this fun project. Once finished, your flower-power ladder makes a great focal point in any outdoor space or as a lovely welcome by your front door.

What you need:

- old rag
- spray primer
- screwdriver
- 120 grit sandpaper
- 1 1/4-inch outdoor screws
- potted plants in different size pots
- wooden stepladder (front and back rungs must match)
- outdoor latex spray paint in your color choice
- 1x10-inch cedar boards to lay between the rungs. Cut them at different lengths for an attractive look.

How to make it:

1. Wipe the ladder off using an old rag.
2. Lightly sand any rough spots.
3. Apply a generous layer of primer to coat the entire ladder and let it dry.
4. Spray paint the ladder in your chosen color. Allow it to dry.
5. Place your ladder in its finished location.

6. Lay the first board on top of the bottom rungs and use a couple of screws to attach it to the ladder.

7. Repeat this process until you have finished laying the last board.

8. Place your potted plants on the ladder so that it is balanced.

Grandma's secret to gorgeous, always-blooming container gardens

Your neighbors will wonder how you keep your potted annual plants looking so spectacular all season long. This easy-to-make, time-tested elixir is the secret.

It has a few unusual ingredients, but don't let that scare you off — this plant potion works wonders. Mix the following ingredients together, and feed your potted plants once a week in the early morning.

- 2 tablespoons brewed black coffee
- 2 tablespoons whiskey
- 1/2 teaspoon unflavored gelatin
- 1/2 teaspoon baby shampoo
- 1/2 teaspoon ammonia
- 1 teaspoon fish emulsion
- 1 gallon of water

The best veggies to grow in pots and planters

Are you ready to downsize your vegetable plot but don't want to give up delicious and fresh veggies or the joy of growing? One of the easiest ways to grow delicious and nutritious vegetables is to put them in pots and planters on your back patio or deck.

As a general rule, hybrid and dwarf varieties of plants do best in containers with adequate soil depth and drainage.

Here are some yummy ones you can grow right on your porch.

Vegetable	Pot size	Tips for success
"Porch Pick" bush beans	at least 12" deep and 15" wide	Place container in full sun. Beans prefer rich, well-draining soil.
"Chioggia" beets	at least 12" deep and 12" wide	Place container in full sun or partial shade. Beets prefer a soil pH between 6.0 and 6.8.
"Rainbow Mixture" chard	at least 8" deep and 8" wide	Place container where it will get dappled sun. Chard prefers rich, well-draining soil.
"Thai Hot" chili peppers	at least 12" deep and 12" wide	Place container in a sunny and warm spot. Peppers prefer loamy, well-draining soil.
"Dwarf Siberian" kale	at least 8" deep and 12" wide	Place container in full or partial sunlight. Kale requires loamy, well-draining soil that is rich in organic matter.
"Slow Bolt" arugula	at least 8" deep and 8" wide	Place container where it will get morning sun and afternoon shade. Snip leaves near base for a continuous harvest.
"Tokyo Long White" onions	at least 6" deep and 24" wide	Place container where it will get at least six hours of sunlight. A tub-type container works best. Provide rich, well-draining soil.
"Cherry Belle" radishes	at least 6" deep and 6" wide	Place container in a sunny or shady location. Radishes prefer a light-weight potting mix that drains well.
"Atlas Hybrid" tomatoes	at least 18" deep and 18" wide	Place container in the sun and feed tomatoes every two weeks with an all-purpose organic feed.

Tricks to get a potted lemon tree to bloom and produce fruit

Although the climate in most parts of the country is not the best for growing lemon trees in the ground, they do quite well in a container if they get what they need. If you are having trouble getting your potted lemon tree to bloom and fruit, here are some essential things to consider.

Maturity. Many types of lemon trees must mature before they produce fruit. In some cases, you have to be patient and wait for your tree to reach its mature size, which can take several years. When you choose your lemon tree, be sure you know how long it might take before it produces. This way, you won't be disappointed by a long wait.

Watering. Too much or too little water can cause a lemon tree to fail to advance to the blooming stage. The trick to successful lemon tree watering is to only water when the top 4 inches of soil are dry to the touch. Lemon trees do not like wet feet, so always check before you water.

Feeding. Giving a potted lemon tree an overdose of feed can result in bloom failure because the plant will put tons of energy into producing new foliage and little into fruit production. A once-a-month application of organic fertilizer during the growing season is generally enough to do the trick.

Sunlight. Lemon trees love the sun, whether they are outdoors on your patio or inside by a sunny window. When your pot is outdoors, it should get full sunlight, not dappled sunlight. If you are unable to provide full sunlight conditions indoors, place a full spectrum bulb about 12 inches from the plant, and leave it on for 12 hours a day.

Temperature. Many times, when an indoor lemon tree fails to bloom, it is because it did not receive the needed chilling hours. Chilling hours are the time spent in 60-degree temperatures.

> Soak clay pots in a pail of water for at least two hours before filling them with potting mix and planting. If you don't do this, your pot will steal water from the soil, which leaves plants dry and stressed.

Lemon trees need several chilling hours per day during the winter and spring that simulate what they would get in their native habitat. Place your lemon tree in a location where you can mimic nature during this time to keep it healthy and encourage fruit production.

Pruning. Lemon trees need good air circulation. However, if you over prune, you may stunt growth and have blooming problems. Always prune conservatively, taking only about one-third of the foliage away per year.

Savvy tips for balcony gardening

All gardeners live in beautiful spaces because they partner with plants to make it so. Living in an apartment or condo opens up exciting opportunities to get creative with container gardening.

You will be amazed by the delightful ways you can create an inviting outdoor space using potted plants. Remember, your balcony is an extension of your living space, so arrange it in such a way that you will use it often.

Plants. Choose plants that you know are hardy and do well in your region and with the amount of sunlight you have on your balcony. Select a variety of colors, sizes, and textures.

Containers. Vertical container gardens are a great way to make use of space. Consider a wall-hanging garden or various heights of hanging baskets. Choose containers of multiple sizes, and group them in sets of three.

Rail huggers. A patio railing is prime plant real estate. Choose long, narrow, sturdy planters that attach to the rail. Fill them with a collection of trailing and upright plants for a dramatic statement. Use caution when you water if you are on an upper level, so you don't accidentally shower your neighbor.

Water feature. Add ambiance to your balcony garden using a small corner or bowl bubbler water feature. If power is an issue, consider solar.

Hummingbird feeder. Many apartments and condo rules prohibit the use of bird feeders filled with messy feed but are OK with hummingbird feeders. Hang one up for hours of enjoyment.

Lighting. Add some soft outdoor lighting on your balcony to enjoy your garden in the evening hours.

Furniture. Don't forget about some comfy chairs or loungers so that you and your friends can enjoy your outdoor haven.

Sweet succulent centerpiece will enhance your home

For your next outdoor dinner party, consider making this adorable succulent bowl for your centerpiece. Succulents are quite at home in containers and require little maintenance once planted. They will reward you with lots of texture, color, and interest.

What you need:

- wide mouth bowl — does not need to have a drainage hole

- cactus potting mix

- variety of succulents

- small gravel

- gloves — nice if you are dealing with sharp-edged plants

How you make it:

1. Put on your gloves.

2. Place 2 inches of gravel in the bottom of your bowl.

3. Fill the bowl three-quarters full with potting mix.

4. Gently remove succulents from their containers by tipping the package into your hand.

5. Plant the largest succulent in the middle for a focal point.

6. Build the rest of your bowl design around your focal

point, planting cascading succulents around the edges of the bowl and filling in the rest of the bowl. Plant tightly, and don't leave gaps.

7. Top the dish with more gravel.

8. Use a mister to water well initially, and water sparingly only when soil is completely dry. Succulents do a great job of retaining moisture.

3 organic fertilizer recipes for stunning plants

Since they cannot extract nutrients from the ground, container plants require regular feedings to grow healthy and beautiful. A weekly dose of organic fertilizer during the growing season will ensure that your plants perform their best.

Veggie-grow-big comfrey elixir. Comfrey leaves quickly decompose and make an excellent tea for potted veggie plants.

1. Squish as many comfrey leaves into a 5-gallon bucket as you can, and place a rock or brick on top.

2. Move the bucket to a sheltered location.

3. Check the bucket regularly as leaves begin to break down into a thick, black liquid. This takes about six weeks.

4. To use on established container veggies, dilute one part comfrey elixir to 15 parts water. Pour into a spray bottle.

5. Spray on plant leaves in the later evening.

6. For young plants, dilute the mixture more to avoid damaging roots.

All-purpose potted granular feed. Use this granular fertilizer for happy and healthy potted plants. Combine the following.

- 2 cups rock phosphate
- 2 cups greensand
- 1/2 cup bone meal
- 1/4 cup kelp meal

Sprinkle around potted plants and water well.

Strange-but-true perennial flower power. This somewhat strange formula will give your perennial flowers an extra beauty boost. Don't let the ingredients put you off — it works. Combine the following in a 5-gallon pail.

- 2 pounds dry oatmeal
- handful of human hair
- 2 pounds crushed dry dog food
- 1/2 cup sugar

Add a handful of this mixture to each planting hole.

How do I know what colors to mix together in my containers?

Although there are no real rules when it comes to color combinations for container gardens, you can create certain moods by choosing a particular color scheme for your garden design.

What mood are you going for?

- Excited and energetic — combine yellow, orange, dark purple, and red-colored plants.
- Romantic — combine pink, tangerine, red, and mauve-colored plants.
- Tranquil — combine variegated plants with white, sage, sky blue, and dark green-colored-plants.
- Cheerful — combine medium blue-green, light green, eggshell, deep violet, and bright orchid-colored plants.

Digging up dirt: soil secrets and transplanting tips

7 strange — but successful — soil hacks grandpa used

If your grandpa was a gardener, he probably added some pretty strange things to his soil to improve texture, drainage, and nutrients. Here are some old-time, unusual, but effective ways to feed your soil for bigger and better plants.

Coffee grounds. Used coffee grounds are rich in nitrogen, potassium, and phosphorus, the three essential ingredients in fertilizer. They also attract beneficial organisms, which in turn attract earthworms to your soil. Work grounds into new garden beds, and place around plants.

Banana peels. Wait, don't throw that banana peel away. Skins are a great source of calcium, potassium, phosphorus, and other minerals critical to soil health. Bury whole peels about 4 inches down in soil, or dry and grind them into a fine powder and sprinkle around plants.

Water from boiling eggs. When eggs are cooking, they release calcium into the water. After you remove your eggs, let the water cool, and pour over your soil.

Cardboard and newspaper. Shred the paper or newspapers and lay flat in layers when building up soil.

This method works great in raised beds where you can layer compost and organic material on top of cardboard and newspaper. As the paper breaks down, it enriches and improves soil texture.

Dryer lint. Dryer lint is composed of hair and fibers, which can improve the soil's texture and nutrients. Bury dryer lint a few inches down for best results, or throw it in your planting holes.

Fish heads and fish parts. Bury fish heads and fish parts about 6 inches into the soil. As the parts break down, they provide a slow release of nitrogen and calcium, which plants love.

Hair. Your hair, along with your pet's fur, can be used to enrich the soil. As it breaks down, it releases nitrogen and improves soil texture. Bury a few inches down for best results.

Feel, squeeze, settle — 3 ways to figure out your soil structure

When it comes to garden soil, one of the most important things you need to do is determine its texture or structure. There are six main soil groups, and each has unique characteristics.

All soil contains a combination of sand, silt, and clay particles in different ratios. Knowing how much of each your soil has will form the basis for future decisions on planting.

Here are three simple tests you can perform to give you a good idea about what exactly is in your soil.

Feel it. Put a little soil in your hand and rub it around. Check the following table to see what the different types will feel like.

Soil type	What it feels like
clay	lumpy and quite sticky when wet and rock hard when dry
sandy	gritty, like salt crystals
silty	soft and soapy when moist
peaty	damp and spongy
chalky	stony
loamy	fine-textured and somewhat damp

Squeeze it. Grab a handful of soil and slowly and softly compact it. Open your hand to see what happens.

Soil type	What it feels like
clay	remains in softball-shape formation
sandy	falls apart but feels gritty
peaty	falls apart but feels spongy
loamy and silty	both hold their shape for a bit but eventually fall apart

Settle it. Add a handful of soil to a mason jar and fill three-quarters full with water. Shake and let the jar sit for at least 12 hours and observe.

Soil type	What you see
clay and silty	water is cloudy with a layer of particles on the bottom of the jar
sandy	water is mostly clear with most of the particles forming a layer on the bottom of the jar
peaty	water is slightly cloudy, and particles are floating on the surface with a thin layer on the bottom of the jar
chalky	water is pale gray with a layer of grit-like, whitish-colored fragments on the bottom of the jar
loamy	water is clear with layered particles, with the finest on top, at the bottom of the jar

To conduct a thorough soil analysis, use a boxed test that is available at your local Cooperative Extension office. This test will tell you precisely what you need to make your soil just right for your planting needs.

Earthworms — a gardening partner worth cultivating

As you work hard to cultivate an excellent planting area and a productive garden, think of earthworms as vital partners in your effort. Worms are the single most essential and hard-working organism in the soil. Although thousands of species of earthworms exist, they all have a few things in common.

Earthworms burrow through even the heaviest ground, creating essential spaces for air, water, and nutrients. They gobble up organic matter and organisms and excrete valuable castings that enrich the soil and feed plants.

Earthworms also secrete mucus as they tunnel through the soil. This mucus is rich in nutrients that

> Is your planting ground compacted? Find out by sticking a wire into the soil and marking the depth at which it bends. If it penetrates the soil by at least a foot or more, your soil is not compacted. If it bends before a foot, consider adding earthworms and work at least 2 inches of organic compost into the soil each year before planting.

further improve soil richness. The bottom line is, worms are good. The more, the better. Here is a simple way to determine if you have an active earthworm population in your soil.

Examine the surface of the soil for earthworm castings and burrows. Dig up about 6 inches of soil, and put the soil on top of a newspaper. How many worms do you see? Three worms are good, but five is better.

If you don't see any worms, it's a good indication your soil does not have enough organic matter for the worms to feed. The only exception is if you live in the Southwest, where earthworm activity is very low. Worms do not like hot soil.

To encourage more worms, here are some things you can do.

- reduce tilling
- add aged manure
- add compost to your soil
- don't use chemicals
- aim for loamy soil
- aim for a neutral soil pH
- water regularly so that soil is moist but not saturated
- add items like grass clippings, leaves, and kitchen compost
- top the soil with organic mulch to keep it cool
- make an effort to keep your soil cool

Fall tips for sweet spring soil

As colder weather arrives, it is a great time to think about how to prepare your garden next season. A little time spent in the fall can make a tremendous difference in the quality of your garden soil. Here are some things you can do.

Mix and add compost to vegetable gardens. Clean up your vegetable bed by removing any debris and leftover plant material. Loosen the planting medium using a garden fork down to about 4 inches, and mix in about 3 inches of organic compost material.

Before the temperature gets too cold, the nutrients and organic matter will work like a flashing welcome sign, attracting beneficial microbes and valuable organisms to the soil. The party will heat up and pave the way for fertile spring soil.

Clean up flower beds and add compost. Fabulous flowers can use compost as well. Fill a bucket with organic compost. As you clean up gardens, pulling out annuals and trimming back perennials, pack compost in wherever you can. Be generous around established plants and shrubs, adding about 2 to 3 inches around the base of each plant.

Add raw organic matter to your veggie bed. After you have mixed in plenty of compost, you may want to supercharge your veggie bed by adding some fresh organic matter that will decay over the winter months. You can add raw organic matter like shredded leaves and animal manure (not dog or cat).

The animal manure can be green as it will break down over the winter months. Sprinkle some organic fertilizer on top of your garden bed to provide plenty of nitrogen for the soil's microbes.

Add other organic amendments. It's a good idea to add additional organic soil amendments like bone meal, kelp, rock phosphate, and greensand to your garden beds in the fall. They will break down slowly over winter and improve the nutrient quality for plants in the spring.

Test and adjust pH. Fall is a great time to test and improve the pH of your soil. Winter allows plenty of time for the slow change of pH, which is best.

Remember, the best pH is between 5.5 and 7.5. If you need to raise pH, add some lime, and if your soil is too alkaline, add some pine needles or peat moss.

> Chicken droppings have a very high level of nitrogen and can quickly burn plants if not composted. If your soil lacks nitrogen, use chicken droppings in your garden beds only after composting it for at least six months.

No. 1 rule when using wood ash in your garden

Do you burn firewood? If so, don't put those ashes to waste. Did you know that for each cord of wood you burn, you will gain about 20 pounds of wood ashes? Wood ashes are loaded with potassium, calcium, and magnesium and are frequently used to alter soil pH in a similar fashion to lime.

To use wood ash effectively in your garden, first understand the do's and don'ts.

- Do take a pH test. If the pH is low (below 6.5), you can safely add wood ash to your soil because magnesium and calcium are low.

- Don't add wood ash to your soil if your pH is greater than 7. It can damage or even kill plants. Similarly, don't add wood ashes to garden beds where you have blueberries, azaleas, holly, or rhododendrons growing. These plants like more acidic soil.

When using wood ash to increase the pH of your soil, note that it works quite a bit quicker than lime. In fact, lime takes about six months to alter the pH while wood ash goes to work right away. Always use twice as much wood ash as the recommended lime amount for your garden soil.

If your soil is already in the optimal pH range of 6 to 7, apply one gallon of hardwood ashes per 500 square foot area. Use caution not to apply more than this each year as it can cause salt injury to plants.

Be sure to wear gloves, eye protection, and a mask when spreading the ash, and do so on a dry day with no wind. After spreading, mix the ashes into the top several inches of soil, and rinse off any that may have landed on nearby plant foliage.

Read the weeds for planting cues

Learn how to read the weeds before determining where to plant a garden. The type of weeds you have growing can tell you a great deal about the nature of your soil and its ability to drain and support healthy plants.

Check the table on the next page for helpful hints.

Good drainage	Bad drainage	Heavy soil	Light soil
dandelion	mosses	buttercups	wild cornflower
purslane	sedges	plantain	yellow toadflax
chicory	horsetail	broad-leaved dock	white campion
pigweed	curly dock	dandelion	sheep sorrels

Try this quick drainage test and fix

How well your soil drains is critical to plant health. This simple drainage test will identify any issues you may have.

1. Dig a hole that is 6 inches wide and 12 inches deep.

2. Fill the hole with water and allow it to drain completely.

3. Fill it up with water again.

4. Set your watch and time how long it takes for all the water to drain out.

5. If it drains quickly, your soil is too light. If the water is still there the next day, it is too heavy. The perfect soil will drain in about 30 minutes.

Add any of the following to fix drainage issues.

- Sand. This is by far the cheapest thing you can add to soil that does not drain well. The small particles in the sand get in between clods of soil and break them apart.

- Perlite. The volcanic rock helps loosen up the soil and keeps it from clumping. It can also retain water, which helps prevent soil from baking and cracking.

- Organic compost. Not only does compost add valuable nutrients to the soil, but it also helps with drainage. Organic matter is spongy and makes the soil attractive to beneficial living organisms, further helping soil quality and drainage issues.

- Mulch. Mulch is fantastic at retaining water and breaks down quite slowly, which protects soil from baking and getting too hot. As the mulch breaks down, it also provides food for worms and other insects. Mulch all garden areas each fall, and over time this will loosen up any poor-draining areas.

- Vermiculite. Vermiculite is a lot like perlite in that they are both volcanic rock. This material looks like glass and is highly absorbent. When combined with compost and perlite, it will break up tough soil and improve drainage tremendously.

Woodworkers: Use leftovers to improve acid-loving soil

If you have a woodworking shop and use it regularly, you likely have a buildup of sawdust. Rather than throwing it out, use it to improve the soil conditions for acid-loving plants like blueberries.

Because sawdust needs nitrogen to break down, you must add nitrogen at the same time you add the sawdust. Use 1 pound of nitrogen for every 50 pounds of dry sawdust.

Put your falling leaves to good use

Who doesn't love colorful fall leaves? But if you're like most people, you could do without them falling all over your beautiful lawn.

Rather than raking and bagging them or letting them sit, consider turning them into a rich — and free — soil amendment, known as leaf mold. Your plants will love it.

Leaf mold is the ultimate soil conditioner. While compost is excellent and adds tremendously to soil texture and fertility, leaf mold is a far better amendment.

Some studies have found that adding leaf mold to soil increases water retention by over 50%. Leaf mold also improves soil structure and provides an excellent habitat for earthworms and beneficial bacteria.

There are two popular and easy ways to make leaf mold. Both require patience as leaves are mostly carbon and take longer to break down than nitrogen-rich amendments like grass clippings. It takes between 6 to 12 months for leaves to break down, but the wait is worth it.

Wire bin method

1. Create a wire bin that is at least 3-feet wide and 3-feet tall.

2. Transport all your leaves into the bin and squash them down.

3. Water the pile well and keep damp during dry periods.

4. Cover the bin with a plastic tarp.

5. Stir the pile a couple of times a month with a garden fork.

Bag method

1. Fill a large contractor-size garbage bag (or two or three) with leaves.

2. Moisten the leaves before tying the bag shut.

3. Cut some slits in the bag to allow for airflow.

4. Give the bag a shake every month or so, and add water if needed to keep leaves moist.

Using leaf mold in your garden is easy. Dig it into your garden beds to improve the soil structure and help with moisture retention. You can also use it as a mulch in vegetable gardens or flower beds. If you plant in containers, use it as a top dressing to help maintain water.

How do I make my sandy soil work for me?

Sandy soil has been referred to as "early soil" because it can be worked and planted earlier in the spring than other soil types. Although this can be an advantage, sandy soil can also be frustrating, mainly because it doesn't retain moisture very well.

Sandy soil is composed of 80% to 85% of various sand types (coarse, medium, and fine) and only about 15% to 20% clay and silt, which improve water retention. Interestingly, in some areas with limited rain, sandy soils can be rich in nutrients, while in wet or humid regions, the quality is quite poor.

Don't fret if your soil is light and sandy. There is hope. With a little time and a few amendments added in the fall, your garden will be productive and ready for planting. Here are some options.

- Add 3 to 4 inches of organic matter such as compost, leaf mold, or well-rotted manure. Work it into the soil thoroughly. Add at least 2 inches of organic matter each year.

- Mulch around plants using leaves, bark, hay, straw, or wood chips to retain moisture and keep the soil cool.

- Work some green manure consisting of grass clippings, wood chips, and plant leaves about 6 inches into the soil.

Fun ways to figure out pH — and why you should do it

Do you know whether your soil is alkaline, neutral, or acidic? If not, you need to find out. The pH of your soil is one of the biggest factors in how well your plants will grow. It affects soil structure and nutrient availability among other things.

Is there a magic number? Soil pH normally falls between 3 and 10 with 7 being neutral. Acid soils are under 7, while alkaline soils have a pH above 7. Scientists have found that nutrients are most available to plants when the soil is between 5.5 to 6.5.

The best way to test your soil pH is to use a test kit. However, if you don't have a kit on hand or don't want to wait for the results, you can do it yourself. Here are a few unique ways to get a good idea of the nature of your soil's pH.

Use baking soda and vinegar. Good old-fashioned baking soda and vinegar can tell you quite a bit about your soil.

1. Gather 1 cup of soil from various parts of your garden bed or lawn.

2. Add 2 teaspoons each into two different containers. Be sure the containers are clean.

3. Chill 1/2 cup of white vinegar, and add it to one of your sample cups.

4. If it fizzes, your soil is alkaline, a pH between 7 and 8.

5. If it does not fizz, add distilled water to the other soil container until it becomes muddy.

6. Add 1/2 cup of baking soda. If it fizzes, your soil is acidic, between 5 and 6.

7. If there is no reaction during the test, the soil is neutral, with a pH around 7.

Try the red cabbage test. Here is a fun way to test your soil's pH using cabbage.

1. Pour 2 cups of distilled water into a saucepan.

2. Cut up five red cabbage leaves and simmer them in the pot for 10 minutes.

3. Allow the pot to set for 30 minutes.

4. Strain off the liquid — it will be purple or bluish. This liquid has a neutral pH of 7.

5. Take soil samples from various locations in your testing site, whether it be your lawn area or garden area.

6. Add about 2 teaspoons of each soil sample to separate clean, glass jars. Label the jars.

7. One at a time, add 2 inches of cabbage water to each jar and observe.

8. Soil samples that turn reddish/pink in color are acidic. Sea blue/yellow-green means the soil is alkaline. Neutral soil will be purple/bluish.

Make your soil pH just right. Add crushed limestone if your soil is too acidic. Add organic compost if it is too alkaline.

2 paths to practically perfect dirt

Growing plants in raised beds creates a unique opportunity to make the near-perfect soil mixture. This growing method is especially useful if you have rocky or heavy clay soil that might take some time to amend before you can plant.

If you are so fortunate to have raised beds, here are two recipes for the best elevated-bed soil ever.

Veggie delight mix

- 1/4 part organic compost
- 1/4 part coconut coir
- 1/4 part topsoil
- 1/4 part organic material such as worm castings or rabbit manure

Combine all ingredients and mix well.

Light and fluffy all-purpose mix

- 1 part coconut coir
- 1 part bulk organic compost
- 1/4 part aged chicken manure
- 1 part vermiculite
- 1/4 part worm casting

Combine all ingredients and mix well.

Stinky ingredient adds beneficial bacteria

It may not smell the best, but animal manure is a valuable conditioner for your soil and garden plants if used correctly. Manure is a fantastic source of nitrogen, potassium, and phosphorus. Plus it is teeming with beneficial bacteria.

Just be sure you don't apply fresh manure to an edible garden. That's the biggest mistake you can make. Fresh manure may cause illness due to pathogens like *E. coli* and salmonella.

Another mistake is using the wrong kind of manure in the garden. Keep in mind that all animal manure is not created equal. Cow manure is an excellent soil conditioner that is not too high in nitrogen but loaded with nutrients. Because cows have four stomachs, food breaks down well, and there are fewer weed seeds to be found.

The best way to compost cow manure is to select a square area where you can build a 4x4-foot pile. This should be away from your home and any outdoor gathering spaces. To make it easier, build a frame to hold the pile.

- Add 2 inches of cow manure on top of the dry organic matter.

- Water the pile so it is damp.

- Repeat until you have a 4-foot-high pile.

- Cover the pile with a 2-inch layer of soil.

- Turn the pile every three days, and keep it moist.

- Check the temperature of the pile in the center when you turn it. It should be 120 to 160 degrees F.

- The compost is ready to use when it stops heating up in the center and is brown and crumbly with an earthy smell.

If your compost has a powerful odor, it is too wet and needs more dry organic material. If the compost does not heat up, it is too dry or lacking in nitrogen. Add water if it feels dry, and add more manure if it is damp and cool.

Use 20 pounds of composted cow manure for every 50 square feet of a new garden. For established and fertile gardens, use 3 inches on top of the bed, and work it well into the soil.

Composted animal manure: Which is best and when?

Depending on what you plan to grow in your garden, the type and timing of manure matters. Follow this chart to make the most of your fertilizer application.

Type of garden	Best manure	Best time to apply
flower	cow and horse	early spring
vegetable	chicken, cow, or horse	fall or spring
potato	chicken, cow, or horse	fall or spring
acid-loving plants like blueberries, azaleas, and mountain laurel	cow and horse	early fall

Surprising secret to better soil and healthier crops

You may think cover crops are only meant for large, substantial garden plots. But you can plant a cover crop in any garden area, even a raised bed. And believe it or not, it will help your garden be even more productive year after year.

A cover crop, also known as green manure, is one that is planted for the benefit of the soil, not for the crop itself. Because it makes soil more fertile without chemicals, it's an essential part of organic and sustainable gardening. And it's quick and easy to boot. Just look at these benefits.

Prevents erosion. Cover crops allow water to drain deep down into the garden.

Improves soil structure. When the roots of cover crops dig deep into the soil, they create spaces for moisture, air, and beneficial insects.

Suppresses weeds. Cover crop roots are sturdy and will deprive weeds of all that they need to survive. They also grow and shade out any weed seeds that try to sprout.

Gathers moisture. These crops protect soil from sun and wind evaporation while sending down deep roots that bring moisture up from down low in the soil.

Adds to organic matter. Cover crops add to the organic matter when they are alive as their leaves drop into the soil and decompose. When they are cut back or die, they become a natural mulch.

So when do you plant your cover crop? As soon as you've finish harvesting your vegetables for the season. Simply scratch the soil with a rake and scatter the seeds fairly thickly, similar to planting grass seed. Then rake the soil lightly to set it, and cover it with straw to protect it.

- For a spring or early summer new garden bed, plant heat-loving cover crops such as buckwheat or beans.

- For a late summer new garden bed, plant ryegrass or oats, which both grow in colder weather.

You can also plant a cover crop during the growing season once you harvest early maturing crops. That will keep the weeds down and the soil fertile and loaded with organic matter.

Once your cover crop is grown, and before planting, simply dig it into your bed to add valuable nutrients.

4 reasons not to till — and what to do instead

Tilling larger garden areas is something people have done for centuries to turn up new ground and help the soil be more fertile. But, surprisingly, modern research says tilling is not beneficial and can be harmful to soil health. Here are a few reasons not to till and what you can do instead.

Expands erosion. Tilling turns everything upside down and leaves soil susceptible to washing out from heavy rain.

Increases weeds. Yes, tilling does chop up weeds, but it also disturbs dormant weed seeds and weed cuttings that will happily sprout.

Dries out the soil. The beneficial living organisms found in soil depend on moisture to survive. Turning the soil so that it dries out quicker in the spring also kills many necessary microorganisms.

Reduces long-term soil fertility. Tilling does make the ground more fertile but only for a little while. The immediate richness comes from the breakdown of soil life. Consistent tilling results in a significant decline in insects, worms, and other beneficial critters, making the soil less fertile year after year.

Sustainable alternatives to tilling include:

- setting some chickens free over your garden area in the fall.

- manually turning soil with a garden fork.

- using mulch to suppress weeds.

- adding plenty of organic matter to your garden bed each season.

- building a layered, no-till garden bed.

How to warm your soil for early planting

Warming up your veggie bed soil for early spring planting makes a lot of sense if you live in an area with a very short growing season. Here are some ways to pre-warm your soil so that it is ready about two to three weeks before the "usual" planting time, depending on your growing conditions.

- Keep your garden beds wet but not soaking all winter long to absorb and hold on to daytime heat.

- Water your garden soil well, and cover it with thick, plastic sheeting for six weeks before planting. Sow seeds or set transplants, water, and re-cover the garden bed if necessary to create | a greenhouse effect.

> Make a simple cold frame by adding an old window to your raised bed. This cold frame will help the soil warm up quickly in the early spring and allow you to start planting well before the official growing season kicks off. Put your cold frame in place at least two weeks prior to planting for best results.

- Keep the soil warm over the winter in more temperate areas by putting a 3-inch layer of dark compost over the surface. You can also cover with a piece of plastic if necessary.

Easy-to-make compost tea features special ingredient

Keep a few rabbits as adorable pets, and they'll do wonders for your garden soil. Many gardeners use rabbit manure fresh from the hutch without composting.

For the most part, this should be OK because rabbit manure is known as 'cold' manure, meaning it does not require composting before use. When spread around the base of plants, the manure acts as a time-release fertilizer.

If you're not using fresh rabbit droppings, you can improve the fertility of your soil with a rabbit compost tea.

What you need:

- 5-gallon bucket with lid

- drill and 1/4-inch drill bit

- long stir stick

- rabbit manure

- water

How to make it:

1. Place the lid on your plastic container, and make numerous holes in the lid using the drill and drill bit.

2. Add 4 gallons of water to your bucket.

3. Add 3/4 gallon of rabbit manure to your bucket.

4. Stir well and put the lid on the bucket.

5. Stir each day for one week.

Ladle out tea and apply it around existing plants, or strain out the droppings and pour the bucket directly on top of existing garden beds.

A great way to enrich your veggie patch is to pour some tea right over the top of the soil — pellets and all — after you have cleaned out the bed for the season.

Edible gardens to make your grandma proud

10 really great reasons to grow food now

Gardening can be an incredibly satisfying hobby, but there are many other practical reasons to grow your own food. Here are some of the top reasons why planting a food garden is a great idea.

- Growing food makes eating healthy effortless.

- Unlike grocery store produce that travels thousands of miles to reach your table, garden-fresh veggies and fruit travel mere steps. The impact on the environment is far less for homegrown food.

- Homegrown produce contains many vitamins, minerals, and antioxidants.

- Growing food can save you money.

- Planting and tending a garden provides rewarding exercise and helps slash stress.

- When you grow a garden, you reduce the risk of contamination.

- Gardening provides an excellent opportunity to expand your knowledge base.

- Creating and tending a food garden is a fun activity for the entire family.

- Garden-fresh food tastes better than grocery store fruit and vegetables.

- Growing food gives you a sense of accomplishment.

The bottom-line best food crops for beginners

Are you a beginner gardener and not sure where to start when it comes to growing food? When setting out on your gardening journey, the key to success is to start small and grow from there.

Your first year of gardening will be a journey and learning experience that will build a solid foundation for the future. One of the best ways to boost your chance of a favorable outcome is to plant crops that are easy to grow. If you could only choose three foods for your garden, it should be these.

Lettuce. Lettuce is super easy to grow and will reward you with a harvest quickly, which will build your confidence. It takes little space to grow lettuce, and you can even plant it in containers if you don't have much garden space.

Harvesting is as easy as snip and enjoy. The best types are the ones you can cut, and they keep coming the more you cut.

Lettuce grows best in loose and cool soil in a partially shady location that has excellent drainage. Add plenty of organic matter like compost or manure, which provides the essential nutrients lettuce loves.

Cucumbers. With enough water, cucumbers will grow fast, like weeds. If you wish to grow cukes in containers, try bush varieties that require a trellis for support.

Most types have good resistance to disease and pests, which makes them super easy keepers.

Plant your cucumbers where they will receive plenty of warm sunlight. Provide lots of rich organic material in the soil, and feed cucumbers once a week during the growing season with a compost tea.

> To grow bigger and better cucumbers, leave only four fruits on the plant at any one time. Remove immature cucumbers as soon as you see them, and you will be rewarded with a bigger and better harvest.

Green beans. You have so many green bean types to choose from — those that vine and climb and those that bush. Green beans are super easy to grow and only require a small amount of maintenance and care to thrive.

You can directly sow green beans in the garden in slightly acidic soil with a pH of around 6. As long as you plant in rich soil, there is no need to feed beans as they feed themselves by fixing their nitrogen. With lots of sunshine and plenty of water, your beans will reward you with a plentiful harvest.

Vegetable friends and foes — what you need to know

Basil — the perfect partner to plant next to your tomatoes. Not only will it protect your tomatoes from pests, but this pair tastes great together on your plate.

Companion plants like these help each other out by supplying nutrients and keeping pests at bay. On the flip side, some plants just don't get along at all. Use this handy chart to figure out what to plant together and what to keep apart.

Vegetable	Best friends	Worst foes
asparagus	tomatoes, basil, dill, cilantro, marigolds, oregano, peppers	leeks, onions, garlic, potatoes
beans	beets, cabbage, potatoes, carrots, cucumbers, cauliflower	onions, garlic, sunflowers, peppers
beets	beans, kohlrabi, onions, cabbage, catmint, lettuce	pole beans, wild mustard
cabbage	chamomile, dill, mints, potatoes, rosemary, sage, thyme, lettuce, kale	cauliflower, strawberries, broccoli, tomatoes
carrots	beans, lettuce, sage, onions, peas, radish, tomatoes, rosemary	anise, dill, parsley
cauliflower	beets, broccoli, chard, spinach, cucumber, corn, radish	peppers, beans, strawberries, onions, peas
corn	beans, cucumbers, melons, peas, potatoes, pumpkins, squash	tomatoes, celery
cucumbers	radish, cabbage, sunflowers, lettuce, peas	melons, potatoes, fragrant herbs
lettuce	carrots, strawberries, peas, corn, tomatoes, carrots, beets, radish	broccoli
onions	beets, lettuce, potatoes, peppers, spinach, cabbage	peas, beans, sage
peas	beans, carrots, corn, radish, cucumbers, turnips	cilantro, cucumbers, mint, carrots, beans, cauliflower, cabbage
peppers	basil, onions, spinach, coriander, tomatoes	beans, kohlrabi
potatoes	beans, cabbage, corn, thyme, parsley	asparagus, carrots, parsnips, melons, squash, turnips, kohlrabi, cucumbers, sunflowers

Vegetable	Best friends	Worst foes
radish	chervil, cucumbers, lettuce, peas	kohlrabi
spinach	strawberries, lettuce, peas, radish	potatoes
tomatoes	basil, parsley, mint, asparagus, thyme, carrots, lettuce, onions, melons, radish	broccoli, kale, potatoes, corn, cabbage, cauliflower, Brussels sprouts

Grandma's tips for tasty and terrific tomatoes

Do you remember grandma's tomatoes tasting better than today's? Here's why — and how you can taste 'em again. These tomato tips will help you grow a bountiful harvest of delicious fruit to make your grandmother proud.

Plant tomatoes on their sides. Increase your tomato harvest by 30% when you make one creative change. You won't believe this, but it works.

Planting tomatoes on their sides helps to increase nutrient absorption, creating a healthy and robust plant. Pinch any yellow leaves off the bottom section of the plant to increase stem length.

When planted on its side, the tomato plant develops a healthy root system towards the soil's surface. This method of planting allows the plant to take in more heat, which increases yield. To prepare young plants for side growing, place them on their sides for a few days before planting in the garden so they get the hang of reaching for the sun.

Here's one secret to a bountiful harvest of beans, squash, cucumbers, tomatoes, or okra. Miss it and your plants will shut down production early. Don't ever leave overripe vegetables hanging on the vine. It lowers productivity, reduces crop yield, and encourages pests and disease. Make sure you harvest when the time is right.

Add something special to your bed. Wondering what to plant with your tomatoes to make them superbly healthy, robust, and tasty? Here's something that won't cost you a single penny and does the job well.

If you love fishing, this tip is definitely for you. After cleaning your fresh fish, save the head for your tomatoes. You can also pick up fish heads at your local fish market for next to nothing. Fish heads add a slow release of nitrogen and calcium that tomatoes gobble up as they grow.

Rotate your planting spots. To keep your tomato plants as healthy as possible, it's critical to switch up where you grow tomatoes each year. Doing this helps avoid disease issues that hide in the soil, such as blight and blossom rot. Also, tomatoes are heavy feeders and can drain the soil of nutrients quickly. Rotating planting spots ensures your plants will get the best of the new soil.

Secret ingredient for the sweetest, juiciest tomatoes ever

Sweet, delicious tomatoes. That's what you'll get when you add a certain something to your watering can. Can you guess what it is?

If you said banana peel, you are right. Bananas contain some valuable things that tomatoes love, such as potassium, calcium, and phosphorus.

To make banana water, soak three banana peels in three cups of water for several days. The minerals in the peel will leach into the water. Feed your tomatoes weekly with this nutrient-rich water, and compost the peels when finished.

3 raised-bed plans for a super-abundant harvest

Many people mistakenly believe you need acres and acres of space to grow food. The good news is there are many ways to reap an abundant harvest, even if all you have is a small balcony or patio.

One way is to plant a raised bed. There are endless types, including elevated beds that reduce bending and twisting. It is astounding how much food you can harvest from a tiny space.

Here are three raised-bed plans that make planting, tending, and harvesting your garden a snap. Each square represents 1 square foot of growing space. Remember to fill your beds with plenty of rich soil and to provide a sturdy trellis for cucumbers and a support cage for tomatoes.

Sensational salad garden			
tomato x 1 small	radish x 5	green onions x 5	cucumber x 2
spinach x 6	leaf lettuce x 4	pepper x 1	arugula x 4
tomato x 1 small	radish x 14	green onions x 5	cucumber x 2
spinach x 6	leaf lettuce x 4	pepper x 1	arugula x 4

Mixed herb and veggie garden			
cucumber x 2	sugar snap peas x 6	tomato x 1	cherry tomato x 1
red bell pepper x 1	yellow bell pepper x 1	basil x 4	Swiss chard x 4
leaf lettuce x 4	beets x 9	kale x 1	cilantro x 1
carrots x 14	radishes x 14	parsley x 1	bush bean x 6

Strawberries and friends garden			
strawberry x 1	strawberry x 1	strawberry x 1	strawberry x 1
spinach x 6	leaf lettuce x 4	garlic x 4	bush bean x 6
strawberry x 1	strawberry x 1	strawberry x 1	strawberry x 1
spinach x 6	leaf lettuce x 4	garlic x 4	bush bean x 6

Take the mystery out of growing watermelons from seed

Nothing tastes quite as wonderful as fresh watermelon on a warm summer day. Although watermelons are mostly water, they also contain potent antioxidants and vitamins C, A, and B6.

Watermelons are not overly difficult to grow — they are just demanding plants. They require lots of water, nutrients, space, and sunny weather. They are not fond of extreme heat or humidity.

Pay attention to these critical details when growing watermelons from seed.

Time to maturity. Watermelons need about three months of warm (70 to 80 degrees) and sunny weather to grow to maturity. Choose a fast-growing type if you have a short season.

Give them space. Watermelons will spare no plant that gets in their way once they start to sprawl. You need enough room for your plants to spread comfortably. If you have a small garden, a sturdy trellis will help send your plant upwards. Be sure to use the smallest variety of melon you can find.

Test if your watermelon is ripe and ready for harvest by knocking on the fruit with your knuckles. Ripe melons generally have a dull and hollow sound, while unripe fruit returns with a higher-pitched sound. Once you get the hang of it, thumping is an excellent way to determine when to harvest.

Seed type. Open-pollinated and heirloom seeds are best. Using heirloom seeds allows you to save some seeds for growing again next year.

Grow in mounds. Watermelons do well when grown in clumps in mounds. Form mounds of organically rich soil about 3 feet wide and 1 foot high. Place three groups of three seeds in each mound. Space groups about 1 foot apart.

Snip weaker plants. Once your seeds start growing, snip off those that look weaker than the rest. Do not pull the plants, as pulling will disrupt the roots of the healthy plants.

Water well. Watermelons have shallow roots, so keep the soil moist at all times, but not soggy.

Mulch. Keep weeds down and moisture locked in by mulching with aged manure around plants.

Feed. Watermelons are super heavy feeders. Provide a high nitrogen organic feed like pelleted chicken manure to help them mature. Once they start to flower, cut back on nitrogen and increase potassium to encourage fruiting.

If you live in a cool or mountainous area, use this neat trick to hurry along the melon's ripening process. Place a piece of tile or flagstone underneath ripening fruit. The warmth that is collected by the tile will not only help the melon develop faster but will also improve the taste of the fruit.

Pinch. Once vines reach about 6 feet, pinch off the tips to encourage a branching habit.

1 little pill will keep your plants healthy

Want tastier tomatoes, peppier peppers, and healthier house-plants? Give 'em an aspirin. Aspirin contains acetylsalicylic acid that boosts the plant's immune system. That in turn allows it to fight disease, pests, and physical damage.

Just follow these super-simple instructions to reap the benefits of aspirin.

1. Place three aspirins in a gallon of water and let them dissolve.

2. Add a tablespoon of liquid dish soap and mix well.

3. Pour the mixture into a garden sprayer. Spray all plants

in your garden once a month with this mixture. Be sure to spray in mid-morning after the dew has evaporated. Coat the leaves and stems.

4. In addition to spraying plants, you can also water them directly, pouring the mixture into the soil around plants. Do this once a month as well.

> ## 5 valuable lessons from a first veggie garden
>
> Years ago, when Diane was just a novice grower, she planted her first vegetable garden. Now that she's a veteran gardener, she remembers the challenges she went through and likes to share what she learned. Here are just five of the many things her first garden taught her.
>
> **Dig in.** While it is a good thing to research before you plant, the best way to learn is to dig in and get your hands dirty.
>
> **Build up your soil.** Rich organic compost and leaf mold are your garden's best friends. Both will build up your soil over time. The better the soil, the healthier the plants, and the more they will produce.
>
> **Simple is best.** When it comes to garden tools and planting aides, simple is best. Don't spend tons of money on things you can make yourself. Don't go overboard on seeds either. Buy just a few types and concentrate on these before expanding.
>
> **Put it on paper.** Nothing can replace a garden planner. This notebook will become your best friend year after year. Record your garden plants and layouts, your success stories, and your challenges. This info will be more than valuable as you grow in your gardening knowledge.
>
> **Get involved in garden groups.** Tap into local sustainable living movements and become part of something great. As you do this, you will find support and friendship with like-minded people — an integral part of a successful garden.

Checklist for growing bigger and better blueberries

Blueberries are a delicious and attractive addition to the land-scape. These easy-to-grow bushes can be grown in every zone in the continental United States and generally don't have any pest issues. Here are some things to check for when growing the best blueberries ever.

Choose the best cultivars. Pick blueberry types that are best for your growing region. Buy at least two varieties to ensure adequate pollination. Choose one to three year old plants from a reputable nursery.

Select a sunny spot. In nature, blueberries grow in semi-shaded locations. However, for heavier fruiting, sunshine is needed.

Plant bushes in the fall or spring. Space them about 2 feet apart up to 6 feet depending on how you want to grow them. Space rows 8 to 10 feet apart. Plant with roots spread out a couple of inches deeper than the depth of their nursery pot.

Test the soil pH. Blueberries like acidic soil in the range of 4 to 5. Use pelleted sulfur to get levels up if needed.

Incorporate plenty of organic matter. Mix into the soil before planting, and use organic matter as a top dress.

Add a handful of coco fiber. Place it in each planting hole to prevent compaction and help with drainage. Blueberries have a shallow surface root system and need adequate drainage to thrive.

Install a drip system. One way to be sure your plants, especially young plants, get plenty of water is to use a drip system. Run the system for an hour or more several times a week during the growing season.

Focus on appropriate feeding. One month after planting, apply half an ounce of 10-10-10 fertilizer in a circle 6 to 12 inches from the crown. Annually, use a balanced organic fertilizer before buds open. If you live in a warm climate, feed again after harvest.

Cover bushes with a net. Doing this during the fruiting season will protect your harvest from hungry birds.

Be prudent with pruning. Don't prune until four or five years after planting, and only prune in late winter.

Keep your harvest fresh for longer

You can keep everything from strawberries to onions fresh days or weeks longer. Here's how.

Green beans. Blanch beans for several minutes in boiling water, let them cool, and place in a freezer-safe bag. Beans will keep up to a year when stored this way.

Strawberries. To keep strawberries fresher for longer, don't wash them or trim off stems. Place them in a glass jar in the refrigerator, and trim and wash when you are ready to use them.

Potatoes. Do not clean the soil off potatoes before putting them in your basement or root cellar for storage. This protects the potatoes from the air and makes them last longer. Stored this way, potatoes will last up to three months.

Onions. Place onions in a single layer on a clean, dry surface. Let them dry for a few weeks until the necks are dry and the skin becomes papery.

After they cure, cut the tops or necks off. Place onions in a nylon stocking, tying a knot after each onion. Hang the nylon and snip off part of the stocking when you need an onion.

Beets. Store beets in a perforated bag in your crisper. Beets will keep up to three months when stored this way. You can also pack beets in a moist sand container and place the container in a cool, dark location.

Kale. Never pre-wash your garden kale before storage. Lay out a paper towel and roll your kale tightly in the towel. Stick the roll in a zip lock bag if you can. Put the bag in the refrigerator.

Never store kale next to apples, apricots, cantaloupe, figs, peaches, pears, plums, or tomatoes in the fridge. When stored correctly, your garden-fresh kale should keep for up to 10 days.

3 easy garden veggies that save you money and 5 that aren't worth it

When you choose produce to grow, it's a good idea to pick the ones that offer the biggest bang for your buck. You'll often pay way too much if you buy these easy-to-grow crops at the store.

- Lettuce. This is quite an easy crop to grow, and an entire pack of seeds costs less than half the price of a single container of spring mix. Lettuce is happy in containers or raised beds, and you can even grow it indoors all year with the right lighting. Grow a variety of cut-and-come-again with leaf lettuce for the most bang for your buck. One plant will continue to provide lettuce all season long.

- Garlic. You may pay anywhere from $1 to $7 for a bulb of garlic at your local grocery store. Growing garlic in your home garden costs about $.50 a clove, which is quite a savings since one clove will grow into an entire bulb. Because garlic is grown over winter, it makes great use of garden space. Keep your garden weed-free as garlic does not like competition in its growing area.

- Bell peppers. Green bell peppers command a hefty price of about $1.50 each. If you want red or yellow peppers, you will pay even more. Young pepper plants cost about $2 each and will bear several single peppers. Peppers are easy to grow and love warm weather.

On the flip side, some food crops offer little, if any, monetary savings when compared to grocery store offerings. Here are five such food crops.

- Corn. Because you must plant enough corn for it to pollinate, it becomes a garden space hog. Both fresh and fresh-frozen corn are relatively cheap at the grocery store or even your local farmer's market, which means you will have more space to grow other crops.

> Pick off any small peppers that form on plants. Removing this small fruit will help the plant grow strong and healthy and bear large fruit. Picking green peppers as soon as they mature will also encourage more fruiting and increase the yield.

- Celery. This long-stalk plant likes cool weather and tons of moisture, which makes it hard to grow in the summer in most locations. The long growing season also makes it difficult for those with only a few months to mature. Better to pick up a bunch of celery at the store instead

- Eggplant. Eggplants easily succumb to heat and pest infestation, and they can quickly become a frustrating crop to grow. If you enjoy eggplant, buy it organic from the store and spare yourself the possible disappointment.

- Carrots. Although carrots are fun to grow, they can be somewhat finicky, especially regarding the soil. Even the smallest obstruction can stunt a carrot's growth. You can pick up a bunch of fresh, organic carrots at your local grocer fairly cheap.

- Cauliflower. This veggie has a long growing season and prefers cool temperatures. Cauliflower requires loads of attention, and pests can be a significant problem. Heads of organic cauliflower are not that expensive at the store and are relatively easy to source.

Why do my carrots always come up deformed?

Carrots are determined little roots. As they push their way through the soil, they route their way around any barrier, be it a rock or a thick clod of dirt. That's one reason they end up with strange shapes. To help clear their way, remove stones and clods before planting.

Here are some other reasons your carrots end up short, fat, or otherwise disfigured, and what you can do about it.

- Planting carrots in heavy, compacted soil generally results in small, stumpy veggies. Be sure to work compost into heavy soil to improve the outcome. You can also choose to plant a shorter variety of carrots like Little Fingers that does much better in heavy soil.

- If your soil has too much nitrogen, carrots tend to branch out in different directions and develop hairy roots. To avoid this problem, soil test before planting, and only use a low-nitrogen organic feed and well-aged manure.

- Planting carrots too close together may result in deformity as they can twist and turn around each other. Be sure to allow each carrot plant ample room to grow. Thin seedlings when they are 3 to 4 inches tall.

- Weeds close to your planted carrots can interfere with growth by competing for nutrients. Keep your garden as weed-free as possible to avoid stunted growth.

Simple growing method yields loads of potatoes

If you love potatoes, you will be amazed at how easy it is to get a massive harvest using a simple bucket growing method. Follow the steps below, and you will have enough potatoes to last all winter long.

Although most potatoes, even sweet potatoes, do well growing in a bucket, some of the best varieties to try include Charlotte, Rocket, Lady Christi, and Anya.

What you need:

- gravel
- seed potatoes
- large bucket, 12-16 inches in diameter. Keep in mind that one potato needs about 2.5 gallons of space. Don't use a black bucket.
- organic soil with compost
- drill and 1/2-inch drill bit

How to make it:

1. Drill holes around the circumference of the bucket towards the bottom to help with drainage.

2. Place about 2 inches of gravel in the bottom of the bucket.

3. Place 4 to 6 inches of soil in the bottom of the bucket.

4. Plant seed potatoes in the soil with the sprouts pointing upwards.

5. Cover potatoes with 3 inches of soil.

   > If your potato has more than one eye, cut it into two pieces, each with an eye. Allow the pieces to cure on an indoor window-sill for several days before planting to avoid mold.

6. If you use a 5-gallon bucket, two potatoes are plenty. If you use something larger, scale up proportionally.

7. Water potato bucket until the water runs out of the drainage holes.

8. Place the bucket in direct sunlight.

9. As the potatoes grow and you see about 4 inches of green, cover them with more soil, so just the tip is peeking out from the soil.

10. Continue this until the bucket is full.

11. Feed your potatoes with a low-nitrogen compost tea once every two weeks.

12. Once the potato plant turns yellow and begins to die, turn your bucket over and dump out your harvest.

Broccoli — a 'smart' addition to your garden

Keeping your brain healthy for the long term can be as simple as going to the garden or your fresh produce aisle. The secret is knowing about one type of incredible plant.

What is this miracle brain booster? It's broccoli — a power-house veggie that contains two essential nutrients that affect brain function. Vitamin K strengthens cognitive functioning, and choline may improve memory.

You'll find countless varieties of broccoli to choose from to help keep your brain and body healthy. Here are some favorite types found in home gardens.

Belstar. This hybrid plant is popular in southern winter gardens and matures in 65 days. Grow this stress-resistant variety for a spring and a fall harvest.

Destiny. Created especially for growing in zones 7 to 11, this hybrid has small to medium heads with a purple tint. Destiny will mature 70 to 75 days from planting.

Green magic. This hybrid plant thrives in zones 3 to 9 and has excellent heat tolerance in southern regions. It has smooth medium-sized blue-green heads and an interesting buttery taste.

Purple sprouting. A cold-hardy heirloom plant with small purple-colored florets on each plant rather than one large head. It does great in zones 2 to 11. A neat feature about this type of broccoli is that you can eat the leaves and stems as well as the florets.

Romanesco. An Italian heirloom broccoli that has beautiful chartreuse florets. This plant grows well in zones 3 to 10, but bolts when temperatures rise. Its nutty flavor is as impressive as its sea coral-like texture. This type of broccoli is quite a conversation piece as well.

7 creative ways to harvest more strawberries

Strawberries are one of the easiest and tastiest crops to grow. The healthier your plants are, the more fruit you will have to enjoy. Here are some tips to help you get the most out of your strawberry plants and enjoy a bountiful harvest year after year.

Pick the correct soil. Plant your strawberries in sandy and well-draining soil. If strawberries are too wet, the crowns will rot and the plant will eventually die.

Get pH levels right. Strawberry plants do best in soil that is slightly acidic to neutral with a pH of around 5.5 to 7. Always test your soil before you plant. If it is too acidic, add some lime. If it is too alkaline, add some organic compost.

Pay attention to moisture. Since strawberry plants have a shallow root system and get most of their moisture from the top 2 inches of soil, it is critical to monitor moisture levels. To keep soil from drying out, add a healthy layer of mulch around each plant.

Feed them right. If you feed your strawberry plants too little, they won't grow well. Too much, and they will develop beautiful foliage but not much fruit. A low-nitrogen organic feed made for fruit and vegetables works best.

Keep runners under control. Strawberry plants send out runners each season. These runners root in the soil and begin to create a new plant. However, when they do this, they zap the nutrients from the parent plant, causing the parent plant to stop producing fruit. Keep runners trimmed up so your main plant can become healthy and productive.

Make your garden pollinator-friendly. The more pollinator-attracting plants you have around your strawberry patch, the bigger and tastier your strawberries will be.

Watch out for problems. Keep a sharp eye out for pests or disease signs, and treat accordingly as soon as you spot a problem.

Secrets to growing veggies in a straw bale

Straw bales can be used just like raised beds and are a practical option if you have poor soil. Keep in mind the difference between straw and hay. Hay is grass, and straw is stalks and should have no weed seeds. Straw is an excellent natural container for growing. As the straw breaks down, it provides valuable nutrients that plants can use.

Here's how to get your straw bale garden started.

1. Source your straw bales carefully to ensure they have no weed seeds.

2. Lay down landscape fabric in your chosen garden location.

3. Place straw bales where they will receive six to eight hours of direct sunlight daily.

4. Position bales side by side in rows with their cut side facing upwards. The strings that hold the bales together should be running along the sides, not the bale's top.

5. Two weeks before you plant, condition the bales. For the first six days, pour 3 cups of organic fertilizer on each bale and water it thoroughly.

   If your bales start sprouting what looks like grass it means you have weed seeds in your bale. To fix it, pour 50% diluted vinegar on top of the bales to keep the weeds from taking over.

6. On days seven through nine, apply 1.5 cups of fertilizer to each bale and water.

7. On day 10, apply 3 cups of phosphorus and potassium

to each bale. Fish meal mixed with 50 percent wood ash works great. Water bales thoroughly.

8. Check bales by sticking your finger down into them — they should be hot and moist. If you see mushrooms growing up out of your straw bales, don't worry, this is a good sign. When mushrooms show up, it means your bale is decomposing as it should. The mushrooms will not hurt your plants.

9. If desired, place 7-foot tall posts at the end of each straw bale row. String sturdy wire between the posts starting about 10 inches from the top of the bales. Drape plastic sheeting over the wire to protect seedlings from chilly weather. As plants grow, the wire acts as a trellis, encouraging plants to grow upwards. This wiring system is great for cucumbers, squash, melon, beans, and other climbers.

When it's time to plant seedlings, separate the straw using a trowel to make a planting pocket. Fill the pocket with a sterile planting medium. If you are planting seeds, spread a 2-inch layer of planting medium over the bale.

Plant some herbs and annual flowers along with your veggies to create a pretty, pollinator-friendly garden. Lay a soaker hose on top of bales to help with watering.

When harvest season rolls around, the bales will be gray and soggy. They will continue to decompose nicely after you harvest your veggies. Use the rich compost next year in other garden areas and even containers.

Perennial crops: Plant once and harvest every year

Although most vegetable plants grow for only a season, some return each year just as luscious and tasty. Perennial food crops are a great complement to annual crops as they extend the growing season on either end. That means more fresh food for your family throughout the year.

Once planted, perennial food crops are low-maintenance and help to enrich the soil. Here are some popular ones you can try.

Rhubarb. During the first year, rhubarb works to put down deep roots. Most rhubarb plants last up to 20 years. Enjoy the stalks year after year, but don't eat the leaves as they are poisonous.

Asparagus. Asparagus is happy in the sun and well-draining soil. When planted in a good location, it will grow tall spears for at least 10 years.

Although kale is typically grown as an annual, it will regrow each season given the proper care. At the end of the harvest season, cut kale plants down to about 1 inch above the soil, and cover with several inches of mulch. In the spring, it will begin to regrow.

Jerusalem artichoke. Also called sunroot, earth apple, or sunchoke, it is a drought-tolerant sunflower species native to central North America. The white tuber that is produced by sunroot can be harvested all winter and eaten raw or cooked.

Horseradish. Grated horseradish adds a nice zip to any meal. As long as the ground will allow, you can harvest horseradish. This plant is in the same family as cabbage, Brussels sprouts, and broccoli but is much hardier than any of them.

Egyptian onions. Also known as walking onions, these plants set small bulbs at each plant. These are small edible onions. As the bluish-green stalks grow and become heavy, they fall over, touching the soil to create new roots and grow another plant. One of these top-set onions can make as many as six more plants each year.

Berry bushes. Don't overlook the bounty in berry bushes such as strawberries, blackberries, and raspberries. Once berry plants get going, you will have an endless supply of tasty fruit each season. Be sure to include a good variety of berry bushes in your home garden.

Feeding secrets: give your plants a natural boost

No. 1 thing to do to keep your plants happy and healthy

If plants could talk, they would remind us that they get hungry, too, and need regular feeding to do their best. Sadly, a recent poll revealed most gardeners don't pay close enough attention to their plants' feeding needs.

The truth is, you have no better way to improve the health, vibrancy, and productivity of your plants than to provide them with a balanced diet that also feeds and builds up the soil. Your plants will be more extensive, produce more flowers and fruit, and better handle drought and other severe weather, pests, and diseases.

In the natural world, plants receive their nutrition from:

- decomposing organic matter that is converted into simple useable elements by a host of microorganisms.

- inorganic materials in mineral form, including rocks, sand, or clay.

Most soil, however, is over-tilled, compacted, flooded, or exposed to chemicals — sapping it of the nutrients it needs to produce healthy plants. Without the necessary elements for survival, plants are unable to complete their normal life cycle.

Even if you have great soil to start with, as plants mature they take up nutrients, leaving the soil less and less fertile. Focus on giving them these super nutrients for a garden you can enjoy year round.

Top 3 nutrients plants need to survive. Plants need three significant nutrients or macronutrients to thrive — nitrogen (N), phosphorus (P), and potassium (K). Together, these nutrients are NPK. When you purchase fertilizer, you will see ratios of each on the product label.

- Nitrogen helps plants make the proteins they need to create new tissues.

- Phosphorus stimulates root growth while helping plants to set both buds and flowers. It also improves vitality by increasing seed size.

- Potassium promotes health and vibrancy. This nutrient is necessary for plants to make carbohydrates. It also regulates metabolic activities and provides disease resistance.

Don't forget these helpers. Plants also need three additional secondary nutrients in smaller amounts, including calcium (Ca), magnesium (Mg), and sulfur (S). Healthy soil, rich in organic matter, often contains the essential micronutrients boron (B), iron (Fe), zinc (Zn), manganese (Mn), chlorine (Cl), and molybdenum (Mo).

Organic vs. synthetic — which should you choose?

Organic and synthetic fertilizers both provide nutrients but in dramatically different ways. Organic fertilizers contain naturally occurring mineral deposits and organic material like bone, composted manure, or plant meal. Synthetic fertilizers contain chemically processed raw materials.

Here are some pros and cons of both types of fertilizers to help you choose the best one for your garden.

Organic fertilizers	
Pros	**Cons**
minimal processing	a slow release of nutrients
sustainable, biodegradable, earth-friendly	nutrient ratios are not guaranteed
enriches the soil	requires warmth and moisture to work
improves the ability of soil to hold water	
safe for children and pets	
very hard to burn plants	

Synthetic fertilizers	
Pros	**Cons**
fast-acting	may require multiple applications
ensures specific nutrient ratios	potential buildup of toxic materials
can be applied quickly to a large area	can deplete nutrients from the soil
	not earth-friendly
	may harm pets and children

Top 3 organic options for healthy soil

So you've decided to go with organic plant food. Now you must sort through all the types of organic fertilizers and choose the best combination to nurture your plants.

While all-purpose chemical fertilizers exist, you won't find one "do-all" organic fertilizer. You'll need a combination of various types of organic matter to get the job done. Here are three that top the list.

Aged compost. Compost makes a dramatic difference in soil health while it adds valuable nutrients. Composting is easy — anyone can do it — and it basically turns scraps headed for the trash into valuable food for rich soil and healthy plants. As a bonus, it is free and good for the earth.

Manure. Cow manure is one of the best things you can add to a large or small garden space. It is also extremely easy to mix into the top several inches of soil. Chicken manure is the perfect superfood for plants in a highly concentrated fashion. Use only well-aged manure and make sure it is free from weed seeds before spreading it in your garden.

Fish fertilizer. Fish fertilizer consists of whole fish and carcass parts, including bones, skin, and scales. Rather than letting unusable fish products go to waste, fish parts become garden nutrients. Fish fertilizer provides essential nutrients for plants and is an excellent source of burn-free nitrogen and the primary nutrients phosphorus and potassium.

> Turn a 5-gallon plastic bucket into an indoor compost station. Drill a few holes in the lid for airflow. Add compostable materials to the bucket along with a handful of shredded paper to keep the compost from getting too soggy. Keep the materials in the bucket well-mixed using a wooden paint stick.

Another fertilizer decision and how to make it

Organic vs. synthetic is not the only decision you need to make when it comes to fertilizing your garden. You also need to decide whether to use plant-based or animal-based foods. Check out these features to help you choose what's best for your garden.

- Plant-based organic fertilizers break down more rapidly than other organic material and offer some quick nutrients along with some trace minerals. They are top of the class when it comes to conditioning the soil. Examples include alfalfa meal, corn gluten meal, kelp/seaweed, and soybean meal.

- Animal-based organic fertilizers add a great deal of nitrogen and are especially valuable for leafy plants and strong growth early in the gardening season. Examples of animal-based fertilizers include livestock manure, worm castings, fish and fish byproducts, and exotic manure from animals like bats, birds, and wild cats.

Potted-plant challenges and feeding hacks that work

When it comes to feeding, container plants need a little extra love because of their own unique set of challenges. These include:

- confined roots. Potted plants do not have the luxury of spreading their roots out far and wide, searching for water and nutrients.

- soilless planting mixes. Many lightweight potting mixes do not contain any soil but are composed of materials such as coconut coir, peat, and perlite. These materials provide good drainage but have few, if any, nutrients to offer plants. Soilless planting mixes contain no beneficial microbes.

Knowing these challenges, it is vital you commit to your container plants' regular feedings. Feed outdoor container plants twice a week and indoor plants once a week with organic, water-soluble plant food.

Need some ideas? Surpisingly, many things you think are garbage make great plant fertilizer. Here are some foods you should toss into your potted plants instead of in the trash can.

- Cooking water. Don't pour your cooking water down the drain. Save it, cool it, and use it to enrich your potted plants. Veggie water or egg water is best.

- Eggshells. Chicken eggshells contain calcium, which is essential for the development of a healthy cell structure. Pour boiling water over eggshells and let them steep for 24 hours. Use the water to supercharge your potted plants.

> To encourage earthworm activity and enrich your soil, grind eggshells into a fine powder, and work them into your garden beds. Earthworms need the grit to digest their food, and ground-up eggshells are an excellent source. Plants thrive on earthworm castings, so being kind to your worms will reap you bigger and healthier plants.

- Used coffee grounds. For a nitrogen punch, dry your used coffee grounds and provide potted plants with 1 to 2 tablespoons, followed by a good, healthy watering once a week.

- Banana peel. Forget expensive fertilizers for your garden. Old banana peels work as well for growing fabulous flowers and yummy veggies. Bananas contain potassium, which helps potted plants become strong and grow healthy roots, flowers, and leaves. Simply add a banana peel to a blender with one quart of water. Feed your container plants with this mixture two times a week and mature plants once a week for best results.

4 strange but effective foods plants will gobble up

It's like five-star dining to your plants. Mix up these simple household ingredients, and treat your plants to a healthy feast.

Unflavored gelatin. It may be surprising, but unflavored gelatin is an excellent plant fertilizer, especially for indoor plants.

It is rich in nitrogen and slowly releases a healthy dose to protect plant roots.

Just be sure you use unflavored gelatin only as the flavored kind contains added sugars, dyes, and chemicals that can damage plants.

Coconut water. Coconut water is an excellent source of calcium, magnesium, and trace minerals that plants love. Additionally, coconut water contains electrolytes that encourage healthy bacteria to thrive within the soil.

Plants that are fed coconut water grow faster and healthier than those watered with plain water. Mix 1 tablespoon of dried coconut powder in 5 gallons of water, and let it sit at room temperature for a day before you water your plants.

Blackstrap molasses. Blackstrap molasses is the byproduct of the sugar cane refining process and a great source of calcium, magnesium, and potassium for plants. Molasses does more than keep plants healthy — it also encourages the growth of garden-friendly microorganisms, which is good for the entire garden.

To use blackstrap molasses as fertilizer, dilute a half cup of blackstrap in a gallon of water. Put the elixir in a spray bottle and spritz on the soil. If crops are flowering, spritz the roots to boost your yield.

White vinegar. This vinegar is a perfect snack for acid-loving plants. While discouraging weed growth, it keeps pests away and helps curtail the spread of fungus.

To amend the pH level of the soil, be sure to test your soil first. If the pH is already low, it is not necessary to add vinegar. If it needs to be lowered, mix a tablespoon of white vinegar in a gallon of water, and feed acid-loving plants like roses, hydrangeas, gardenias, azaleas, and rhododendrons.

My plants are wilting — could I be fertilizing too much?

Like anything, too much of a good thing can end in disaster, and fertilizing is no exception. Yes, you can love your plants too much.

- Plants that are slightly damaged from too much fertilizer will look wilted or just generally unwell.

- Burned plants that have been seriously compromised will have brown leaves that collapse from the outside edges inward. You may also notice a salty crust forming on the soil surface. That's because fertilizer salts have built up in the tissues, and there has not been enough water to flush them out because the roots are damaged.

What can you do? At this point, it is essential to flood your garden with long and deep waterings. But don't let the water run off, as it could contaminate local water sources for wildlife.

Flush potted plants that have been overfed as well using the same method — long and deep. Repeat the long and deep waterings daily until you see improvement in your plant's health.

To avoid overfeeding plants, you must know what your plant's feeding needs are. Pay careful attention to not only the type and amount of feed but the timing of feedings.

You can also try a slow-release fertilizer that does not shock the plant all at once. One of the best ways to prevent fertilizer burn is to use an organic feed such as compost.

---

5 kitchen scrap throwaways plants love to eat

Americans live in a throwaway culture where reusing and recycling things is not second nature. The United States wastes about 1.3 billion tons of food annually — about one-third of all the food produced in the world.

If you'd like to help solve this problem, think about turning your trash into treasure. Here are five common kitchen scraps that can save you money and reduce food waste while providing a safe, natural alternative to store-bought fertilizers.

Tea bags. Tea leaves contain tannic acid and other nutrients that are natural fertilizers for your garden. As the bag decomposes, it releases nutrients into the soil. You can also rebrew a tea bag to create a weak tea to pour on potted plants.

Vegetable scraps. These make a great addition to any compost pile, but there are other ways you can use them to feed hungry plants.

One easy way is to make a veggie scrap plant food tonic. Cut peels into small pieces and liquefy in a blender with water. Pour this solution into the soil around plants. As everything decomposes, the nutrients will become available for plants to use.

Leftover coffee. You hear a lot about using spent coffee grounds in the garden, but you can also use the leftover coffee that has sat in your coffee pot for a few days.

Just like coffee grounds, that old coffee is an excellent source of nitrogen. It also contains calcium and magnesium, which are both beneficial to plants. Combine a quarter cup of old coffee with a cup of water, and use it to feed container plants and plants in your veggie garden.

Greywater. How often do you think about the thousands of gallons of water that trickle down your drain daily? Greywater is the wastewater from sinks and bathtubs, and plants and lawns love it.

But it only works if you use all-organic soap and personal care products. The water used to wash fruits and vegetables is best because it contains valuable nutrients plants need to thrive. Use dishwashing water on ornamental flowers and lawns.

Sardine juice. Do you love to eat sardines? If so, your plants are in luck. Keep the juice when done eating these fish, and use it to fertilize your garden plants.

Only purchase sardines packed in water, and go for the highest quality product you can find. This fish fertilizer is rich in organic elements that feed not only plants but also soil microbes.

Save by making your own bone meal fertilizer

Bone meal is a nutrient-dense substance that is usually made by steaming and grinding animal bones. It is useful for fortifying soil with trace amounts of potassium and nitrogen and high amounts of calcium and phosphorus.

Vegetable plants will benefit from an annual application of bone meal at a rate of 10 pounds per 100 square feet. It is especially beneficial for root crops such as onions, carrots, radishes, parsnips, and turnips.

Bone meal is an excellent part of a blanched organic fertilizer program for bulbs, roses, and other plants that benefit from phosphorus's slow release. One application will feed plants for four months.

> Make bone meal tea by mixing 2 tablespoons of bone meal to 1 gallon of steeped manure or compost tea. Allow the mixture to sit overnight and apply it to plants. This healthy drink is perfect for plants deprived of nitrogen and phosphorus.

Here's how to make your bone meal at home.

What you need:

- pressure cooker
- large container with a lid
- soil tester
- mallet
- tool to remove fat
- grinder
- bleach
- lots of bones — turkey, beef, chicken, pork

How to make it:

1. Remove all meat and fat from bones.

2. Bake bones at 450 degrees F until they are dry and brittle — about one hour. Let them cool.

3. Transfer bones to a bag or sack, and beat them with a mallet to crush.

4. Transfer pieces to a grinder, and grind until they become a fine powder.

5. Store in a container with a lid.

6. Test your soil before applying.

Winter trick for super summer fertilizer

How often do you clean the hair off of your brush? What do you do with your shaving clippings? If you save them for your garden, your plants will love you.

Human hair has more nitrogen than manure and is incredibly beneficial to plants. It provides structural support for roots, breaks up clay soil, and slowly releases nutrients and nitrogen into the soil.

Gather hair from your family members all winter long, and keep it in a container. You'll have lawn and garden fertilizer all summer for free.

But be careful. Unless you use organic hair products, this plant food is best for ornamental — not food — plants.

Energize your garden with a sweet treat

Treat your soil to this "sweet" and it will reward you with a bonanza of blooms come spring.

Everyone loves honey, and your soil and flowering, fruiting, and annual plants are no exception. This sweet feed has antibacterial and antifungal properties that will help keep disease at bay while giving plants a valuable energy boost.

Honey also feeds beneficial bacteria and fungi in the soil. Using honey on fruiting plants will result in a sweeter harvest — literally.

Whisk 2 tablespoons of raw, local honey into 8 cups of water. Apply it the same way you would water your plants. For potted plants, pour into the soil until you see it draining out the bottom. Apply once every two weeks.

Warning — do not use this honey treat if you are dealing with ants in your garden. They love it too.

Nutrient cravings: What your plant is trying to tell you

When your plants crave a particular nutrient, you'll see a few telltale signs. Knowing what to look for will help you provide the perfect snack to satisfy your plant.

Deficiency	Symptom	Fix
nitrogen	pale and yellow leaves along with stunted growth	add used coffee grounds to soil, or plant nitrogen-rich plants next to nitrogen-deficient plants
phosphorus	darkening around leaf edges, small or negligible leaves, and stunted growth	add bone meal or fish tank water (freshwater) directly to the soil
potassium	leaves develop brown spots, brown and yellow veins, or yellow edges	bury banana peels into the soil
magnesium	veins and edges of leaves become yellow and sometimes marbled in appearance	sprinkle Epsom salts on top of the soil and water well
calcium	yellow spots develop between leaf veins, and stems become weak or die; stunted growth and blossom end rot may develop	work crushed eggshells into the soil

How to use this 100% free fertilizer for beautiful plants

An organic garden has a wonderful cycle of life where nutrients stored within plants can be returned to the soil to be used by other plants. Creating a nutrient-dense tea from plants and weeds is an easy and effective way to nurture your garden.

Here are three tea recipes that upcycle green material and provide loads of nutrients for hungry garden plants.

Dandelion tea. If you have spent much time trying to rid your yard of dandelions, you know just how hard they can be to pull out. Their hardy tap roots go deep and fill up with an abundance of nutrients.

Even though they are considered weeds, dandelions are highly valuable plants that are also edible. They are rich in potassium, which is excellent for fruiting plants.

Yarrow tea. Yarrow also has an incredible storage tank of nutrients. It attracts pollinators and has useful medicinal properties. Yarrow is a gold mine of nutrients including phosphates, copper, sulfur, potassium, and others that plants love.

Comfrey tea. Growing comfrey in your garden for the sole purpose of making plant tea is an excellent idea. Comfrey is a fast-growing plant whose roots and leaves have been used in traditional medicine for centuries. Comfrey is rich in potassium and other essential nutrients.

To make these teas:

1. Add plant material to a bucket.
2. Cover the plant material with water, and let the tea steep for two weeks.
3. Strain the mixture, tossing the solids into your outdoor compost pile.
4. Dilute teas with 10 parts water, and feed plants.

Triple your tea's nutritional power

Want to make your tea even more powerful? Brew it with multiple plants. Using three or more plants to make the tea offers a greater diversity of nutrients. Here are some options for a mixed-brew tea made of plants often considered to be weeds.

Plant	Nutrients
alfalfa	nitrogen and iron
purslane	calcium, potassium, and iron
tansy	phosphorus
burdock	iron
lamb's quarters	nitrogen, phosphorus, and potassium
chamomile	calcium, potassium, and phosphorus

Easy-to-make plant food does the trick

You won't believe what you can put in your garden soil that works just like expensive organic fertilizer you can buy.

This all-purpose food does wonders for both potted and garden plants of all kinds. It contains just the right balance of nutrients that plants need to grow big and beautiful. Here's what you'll need.

- 4 parts seed meal
- 1/4 part gypsum
- 1/2 part dolomite lime
- 1 part bone meal
- 1 part kelp meal
- 1/4 part calcium carbonate, finely ground

Mix all parts and apply them. For best results, add 4 to 6 quarts per 100 square feet or half a cup per 10-gallon potted plant.

Super feeding secret for bigger and better roses

Roses add a delicate and beautiful elegance to any garden space. To maximize the blooming potential of your roses, it is essential to keep them healthy and well-fed.

Along with the primary nutrients that all plants need — nitrogen, phosphorus, and potassium — roses benefit from micronutrients, including calcium, sulfur, boron, copper, iron, manganese, zinc, and magnesium.

Your roses will be gorgeous when you know this fertilizing secret recipe.

What you need:

- 3 cups of water

- 2 tablespoons powdered fish

- 1 tablespoon Epsom salts

- 1 tablespoon kelp extract

- 2 tablespoons molasses

- 2 tablespoons apple cider vinegar

How to make it:

1. Combine all ingredients.

2. During the summer months, apply a half gallon of this mixture in the evening after you have watered your roses. Repeat every six weeks until the end of summer. This will keep your roses blooming right up until frost.

Unique way to feed your plants

Have you heard of foliar feeding? It's a technique of feeding plants by applying liquid fertilizer directly to their leaves. Plants absorb essential elements through their leaves and bark. Here are some best practice tips for foliar feeding.

- Apply foliar feed in the early morning when the air is cool.

- Spray plants until you see the spray dripping from the leaves.

- Add a tiny bit of horticultural oil to your foliar spray to help it stick better to the leaves.

- Use a foliar spray as a short-term solution for stressed plants.

For a quick-mix foliar feed, try Epsom salts. This magnesium sulfate compound encourages healthy plant growth by helping plants take in valuable nutrients like nitrogen and phosphorus. It will improve blooming and make your plant a beautiful vibrant green.

To make an Epsom salts foliar spray, dissolve 2 tablespoons of plain Epsom salts in one gallon of water. Pour into a spray bottle, shake well, and spray plants once a month.

Grass and groundcovers for a beautiful lawn

4 'good' things that may harm your grass

Sadly, many of the "good" things you have been doing to your lawn are counterproductive and can cause harm. Have you been guilty of any of these while trying to cultivate the perfect lawn?

Raking leaves. If you think that not raking leaves is better for your lawn and trees than picking them up, you are right. Many people spend countless hours raking leaves into big piles and disposing of them, so their grass looks neat and tidy.

Thankfully, you can spare yourself this back-breaking chore because leaves are loaded with organic material that breaks down like a slow-release fertilizer, feeding your lawn all winter long.

Leaves can even help suppress annoying weeds. For best results, use a mulching mower to break leaves down, giving them a head start.

Mulching lawn clippings. While mulching leaves is a good thing, mulching lawn clippings is not. Contrary to what you might have heard, leaving grass clippings on your lawn does not result in thatch buildup. Leaving the clippings on is quite useful for your grass, returning much-needed moisture and nutrients to the soil.

Overfeeding. Yes, too much of a good thing is bad when it comes to fertilizing your lawn. Testing your soil is the perfect way to know just how much fertilizer your lawn needs. Overfeeding your yard can cause nitrogen and salt levels to increase, which damages or even kills grass.

Forgetting to top-dress. Even established lawns benefit from a healthy top-dressing of organic mulch. Just one teaspoon of organic compost contains a billion beneficial microorganisms that improve soil structure and texture while increasing nutrient, water, and air retention.

Spread a half inch of compost over your grass, and work it into the turf using a leaf rake. Any leftover mulch can be applied to your garden beds.

Winter lawn care steps for the best spring grass ever

One of the biggest mistakes you can make with your lawn is to forget about your grass once the cold temperatures hit. Depending on the part of the country you live in, you may have a combination of warm-season grasses such as zoysia and Bermuda, or cool-season types such as fescue, perennial rye, and Kentucky blue.

When you shovel your driveway, don't pile snow on your grass as it causes compaction. Also, the snow close to the road may be contaminated with salt and other chemicals that can kill your grass. To save the grass along walkways, use cat litter to de-ice as it will not kill your grass like other de-icing products.

Warm grasses thrive in the spring and summer and go dormant in the winter. Cool-season grass does best in the spring and fall and stays on the green side even during the coldest months.

No matter what kind of grass you have, there are some things you can do before and during the winter months to keep your lawn looking its best.

Do this	When	Why	How
aerate	prior to the first frost	to relieve compaction caused by foot traffic and improve nutrient uptake, water retention, and airflow	Use an aerating tool or pitchfork for a small-size yard.
final mow	before it gets too cold	to reduce rodent damage and keep snow mold at bay	Mow summer grasses to 1 to 2 inches and cool-season grasses to 1 to 2.5 inches.
feed	before the ground freezes	to help spring grass look its best	Apply a slow-release winter fertilizer or lime if a soil test shows it's necessary.
remove debris	before snowfall	can hinder drainage and cause compaction, which can lead to damage	Grab a wheelbarrow and pick up and dispose of any debris on your lawn. Repeat if necessary to keep your lawn clean.
seeding/ sodding	when temperature is above freezing	to reduce erosion and compaction	Lay sod or spread seed to cover bare spots and water well. In the South, overseed with ryegrass for a green lawn all winter.
water	when temperature is above 40 degrees F	to reduce the chance of winter drought damage	Water the grass deeply during a winter drought.
weed	on a mild and wet winter day	to reduce the number of weeds in the spring	Pull by hand if in a small area or apply a pre-emergent weed killer.

Consider the pros and cons of installing sod

Are you trying to decide whether to restore your existing lawn or tear it out and start from scratch? If sod is on your radar, it is important to consider both the advantages and disadvantages.

Advantages:

- Quick to establish. When appropriately installed, new sod takes only a few weeks to root and become established.

- Erosion control. Sod offers immediate erosion control when installed on slopes or other trouble spots.

- Flexibility in planting time. Sod can be planted any time during the growing season except when it is super hot.

- Limited weeds. High-quality sod will have few or no weeds and can quickly push out any weeds that sneak in.

- Quick access for foot traffic. As soon as sod sets some roots it is ready for foot traffic, kids, and pets.

Disadvantages:

- High product cost. Sod is more costly when compared to seed for the same area.

- Labor intensive. Proper sod installation is essential to its success, and it can be quite a physical task.

- Restricted choices of grass. You are limited to whatever type of grass local sod farmers are growing.

- Limited transplant time. Fresh sod must be planted as soon as possible after harvest, ideally within 24 hours.

- Different growing conditions. Growing conditions in your yard may be different from what the sod was grown in.

Make your own lawn feed on the cheap

Lawn fertilizer can be costly and, if misapplied, can even cause damage to your grass. Skip the commercial feed and go for something a little more unique. You can make a natural and effective fertilizer from ingredients you probably already have.

Lawn tonic No. 1

- 1 can of beer
- 1 cup baby shampoo
- 1 can regular soda, any kind
- 10 gallons of water

Combine ingredients and pour them into a yard sprayer. Spray weekly throughout the growing season.

Lawn tonic No. 2

- 1 can tomato juice
- 2 cups of water
- 2/3 cup orange juice
- 1/2 cup liquid fabric softener

Combine ingredients and pour them into a yard sprayer. Spray weekly throughout the growing season.

Lawn tonic No. 3

- 1 can of regular beer
- 1 can of regular soda
- 1/2 cup ammonia, household strength
- 1/2 cup mouthwash
- 1/2 cup non-antibacterial dish soap

Combine all of these ingredients, and pour them into a 10-gallon rated hose-end sprayer. Spray the lawn after mowing just enough to get it wet but not saturated. Repeat every three weeks during the growing season.

Best groundcovers for stubborn shady spots

Do you have parts of your lawn that grow well and other parts that disappoint year after year? Likely, these spots that won't grow beautiful green grass are under the overhang of trees or other shaded areas where light is compromised.

The good news is you don't have to struggle with grass that won't grow as you'll find numerous made-for-the-shade groundcovers that will thrive in shaded spots. Here are just a few perennial groundcovers to consider in those hard-to-grow grass areas.

Japanese forest grass. Hardy in zones 4 to 9. The graceful sway of this ornamental grass in the wind is striking. The bamboo-like stems reach a height and width of about 18 inches. This plant is fantastic up against a wall or a fence where grass won't take. As a bonus, Japanese forest grass is deer resistant.

Spotted deadnettle. Hardy in zones 3 to 8. This attractive low-growing plant has beautiful foliage that is topped by pretty pink, purple, or white flowers. Growing to about 6 to 9 inches in height, this hardy perennial boasts thick mats of foliage that quickly fill empty landscape spots.

Creeping liriope. Hardy in zones 4 to 10. Although this liriope can sometimes be invasive, it is perfect for a large shady spot that is troublesome. Attractive variegated foliage surrounds beautiful purple flower spikes that add color and interest to the landscape. Liriope grows up to 18 inches tall and wide and will cover a large area quickly with its grass-like clumps.

Pachysandra. Hardy in zones 5 to 9. This evergreen subshrub has many varieties, with Japanese pachysandra being the most useful landscape plant.

Often called spurge, pachysandra grows up to 12 inches in height and will quickly fill in areas that receive part to full shade. It grows well under large trees and will happily form a thick green mat. Monitor spread by digging and transplanting as necessary.

2 common turf problems you can fix naturally

Even the prettiest and healthiest turf is not immune to problems. Here are two commonly reported issues with grass and what you can do to eliminate the problems naturally.

Dog urine. You love your dog, and you love your grass, but sometimes they don't mix well. If you have small brown spots surrounded by dark green lawn, dog urine is likely the culprit.

Repair the damaged lawn by raking out the dead grass with a hand rake, and drench the entire area with water to get rid of any remaining urine. Add some organic compost to the urine spot and scatter grass seed. Then top with compost and water thoroughly.

One of the best ways to prevent this problem is to create a special place for Fido to urinate. Provide a small graveled, mulched, or even artificial turf area, and train your dog to relieve himself only in that spot.

This easy activity is the simplest and least expensive way to keep your lawn looking lovely. Send for a soil test. It costs as little as $20 and reveals the truth about what is under your grass and what your lawn needs to look its best. Do a test each year and you will have the blueprint to a fantastic-looking lawn.

Grubs. Also called white grubs, lawn worms, or grub beetles, grubs are the larvae of beetles such as Japanese beetles and June bugs. These pests feed on grass roots and organic soil matter.

Doing so can leave brown, dead patches of lawn that are easy to pull out. Here are some things you can do to control the grub population in your yard naturally.

- Encourage more birds to come to your yard. Birds love grubs and will happily peck them up for you.

- Treat your lawn with milky spore, a bacterial disease

that will eliminate grubs from Japanese beetles. Treat your yard a couple of times a year for a few years, and you should be grub-free for up to 15 years.

- Introduce beneficial nematodes. This is an excellent nontoxic grub-removal strategy. Nematodes are parasitic worms that eat a wide variety of garden insects, including grubs. Applying nematodes a couple times a year for a few years will help establish a hardy population to keep grubs at bay.

Natural weed killer gets power from essential oils

You don't have to rely on toxic products to control your weed population. Make your own natural weed killer from these powerful essential oils.

- 1 3/4 cups white vinegar

- 1/4 cup liquid Castile soap

- 3 drops wintergreen essential oil

- 3 drops clove essential oil

- 3 drops cinnamon essential oil

- 3 drops orange essential oil

Combine ingredients in a spray bottle. Spray some of the solution on a clean rag or paper towel, and wipe down any lawn weeds. Spray directly on weeds in cracks in patios or other areas where you don't have grass.

How can I kill weeds without harming my pets?

Pets and poisonous herbicides don't mix. The good news is you have plenty of ways to control weeds and pests in your lawn without harming your furry friends. Here are some of the most popular methods you can safely try.

Pull them out by hand. Get your exercise by pulling weeds by hand as they pop up. The trick is to not let any weed go to seed before snatching it out of the ground. Use a wig digger tool for troublesome and deep weeds.

Vanquish them with vinegar. Pure white vinegar sprayed directly on weeds in the heat of the day will kill them. To keep from damaging delicate grass surrounding the weed, dampen a rag with vinegar, and carefully wipe over the entire weed.

Mix up a spray. Eliminate broadleaf weeds like dandelions that thrive in the sun. Mix 1 cup of vodka with 6 cups of water and a teaspoon of dish soap in a spray bottle. Spray directly on weeds, being careful not to spray anything else.

Cover them up. Covering low-growing weeds like crabgrass and clover with newspaper will starve them of sunlight and stop their spread. You can also use mulch to do the same thing.

Create a barrier. Sprinkle some baking soda along the edge of the grass and planting beds to create a weed buffer, keeping the powder at least 6 inches away from plants you want to keep.

Organic weed control? Try this super corn byproduct

As more people search for a nontoxic way to control weeds before they happen, corn gluten meal has become a popular choice.

Corn gluten meal can be found at most local garden shops.

But they're not all the same. Look for one that contains 60% protein and is labeled as an organic herbicide.

The key to success is to use corn gluten meal as a weed suppression agent before weeds start to grow. Annual and perennial weed seeds generally sprout in late spring to early summer, so it is crucial to get the cornmeal gluten on the lawn before this happens.

An application in late spring and early summer will help control weeds when used over time. Be patient — it may take a couple of years of treatment before you see results.

Be sure to water deeply after applying the cornmeal gluten to activate the oils that suppress weed growth.

Choose the best type of grass seed for your yard

How should you decide what type of grass to grow in your yard? It depends mostly on the region you live. (See map below.) You also need to consider the amount of sun in your yard and the type of foot traffic you will have on your turf.

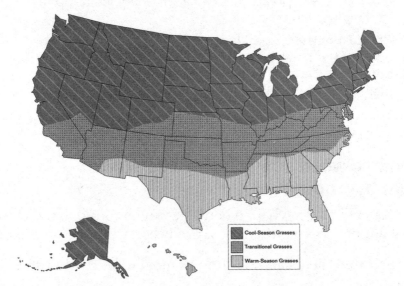

Cool-Season Grasses
Transitional Grasses
Warm-Season Grasses

Basically there are two broad categories of grass — warm-season grass and cool-season grass. Some areas of the country, as seen in the map on the previous page, are called transitional zones and require a mix of both types of grass. But generally cool-season grasses do best in this area.

Cool season grasses			
Grass type	**Soil**	**Light**	**Foot traffic**
tall fescue	any	full sun, part shade	high tolerance
fine fescue	any	full sun, full shade	light tolerance
Kentucky bluegrass	neutral pH	full sun	light tolerance
perennial ryegrass	any	full sun	high tolerance

Warm season grasses			
Grass type	**Soil**	**Light**	**Foot traffic**
Bermuda	light	full sun	high tolerance
St. Augustine	sandy	full sun, partial shade	high tolerance
centipede	tolerates acidic	full sun, partial shade	light tolerance
zoysia	slightly acidic	full sun, partial shade	high tolerance
bahia	any	full sun, moderate shade	moderate tolerance

Water hacks keep your grass green and your bills low

When it comes to grass, there is nothing more important than understanding how, when, and how much water to use. If you have water restrictions in your area or just want to cut down a huge bill, it's essential to learn how to water less while still keeping a green lawn.

Thankfully, several simple water practices help you give your lawn the water it needs without the significant expense and wasted water you don't want.

Install an irrigation system. A simple irrigation system for a small lawn is not difficult to install. Even if you have someone else install it, you'll quickly recoup the money you spend over a couple of seasons with all the water you'll save.

Irrigation systems deliver water only where your landscape needs it, so there is little water waste. You can even get an irrigation system with smart technology based on your local weather forecast. For instance, if it rains one day, irrigation will skip a day because water is not needed.

Capture the rain. One of the best ways to save money on your water bill is to capture your water from the sky each time it rains. Carefully positioned rain barrels around your home can yield a tremendous amount of valuable water when installed correctly.

Rain barrels placed under the downspouts coming off your roof will fill up quickly with just one good rain. For example, a 2,000-square-foot roof in an area with an average rainfall of 25 inches per year can yield as much as 28,000 gallons of water per year.

You can tie your water collection system into your irrigation system to offset city water use.

Water at the right time. When it comes to lowering your utility bills, it's all about timing. For example, wind can cause up to 300 gallons of water to evaporate from your lawn. So you're better off waiting for a calmer day to water.

The time of day matters too. The absolute best time of day to water your grass is early in the morning between 6 a.m. and 10 a.m. If you water in midday, much of it will evaporate. Nighttime watering can cause small droplets to cling to the grass overnight, which can encourage lawn disease to develop.

Make your own super-easy seed spreader

Commercial spreaders, found at the store, can be expensive. This upcycled homemade grass-seed spreader can save you money and is super easy to make.

What you need:

- large empty coffee can with plastic lid

- safety glasses

- nail and hammer

How to make it:

> Supercharge grass seed's sprouting power. Dissolve 1 tablespoon of Epsom salts in a gallon of weak tea water, then mix in 1/4 cup baby shampoo. Add the seeds, and soak them in the refrigerator for 48 hours.

1. Put on your safety glasses.

2. Turn the coffee can upside down on a flat surface.

3. Make one row of holes using a small nail and hammer.

4. Make a second row of holes that offsets the first row.

5. Put the lid on the bottom of the can and turn it upright.

6. Pour a little grass seed into the can.

7. Remove the lid and test the spreader by sprinkling the seeds over a newspaper. Adjust the holes as necessary.

Earth-friendly alternatives to a grassy lawn

Water restrictions, coupled with increasingly warm and dry weather in many parts of the country, have led people to seek different, eco-friendly options to a sprawling and thirsty turf lawn.

Native and eco-friendly plants are becoming the new lawn as more and more people embrace their beauty and resistance.

Here are some great natural options for making your yard more attractive. The best part? They will cut your watering bill in half.

Corsican mint. Hardy in zones 7 to 9, it will freeze in other areas but will self-seed in springtime. This mint not only smells fantastic, but it is a great flowering turfgrass alternative.

Small green and rounded leaves set a beautiful backdrop for tiny purple flowers. Mint is known to be incredibly invasive. However, this type is a fairly well-behaved creeper that won't take over overnight.

As a small lawn alternative, plant Corsican mint in areas that don't receive a lot of foot traffic in fertile soil in either sun or part shade.

Creeping thyme. Hardy in zones 4 to 9, creeping thyme can be planted as a turf alternative in areas that receive a lot of foot traffic. This low-maintenance herb grows 2 to 4 inches high and requires no mowing and very little water.

Creeping thyme will grow in full sun, partial sun, or even full shade, making it a highly versatile alternative to grass.

Clover. Hardy in zones 3 to 9, perennial clover is often planted as a nitrogen-fixing cover crop, but it is also an ideal eco-friendly turf alternative.

Clover has many things going for it, such as its ability to aerate the soil with its deep roots while choking out weeds in its way.

Although clover requires water a couple of times a week when young, once established, it begs for little and stays green all year without the need for fertilization.

For a wild, color-infused ground cover, plant red clover and yellow blossom types. They will grow up to 36 inches and provide a beautiful and tall wild look. Dutch white clover has a neater appearance so you may want to use it in place of a traditional lawn.

Evergreen moss. Hardy in all but the coldest places like Antarctica, moss stays green all year long and is perfect for shady areas where common lawn grass won't grow.

Moss prefers compacted soil and requires no water, no weeding, and no feeding. Just let it be and it will please. As a bonus, moss is pest resistant.

If moss appeals to you, you'll find many varieties to choose from. Some grow in clumps and others spread like a lush carpet. They come in various shades of green from golden to pale and even deep emerald shades.

No. 1 mowing mistake leaves your yard vulnerable

While mowing your grass regularly will keep it looking neat and tidy, mowing too low can cause stress, making it susceptible to weeds, insect damage, and disease. Shaving too much off your turf can damage crowns of the grass plants.

Damaged plants draw energy into healing from the injury, which opens up its weakness. Widespread damage to the plant's crowns makes it hard for a lawn to battle grub and weed infestations.

What's more, short grass offers little shade for the crowns, making it susceptible to heat stress, damaging the grass's natural defenses further.

As a general rule, aim to leave your grass as high as you can to keep it healthy and strong. Mow no more than one-third of the grass's length with each cut, letting the grass grow to at least 4 inches before cutting again.

Maintenance to-do list you don't want to skip

The performance of your lawnmower is critical to the health of your grass. Looking after your mower will help ensure it can do its job to keep your lawn looking its best. Here are some vital tasks to add to your to-do list.

Get your lawnmower a professional tune-up once a year. The money you spend on a tune-up is well worth it and can help you get the most out of your mower.

Sharpen and balance the blades regularly. Dull blades can injure the grass, so keep them sharp and well-balanced for an even cut every time.

Clean grass from under the deck. Every time you mow, it is essential to clean out the undercarriage of your mower to clear it from debris.

Check the oil levels. A mower that is low on oil or has dirty oil will not perform well. Keep the oil clean and topped up according to your owner's manual.

Check the air filter. A dirty air filter can hinder your mower's ability to cut efficiently. Always be sure you operate your mower with a clean filter.

Change the spark plug. Replace the spark plug each year to ensure your mower quickly starts.

Drain the gas before winter. Never let your mower sit all winter with gas in the tank. Run your mower gas out or drain the gas before storing your mower for the off season.

" Tackle hillside erosion like a champ

Dave bought a new house and was excited to cultivate a thick, lush turf. With the front lawn thriving, Dave turned his attention to the moderately steep hillside at the backside of his home.

Every time it rained, more mud and soil washed down the hill. Dave's main concern was to establish erosion control so his entire hillside did not wash away.

He knew he did not want to plant grass that would require mowing or intense maintenance, so he turned his attention to a variety of easy-to-grow groundcover plants that would make the hillside attractive and act as natural erosion control.

He chose English ivy, mondo grass, creeping phlox, and vinca minor to cover the hill — groundcovers that are not only attractive but also practical because of their ability to root and spread easily.

In just two full growing seasons, Dave no longer has erosion issues on his hillside, and the groundcovers he planted are thriving with minimal care. Dave offers this advice for others facing similar challenges.

"Tackling a hillside erosion problem takes a little planning but don't let it scare you. If you are able, select and plant a variety of groundcover plants that will not only help keep the soil in place but also add beauty to your hillside.

"Keep in mind the amount of sunlight your hillside gets, and choose plants that require little maintenance once planted." "

Herbs that heal and add zip to your meal

8 amazing reasons to grow an herb garden

An herb is any plant whose leaves, seeds, or flowers are used for flavoring, dye, food, medicine, or beauty. Herbs are not only beautiful, they are also functional and the perfect addition to your landscape. Here are just some of the reasons why you should consider growing these unique garden plants.

Attract pollinators. Birds, bees, and butterflies love sweet nectar-producing herbs and happily visit your garden when you plant flowering herbs like thyme, rosemary, lavender, and fennel.

Use your homegrown herbs to make a soothing foot soak. Add 1 ounce of dried herbs to 2 cups of water and bring to a boil on the stove. Simmer just below boiling for about 30 minutes. Add to a warm tub of water to relieve your tired and achy feet.

Lure beneficial insects. Herbs attract insects such as lady-bugs and lacewings that keep pests like aphids away. Planting herbs among your vegetables is a great way to keep them healthy and pest-free.

Act as health remedies. Several easy-to-grow herbs have powerful medicinal properties. Some great choices include lemon balm, yarrow, echinacea, and peppermint.

Save you money. Fresh herbs are quite expensive to buy in the grocery store, so growing your own is a cost-effective option. Keep in mind, even herbs at the grocery that are labeled fresh have traveled some distance to reach the store and have lost flavor and nutrition.

Spice up your dinner. What could be better than plucking delicious herbs from your homegrown plants to add fresh and delicious flavors to your culinary delights?

Provide curb appeal. If you want to increase the curb appeal of your home in a practical way, plant herbs. They are beautiful plants that offer high interest and value in the landscape.

Boost your health. Herbs are a fantastic addition to your diet and provide antioxidants, vitamins, and other beneficial properties.

Relieve stress. No doubt about it, cultivating an herb garden with all of its sensory delights is a great way to let down and relax. Merely walking by an herb garden and taking in all the sights, textures, and aroma can wash away your cares.

Warning: Avoid these 9 common mistakes

Although most herbs are pretty easy to grow and fairly forgiving, being aware of these common mistakes will help you produce the healthiest herbs possible.

Choosing unhealthy plants. To increase your chances of success, select healthy and happy plants. Healthy plants are brightly colored, have lots of foliage, and are bug and disease free.

Planting herbs where they are not happy. Herbs, like other plants, have specific requirements for sun, shade, and moisture. For instance, rosemary prefers drier soil and will die if it gets wet feet. Planting herbs that like sun in shady spots will result in disaster.

Improper pruning. Pinching and pruning herbs is an essential part of keeping them healthy. If you don't prune, plants will become tall on just a few stems, and leaves will age and fall off, leaving only the stem. Pruning, pinching, and using herbs keeps the plant in its growth cycle for as long as possible.

Overcrowding. It is critical to know how far apart to plant herbs to accommodate their mature size. Planting too close will stunt growth and interrupt the development of a healthy root system.

> Perk up herbs instantly with this organic and straightforward molasses elixir. Organic unsulphured blackstrap molasses contains micronutrients that herbs love. A bonus is that this formula is also a great way to keep pests at bay. Combine 1/2 cup molasses to 1 gallon of water, and feed tired herbs 1/4 cup once a week.

Using chemicals. Because you are most likely using and eating herbs, it is not good to use any chemicals around or on the herbs. Choose organic pest and weed control only.

Letting flowers go to seed. Although many herbs have beautiful and edible flowers, don't let them go to seed during the growing season. It will stunt the plant's life cycle. If your herbs start to bud, pinch them off to redirect the energy to the foliage.

Watering improperly. Most herbs require minimal water, but it's crucial to know your plants' exact water needs. Water herbs in the early morning and avoid getting the foliage wet.

Neglecting to feed them. Once your herbs are up and growing, it is critical to feed them using an organic fertilizer. Compost tea is an excellent option and provides a significant nutritional boost for the growing cycle.

Ignoring signs of distress. Although most herbs are not difficult to grow, once planted, it is good to keep an eye on them as they mature. Check the soil for any leaf debris and the foliage for signs of distress. Leaves and stems that are brown, curled, or wrinkled may be a sign of trouble that needs immediate attention.

Save cuttings in fun-to-make fat bombs

Make delicious herb bombs using ice cube trays, and enjoy your fresh herbs all year long. Here's what you'll need.

- fresh herbs such as rosemary, thyme, basil, oregano, and thyme

- olive oil

- silicone ice cube tray

Wash and pat herbs dry, and chop them into small pieces. Pack the herbs into the ice cube molds. Fill about three-quarters full. Pour oil on top, and use a fork to press the herbs into the mold.

Cover the tray with plastic wrap, and put it in the freezer for several hours or until solid. Pop the fat bombs out and place them in a freezer-proof container.

When ready to use in your favorite dish, grab a couple of bombs and drop them in to add a burst of flavor.

Spiral garden gives herbs the perfect spot to grow

Spiral herb gardens became popular years ago when living a self-sufficient life became popular. This space-saving design allows sun-loving herbs to grow on one side and those that prefer more shade to grow on the shadier north side.

Constructing a spiral herb garden is relatively cheap and easy. And who can resist the creative spiral design?

What you need:

- cardboard

- fine gravel

- bricks

- stake with 3 feet of string tied to a lightweight piece of bamboo

- organic matter such as mushroom compost, worm castings, straw, coconut coir, and mulch

- organic compost

- rock minerals and organic fertilizer

- herb seedlings

- rake and shovel

How to make it:

1. Select a location. A flat spot that receives at least five hours a day of sunlight is best. Orient the bottom of your spiral on the northern side. This will allow you to place plants to meet their sun and water requirements.

2. Bang the stake into the central part of your spiral. Stretch out the attached string and mark the circle. The average diameter is 6.25 feet or 3.25 feet from the center.

3. If creating the spiral on a grassy or weedy area, you will need to kill the weeds first. Using cardboard is an inexpensive way to do it. Overlap the edges and fill in the entire circle. Soak the cardboard thoroughly.

4. Cover the cardboard with several inches of fine gravel and rake it flat.

5. Start laying bricks on the outside edge, working inwards. Leave a 1.5-foot width for planting as you make the spiral shape. Remember that your spiral's outer wall is the lowest point and should increase as you reach the center of the spiral.

6. Once you have the basic shape complete, begin adding organic materials and compost. Mix in some rock minerals and organic fertilizer as you go.

7. Plant moisture-loving herbs at the bottom of the spiral. Plant those that are heat-loving at the top of the spiral.

8. Water all plants well, and top with compost for a beautiful finished look.

Delicious rosemary butter adds zip to your dishes

Once you make homemade herbal butter, you won't want anything else. With only three ingredients and easy directions, this herb butter brings a zip of flavor to rice, pasta, meat dishes, and more.

Mix the following ingredients.

- 2 cups cream, preferably fresh

- salt

- dried rosemary (or herb of your choice)

Add cream to a blender and blend well. The cream will turn into whipped cream first and form stiff peaks before finally turning into butter. When the solids separate from the liquids, it is ready. The liquid part is buttermilk, which you can save to use later.

It's essential to take out all the buttermilk. If you don't, your butter will spoil sooner than it should. Drain the buttermilk from the butter before rinsing it with ice-cold water. The water will look milky, so repeat this until it turns clear. Add salt and dried rosemary.

Roll the butter into a log or pop it into a butter dish and chill. This butter will keep for up to three weeks in the refrigerator or frozen for six months.

Herbal pest control secret you need to know

Herbs that have a strong fragrance are the best bet when it comes to natural pest control. Plant these odiferous herbs in between your veggie rows to keep pesky pests at bay.

Herbs	Insects and pests deterred	Plant close to
hyssop	cabbage moth	cabbage family, orchards, grapevines; avoid planting near radishes
basil	flies, mosquitoes	tomato; avoid planting near rue
garlic	Japanese beetle, aphids, other insects and blight	tomato, eggplant, cabbage family plants; avoid planting near peas, beans, and other legumes
rosemary	cabbage moth, bean beetle, carrot fly	beans, cabbage family plants, carrots
sage	cabbage moth, carrot fly	plant with perennial vegetables; avoid planting with cucumbers and rue
peppermint	cabbage moth, ants	cabbage, tomato
thyme	cabbage worm	eggplant, cabbage, potato, tomato, almost all vegetables and herbs
catnip	flea beetles, spittlebugs, ants, Japanese beetles, weevils	all plants

Repel moths with a quick-and-easy sachet

Keeping moths out of your attic or wardrobe can be challenging. Instead of using mothballs, try this spicy herbal moth repellent that works.

Combine the following ingredients.

- 1/2 pound lavender leaves

- 1/2 ounce each of dried thyme and mint

- 1/4 ounce each of ground cloves and caraway

- 1 ounce sea salt

Pour the mixture into a linen bag, tie it, and hang in your attic, hope chest, or wardrobe to protect your clothing and linens.

Mint: Ancient herb that does it all

Mint is a beautiful herb to include in your herb garden and home landscape. You can pick from over 600 types, including chocolate mint, pineapple mint, spearmint, orange mint, apple mint, and peppermint.

This ancient herb is amazingly easy to grow and good for so much more than cooking. From improving digestion to repelling pests, mint packs a mean punch against your biggest bothers. The secret ingredient — menthol.

Plant mint in your garden and you'll not only ward off pests like aphids, cabbage moths, and ants, you'll be ready whenever these health problems crop up, too.

Head throbbing? Soothe it with a minty blend. Menthol helps relieve both tension headaches and migraines. So instead of popping a painkiller every time a headache crops up, try dabbing one of these mixtures on your forehead.

- Add peppermint essential oil to a carrier oil like sweet almond. It will tone down the blend so it doesn't irritate your skin.

- If you don't have an oil, make some peppermint tea. Wait for it to cool, then apply with a wash cloth.

Tea takes the heat out of sunburn. Summer fun can come to a standstill when sunburn comes to town. But menthol calms a sunburn by cooling and refreshing your skin. To take the sting out of the burn, make a strong peppermint tea. Apply the cooled mixture to the burned area with a cloth.

Mint cools off cold symptoms. Menthol relieves your cough and sore throat by interfering with cold-sensing nerves and the cough reflex. But it does more than that. It also acts as a decongestant, thinning mucus and breaking up phlegm.

Make a mint steam treatment for instant relief. Boil a pot of water, turn off the heat, and add a few drops of peppermint essential oil or a handful of mint leaves. Then lean over the pot and breathe in.

Help, how can I keep mint from taking over my garden?

Although they vary in different ways, mint plants all share one common thing — they can be aggressive.

When you first plant mint, it develops bushy upright clumps. However, if left alone, it will spread rapidly via underground horizontal runners and rhizomes. A small peppermint plant can turn into a significant sprawling plant within just one year.

Here are four ways to handle mint's aggressive growth habit.

Plant it in containers. All mint plants do well in container gardens requiring moist soil and protection from the hot afternoon sun. One advantage of planting mint in containers is that you can grow it where it will be accessible, including in a sunny window indoors.

Bury the container in the ground. You can also pot mint and bury the container, leaving at least 1 inch of the pot above the ground. Doing this helps train mint to grow upward rather than outward.

Put up barriers. Walls or sidewalks that are at least 6 inches underground can also slow the spread of mint in the garden.

Prune regularly. Regular pruning and use can keep mint in check and slow the spread via stem to ground contact.

---

6 reasons you need to plant Hippocrates favorite herb

Did you know there is a plant that can attack atherosclerosis, clobber cholesterol, bring down blood pressure, banish bacteria, and crush blood clots? Plus it can keep aphids out of your garden.

What is this wonder food? Garlic. Hippocrates, known as the father of medicine, used it as a remedy for many medical conditions. Modern science has indeed confirmed that garlic is a mighty plant with tremendous therapeutic value.

Garlic belongs to the onion family and grows in many parts of the world, where it is enjoyed for its strong smell and delicious taste. However, in ancient days garlic was mainly used as an herbal remedy. Its therapeutic benefits come from sulfur compounds that form when a clove of garlic is chopped, crushed, or chewed.

> To keep pests from damaging your plants, combine 1 small head of garlic with 2 cups of water in a blender until smooth. Pour the mixture into a glass container, cover, and let sit in a dark space for 24 hours. Strain out solids and add enough water to make a 1-gallon mixture. Spray on foliage to deter aphids, whiteflies, cabbage worms, and many others.

Here are just some of the reasons why everyone should plant and use garlic.

- Studies show that garlic extract is just as effective as popular drugs at reducing blood pressure.

- Garlic can lower total and LDL cholesterol.

- Animal studies indicate that garlic may reduce bone loss by increasing estrogen in females.

- Eating one raw garlic clove each morning can relax your arteries, which lowers blood pressure and prevents clots in those at risk.

- A molecule within garlic interferes with the defense mechanism in bacteria, which boosts your immune response.

- Garlic is nature's gift of a powerful fungicide and pesticide, keeping pesky insects like aphids away.

And it's so easy to grow this wonder food. In fall, when temperatures are cool, plant cloves 4 to 8 inches apart in fertile, slightly moist, well-drained soil. Place individual cloves 2 inches deep with the flat end down and pointed end up. Space rows about a foot apart. After planting, mulch with chopped leaves, grass clippings, or straw.

The best time to harvest garlic is when the bulbs are at their biggest and the cloves have not yet separated. This will usually happen when the lower leaves turn yellow or brown. To check, dig up a few test bulbs, and cut them in half to see if the cloves fill the skins.

Banish headaches and tension with herbal teas

Headaches range from mild and annoying to severe and debilitating. Brought on by stress, dehydration, fatigue, hormonal imbalances, and other health issues, they are no fun to experience.

Headache relief is just a leaf away if you grow these herbs in your garden.

Feverfew. Feverfew is an ancient medicinal, perennial herb valued for its therapeutic properties, especially its ability to fight off migraines. Feverfew is a tender perennial in the aster family that is often grown as an annual in colder areas.

Dense clusters of daisy-like flowers perch at the top of stalks with light, hairy green leaves. It is easy to grow along with other herbs or flowers and also fares well in containers.

To enjoy as a tea, place a tablespoon of leaves into a tea ball, and place the ball in a teacup. Fill the cup with boiling water, and allow the tea to steep for five minutes. Remove the ball and add raw honey if desired.

Roman chamomile. Also called Russian chamomile or English chamomile, this herb is well known for its calming, anti-stress and anti-inflammatory properties. This perennial creeping groundcover spreads out like a mat. It has small daisy-like flowers with yellow centers and white petals.

Chamomile grows best in cold conditions and planted in part shade, but it will also do well in full sun. Soil should be dry, and once established, this pretty herb needs very little care. A drought-tolerant plant, chamomile only needs to be watered in times of prolonged drought.

The best tea uses fresh chamomile flowers. Ideally, make your tea the same day you harvest. Add 3 to 4 tablespoons of fresh flowers (no stems) to an infuser teapot and a sprig of peppermint or chocolate mint. Pour boiling water into the teapot, and let the tea steep for five minutes. Add honey if you'd like more sweetness.

Homemade herbal sock helps with anxiety and sleep

Don't throw your old tube socks out — make your very own soothing herbal sock buddy instead.

Lavender is a popular herb that has some powerful medicinal properties. This aromatic herb is known for its ability to relieve anxiety and induce sleep. It may also help reduce blood pressure.

This easy-to-make sock buddy will calm your nerves and help you relax in an instant.

Even though it's a kitchen herb, marjoram can also pull its weight in aromatherapy. It's another herb that could help lower high blood pressure, relieve anxiety, and bring on restful sleep.

- Add 2 cups of uncooked rice to one sock along with 3 drops of lavender essential oil, 3 drops of eucalyptus essential oil, and 1/4 cup dried lavender buds.

- Tie a secure knot at the top of the filled sock, and place it knot-side down into the other sock. Tie the second sock securely so the rice can't leak out.

- Microwave for one to two minutes, and lay your sock buddy on your neck or your forehead for instant relaxation.

Herbed vinegar — a special treat you can make yourself

Making herbed vinegar could not be easier. Vinegar infused with herbs makes a beautiful decoration in any kitchen and tastes great on your favorite salad and in sauces and spreads.

Here's what you'll need.

- fresh herbs (tarragon, thyme, and chives work well)

- white wine vinegar

- glass jar with lid

- decorative glass bottle with cork

Crush fresh herbs lightly to release their scent and flavor. Pack the herbs loosely into a clean glass jar.

Pour vinegar over the herbs until they are completely covered. Cover the jar and label it. Store jar at room temperature away from heat and direct light for two weeks.

Strain the vinegar into a decorative and clean glass bottle. Leave a few herbs floating for decoration. Cork the glass bottle tightly.

How do I harvest my herbs without damaging the plant?

To get the most out of your herbs, you need to harvest them properly so they continue to produce. Here's the best way to pick these favorite kitchen herbs without hurting the plant.

Basil. When harvesting basil, it is crucial to know how much you need. If you only need a few leaves, you can use your fingers to pinch them off.

To harvest lots of herbs, cut from the top down using clean kitchen shears. Cut up to a third of the total plant height. Make sure you cut or pinch above a leaf pair. Doing this will ensure that you will have more basil to harvest in a few weeks.

Mint. If you only need a few mint leaves, pinch them off with your fingertips. For a larger harvest, snip mint sprigs at soil level. Remember, mint is a prolific grower and harvesting often will keep the plant healthy.

Rosemary. For cooking purposes, cut the top 2 to 3 inches of sprigs from established plants. Don't cut too close to the plant. You need to leave some green leaves so the plant will continue to produce. If you are planning to dry the rosemary, don't harvest until the plant starts to bloom.

Parsley. For a small amount of parsley, cut a sprig or two starting with outside stalks. Be sure to snip stalks at soil level using clean kitchen shears. For a more substantial amount, bunch the stems and leaves together before clipping them close to the ground.

Try these cholesterol-busters you grow right in your garden

Did you know certain herbs can help slash your cholesterol without drugs? Of course, before using an herbal remedy, it's always wise to check with your healthcare provider. But if you're following a healthy lifestyle, these herbal remedies just might give your arteries an extra boost. And they're easy to grow in your home herb garden.

Yarrow. This perennial herb goes by the names of nosebleed plant, old man's pepper, and gordaldo. In the Southwest United States, it is often called plumajillo, meaning "little feather" in Spanish, because of its fern-like leaf shape and texture.

Yarrow does not like soggy soil and will thrive in dry conditions. When planting, be sure to include plenty of organic matter in the soil and space new plants about 2 feet apart.

> Keep animals like deer, moles, and mice out of your garden by planting these herbs as a border. Try lavender, dill, thyme, garlic, catnip, oregano, rosemary, or sage.

The beneficial phytosterols in yarrow help block the absorption of cholesterol, making it a great choice for natural cholesterol balance.

One of the best ways to enjoy its health benefits is to make herbal tea. Place a few fresh leaves in a cup, and pour boiling water over them. Add a squeeze of lemon and a teaspoon of honey and enjoy.

Holy basil. This annual shrub can reach almost 2 feet tall when mature. Its leaves give off a spicy clove-like scent and add flavor to cold culinary delights such as salads.

Basil does best in full sun and well-drained and moist soil. Provide water only when the plant is dry to touch, and be careful not to water the foliage. Provide plenty of organic matter, and space young plants about 24 inches apart.

Well known for relieving stress, holy basil may also have some cholesterol-lowering effects, although evidence is limited. Animal studies have shown that the herb raises good HDL cholesterol and decreases bad LDL. Other studies show that the herb may lower stress-induced cholesterol levels.

Enjoy holy basil as a tea using leaves, flowers, or dried leaf powder. Place 2 to 3 teaspoons of holy basil in a cup of boiling water and let it steep for five minutes or so. Add lemon and honey if desired.

Herb-drying hacks that work

Herbs are prolific plants that grow more as you cut and use them, which presents a perfect opportunity to collect and dry them for future use.

Store-bought dried herbs can be expensive, so drying and preserving your own can save loads of money in the long run. Here are some of the best ways to dry and save your herbal harvest.

> Mints and parsley lose their flavor when dried, but you can preserve their flavor with a salt solution. Add 8 teaspoons of salt to 2 cups of water and bring to a boil. Put herbs in a strainer and immerse in the boiling salt water for three seconds. Place on a screen to dry.

Microwave. Drying your herbs this way is a speedy method for those who are short on time. Place a single layer of herbs on a paper towel on a microwave-safe plate. Cover them with another paper towel and microwave for one minute. If the herbs are not dry after a minute, continue heating in intervals of 30 seconds until they are completely dry.

Air dry. If you live in a dry climate, air drying is the perfect way to dry your herbs. Clip the stems of your herbs, and bundle them together with twine or a big rubber band. Hang them upside down in a dry and warm place. An attic is excellent.

You can also lay herbs on an old window screen and place it where it will get airflow from above and below in a warm and dry location.

Oven. Oven drying is an easy way to preserve your herbs and requires just a cookie sheet. Spread your herbs out over the cookie sheet, and cook at the lowest possible temperature for two to three hours.

Refrigerator. As strange as it may seem, the fridge is a great place to dry fresh herbs. Pile up about six sheets of paper towel and place the fresh herbs on them. Roll up the herbs in the towel and set in the fridge for a few weeks, and you will have nicely dried and preserved herbs.

DIY salt scrub invigorates dry and tired skin

Get silky smooth skin with this homemade herbal skin exfoliating scrub. This recipe makes enough for one application.

Here's what you'll need.

- handful of dried mint leaves

- 2 to 3 tablespoons sea salt

- 4 tablespoons water

- 1/2 teaspoon olive oil

Place your mint leaves in a coffee grinder and grind into a powder. Add water and olive oil. Mix well. It will have a crumbly texture.

To use, massage the salt scrub into your skin and allow it to stay on for 10 minutes before rinsing with cold water.

If you love onions but hate the way your breath smells after eating them, parsley can come to the rescue. Instead of reaching for a breath mint, grab a few parsley leaves and munch on them for instant fresh breath.

How do I know if I'm overwatering my herb garden?

Regular watering is necessary for vigorous and healthy plants, but even too much of a good thing can turn bad. Here are a few signs that your herb garden is getting too much water.

- Leaves turn yellow and fall off.
- Leaves become dark black.
- Herb is not growing.
- Stems are soft and break easily.
- A fuzzy mildew-like substance appears on leaves.
- Blisters, lesions, or indentations appear on leaves indicating edema.
- The plant does not perk up when watered. A thirsty plant will thank you by standing up tall.

To avoid overwatering, do the following.

- Check that plants have proper drainage.
- Don't water on a set schedule but instead wait for the plant to show you it needs water.
- Check the soil for moisture when plants first start to show signs of wilting. Stick your finger about an inch or so into the soil, and if it is dry, provide water.
- Water only the soil area around the plant. This will help prevent evaporation and reduce disease.
- Group plants according to their water needs.
- Water deep but infrequently.

Indoor gardening: handy hints to keep your houseplants healthy

5 clues to the perfect houseplant

Houseplants do more than add color to a room. They can help improve your mood, your mental health — even your home's air quality. That's why more and more people are including them in their decorating.

If you find them intimidating, don't worry. Most plants are pretty forgiving, and if you know what to look for, you can find the perfect plants to fit your needs.

Here are a few things you should look for when shopping for a houseplant.

Shape. Seek out uniformly shaped plants, and avoid those that are leggy or overly bushy.

Potting medium. Don't be afraid to stick your finger into the potting mix. It should be moist. If it is soggy or overly dry, it could be a sign the plant has been incorrectly watered.

Roots. Do you see roots on top of the potting medium or peeking out of the plant's bottom? If so, there is a good chance the plant is root bound and struggling to survive.

Leaves. Check that leaves look fresh and have no signs of browning or yellowing. Check the underside of the leaves for signs of disease and pests.

Flowering plants. When choosing flowering plants, make sure the plant has both flowers and buds. Having buds is a good thing because they will open and replace spent flowers. Avoid plants with tightly closed buds because they may not open when you get the plant home.

How do I start indoor plants from cuttings?

Believe it or not, you can share your houseplants, give them as gifts, or expand your collection without spending another cent. All you need are some cuttings.

Houseplants can be rooted and grown in several different ways, such as root division, leaf cuttings, and stem cuttings. Here's how to do it.

Find a sharp knife or pair of scissors or pruners. Choose one of your houseplants with new growth, and snip off about 5 inches, right below the leaf joint.

Fill a glass with water, submerge the stem of your cutting, and place it in a warm, sunny location. Make sure that no leaves are touching the water. Keep the water topped off, and within a few weeks, you should notice roots extending from the bottom of the stem.

Once the root system is established, plant your cutting in a pot with nutrient-rich soil, and enjoy.

While most common houseplants, such as pothos, philo-dendrons, and monsteras, do well when rooted in water, some prefer to be rooted directly in the soil. Spider plants are a good example. Be sure to research your particular plant before propagating to increase your chance of success.

Simple steps to repot your favorite plant

Repotting indoor plants as they mature is an essential part of keeping them healthy and happy. Plants that have been in pots for some time can become root bound and require a new home. You may decide it's time for a change in pot color or style as well.

If you are unsure whether your favorite houseplant is ready for a new home, check out the list below.

- The plant visibly has outgrown its pot.

- You can see roots pushing out the drainage hole.

- Water is just sitting on top of the soil and not absorbing.

- The soil is crumbly and falling apart. Many plants that you bring home from the store require repotting because the soil lacks nutrients.

- You have not repotted your plant in years.

If your plant needs repotting, you'll need a new container that is wider and deeper than the old pot. Be sure that it has drainage holes.

Lay some newspaper down on a flat and level working surface. Place a coffee filter inside your pot to cover the drainage hole. Add a layer of fresh potting mix to the bottom of the container.

> Moving cacti to a new home can be a bit tricky. When transplanting a cactus, protect your fingers by using a pair of kitchen tongs to lift the plant and place it into its new home.

Water your plant in its old container. Turn the old pot upside down and place your hand gently on the plant. Rotate the plant in both directions to encourage it to fall out. If you have a hard time, use a knife to cut around the edges, and gently pry the plant out of the pot.

Use scissors to prune the old roots a bit, and spread them out to grow outward. That will help your plant thrive in its new pot.

Place the plant in the new pot and be sure it is centered. Push it down gently and fill in all the spaces with a fresh potting medium.

Water your plant frequently as it adjusts to its new home. Keep it out of full sunlight for at least a week, and hold off on feeding for about a month.

Air alert: Plants that protect you while you sleep

Your bedroom should be a safe, comfortable, and restful space. One way to create a relaxing sleep sanctuary is to add some key houseplants to keep the air you breathe as fresh and clean as possible.

While you sleep, these plants are working the night shift to clean your air. Discover the perfect bedroom plants below.

- Rubber plant. The large leaves of this majestic plant gather dangerous air particles and break them down.

This plant needs moderate bright light and consistent moisture to thrive.

- Boston fern. Ferns are at the top of the list when it comes to cleaning air. To water, place the pot in a tray filled with water and pebbles once a week.

- Rosemary. Place in a south-facing window and enjoy the fresh and relaxing aroma of this powerful toxin-catching plant.

- Lavender. This beautiful and aromatic plant also needs a south-facing window. Lavender has soothing properties and is a bright addition to any bedroom space.

Make this special indoor water garden in a snap

If you love the look of water plants but don't want to go through the effort of caring for fish and dealing with the hassle of an aquarium, check out this easy indoor water garden. You can personalize it however you like and put it together in under 15 minutes.

Here's what you'll need:

- a container of your choice. Large bowls, terrariums, unused fishbowls, vases, or any large, glass container will work fine. Try checking out thrift stores for a unique container and to help cut down on costs.

- stones, gravel, or rocks. A mix of plain and colored stones of different sizes will help your water feature pop and make it an eye-catching addition to your decor.

- aquatic plants. Aubias, java moss, coontail, Christmas moss, bolbitis, and marimo moss balls are great options.

- distilled water

- sea fan or other coral

Add the rocks to the bottom of the container. You don't need many, just enough to hold up the plants and add some color. Include as many plants as you want. Lightly press them into the rocks to help them stay in place while you add the water.

Fill with water and voila. You now have an aquatic plant feature for your home. It's that simple. Change the water every month with new distilled water, and keep your water garden in a room with indirect sunlight.

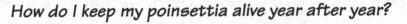

How do I keep my poinsettia alive year after year?

While most people don't think anything of spending $10 every year on a new poinsettia plant, it seems like a waste to let this vibrant beauty die off just because the Christmas season is over.

Don't toss it out. Here's how you can have perfect poinsettias year after year and keep the holiday cheer alive and growing.

Give it lots of light. Keep your poinsettia in direct sunlight but avoid drafty windowsills as they don't like it when temperatures drop below 65 degrees.

Water well. Don't allow the soil to dry out between waterings, especially when it's still in bloom during the winter months. Avoid standing water but check the soil daily and be sure to keep it moist.

Adjust care in spring. Around April, slowly reduce how often you water your plant, letting it dry out slightly between waterings. You should also cut off about 4 inches from each stem and begin fertilizing. Move the plant to a larger container, if needed.

Build in a blackout period. Continue to fertilize until the fall. During this time (starting the first of October), the plant must receive 12 hours of total darkness at night for about eight weeks to cultivate a bloom for Christmas time.

Around the first of December, the plant will start to bloom again, producing a gorgeous flower with a vibrant red hue that will match your Christmas decor and help get you in the holiday spirit.

Unmistakable signs it's time to water

Yellow leaves on a houseplant can mean too much water — or not enough. Doing the wrong thing can kill your plant. Your plants will give you signs that they need a drink. Here are some things to look for.

Yellow or brown leaves. This could mean that your plant is quite thirsty. Leaves of dehydrated plants may become crispy around the edges. But sometimes yellow, brown, and dry leaves can be a sign of something else like overexposure to sun, disease, or too much water.

If your plants have split leaves don't fret. Simply take a little clear nail polish and paint both sides of the damaged leaf. You won't even be able to see that the leaf is torn.

Wilting or drooping leaves. Indoor plants will develop wilty leaves because they lack the water to make them thick and plump. If the leaves on your indoor plant droop, it may mean that you are behind on watering.

If you think a lack of water is the cause for the droop, water right away. The leaves should perk up quickly. Keep in mind other things such as overfeeding, overexposure to sunlight, insect or disease issues, or even overwatering may also cause leaves to droop.

Leaf drop. Many mature plants will drop leaves as part of their cycle of renewing foliage. But if your plant is dropping an excessive or abnormal amount of leaves, it may be a sign of thirst. Similarly, if you have a young plant that is dropping leaves, it may lack water.

Change in soil color. The soil in your plants' pots can be a good indicator of the amount of moisture available to your plant. Moist soil is dark in color while dry soil tends to be lighter.

Checking the soil color in your potted houseplants on a regular basis will help you determine when it's time to water. This check is also useful if you're not sure whether another sign like yellowing or wilting leaves is due to lack of water or something else.

3 foolproof ways to revive dry plants

Oh no. You forgot to water your houseplants, and now they're dry as a bone. Do this to bring them back safely.

Place plants in a sink or tub filled with room temperature water for at least an hour or until the soil is wet to the touch. Make sure the water comes about halfway up the side of the pot.

To avoid plants becoming too dry, use the following techniques to water from the bottom.

- Place potted plants in your sink or a tub filled with room temperature water for a couple of hours weekly. Doing this provides a deep and thorough watering.

- Position a saucer or tray filled with water under your plant. Allow plants to sit in the saucer or tray for several hours. Remove the saucer and discard the remaining water.

- Put your plants in self-watering pots. This type of pot is one of the best investments you can make if you often forget to water your plants because it does all the work for you. All you have to do is fill the water reservoir about once a month, and your plants will happily drink only the water they need.

Share the love: Indoor care hacks that work

You don't have to spend a fortune to make sure your plants get what they need. Follow these easy hacks for healthy and happy plants throughout your home.

Share your morning coffee. You've probably heard of saving your coffee grounds to add to your acid-loving plants' soil. But did you know you can also give your plants a sip of your morning brew?

If you don't drink the whole pot, dilute your coffee a bit and use the less concentrated version to water your acidic plants such as ferns, gardenias, azaleas, begonias, and African violets.

Remember, don't water your plants with this watered-down coffee every time, or you'll run the risk of the soil becoming too acidic. Limit it to about every three or four waterings.

Don't throw out the egg water. Instead of dumping out the water you used to hard boil eggs or cook veggies, let it cool to room temperature, and use it to water your plants.

This water contains beneficial nutrients such as calcium that will help feed your houseplants, keep the pH balance in check, and encourage healthy growth.

Turn your pots weekly. You may not think to do this, but it's essential for a full, lush plant. Each time you water (or about once a week) turn your plant slightly to allow leaves on all sides to get full sun exposure and avoid uneven growth.

Turning is especially critical if you notice your plant getting leggy or leaning towards the window.

How to spot and fix deadly diseases

Houseplants don't come into contact with as many disease-promoting substances as outdoor plants. However, they can still develop various molds, rots, and fungi that can seriously hamper growth and even kill your plant.

Before you give up hope on your struggling, sick house-plant, see if you can identify the infection. Here are some possibilities, along with possible fixes.

Powdery mildew. Leaves may start to grow a white, pow-dery substance and begin to fall off. The plant will become weak and may struggle to grow. Carefully remove affected leaves and dust the plant with sulfur. Increase air circulation and avoid overwatering.

Crown, root, and stem rot. The base of the plant may become blackened and rotted. This could hamper nutrient delivery, causing yellowed foliage, and the roots may start to rot. It's fatal for plants if left unchecked.

If the rot is advanced, it may be impossible to save the plant since it affects the base. Instead, try to repot cuttings of the plant. Often caused by overwatering and poor drainage, severe root rot could be avoided if you repot early enough.

Gray mold or botrytis. This is a fuzzy mold that can spread and cause leaves to fall off or stems to rot. Prune off any infected areas and improve air circulation. Larger plants may need to be staked to increase circulation and prevent a moist environment from developing.

Leaf spot. Yellow or black spots appear on leaves and start to spread, eventually killing the leaves. It's often caused by excessive humidity and heat. Avoid getting water on the leaves and remove any infected foliage.

Remember, isolate diseased plants as soon as you notice the infection. Many diseases can quickly spread between plants, so it's important to quarantine the sick plant while you attempt to treat the condition.

Grow the perfect indoor lemon tree

While it's undoubtedly satisfying to grow a dwarf lemon tree in your living room, it isn't as easy as you may think to get it to bear fruit. These simple tricks will set you on the path to success and help you enjoy a thriving Meyer lemon tree in no time.

Buy a mature plant. To save yourself a little disappointment and stress, buy an established lemon tree from a reputable nursery, ideally, a plant that is at least a few years old. Citrus plants take a while to produce fruit, so this is especially important if you don't want to wait years to harvest your first lemon.

Consider the soil and container. While you won't need to worry about this if you buy an established plant, it is still a good idea to ensure that your lemon tree has what it needs.

Choose a large, well-draining clay, plastic, or ceramic pot, and a potting mix designed specifically for citrus. Remember to fertilize your tree as often as the package recommends.

Keep it warm. Place your miniature citrus plant in a bright, warm spot in your home that receives at least eight hours of sunlight each day. Don't let it be exposed to drastic temperature changes like a drafty door or blazing heater. Consider adding a grow light in the winter if sun exposure is limited.

Water well, but not too much. Water your lemon tree thoroughly about once a week, making sure not to let it sit in water or dry out too much. A water meter can help you achieve this perfect balance, while a humidifier will help mimic the tropical climate where citrus trees thrive. This is especially important in the dry winter months.

Move it outdoors. After all threats of frost have passed, begin leaving your tree outside in a sheltered area like a porch or patio for a few hours at a time. This will help give it some fresh air, improve circulation, kill off any indoor pests, and allow it to survive another winter indoors. Reverse the process by gradually returning it indoors as the weather cools.

It's worse than mold — but this plant can fix it

Are you breathing in mold or something even worse? You may not believe it, but every time you flush the toilet, some feces enter the air. These particles can land on countertops and even your toothbrush.

Thankfully, you can place one beautiful and easy-to-care-for plant in your bathroom, and it will tackle not only mold but also those nasty particles in as little as 72 hours.

According to the American College of Allergy, Asthma, and Immunology, that hardworking plant is English ivy. It's been shown to remove 78% of airborne mold and 94% of other harmful particles.

English ivy loves the humidity found in the bathroom as well as bright light. This vibrant trailing plant will keep the air in your bathroom clean and fresh. Try it and see.

Clever way to get rid of fruit flies — for good

Sometimes you may notice tiny flies, known as fruit flies, hanging just above your potted plants' soil. Although these flies don't damage plants, they are a nuisance.

These pesky critters need rotting organic matter to complete their lifestyle. They lay their eggs in the soil where they hatch.

Fruit flies love damp soil so make sure you don't overwater your plants. Also, keep plant saucers empty so the standing water won't lure the flies.

The great news is you can quickly rid your home of fruit flies without harsh chemicals. Here are two simple solutions to try.

- Cover the soil. Spread a thin layer of aquatic gravel over the top of the potting soil. The gravel will keep the larvae from getting out of the soil, which interrupts the life cycle.

- Set a trap. Pour 1/4 cup of apple cider vinegar into a small disposable plastic cup. Add one drop of dish soap and stir well. Place some plastic wrap loosely over the top of the cup, and secure it with a rubber band. Poke some holes in the plastic wrap using a toothpick. Set this trap near infested plants. Fruit flies will fly into the trap and not be able to escape.

Odor-absorbers keep your home smelling great

You want to keep the air inside your home smelling great but hate using those artificial chemical air fresheners. Why not use beautiful plants instead?

Not only are some plants great at scrubbing the air, they grab odors too, leaving their sweet-smelling aroma behind. The plants below are the perfect, nontoxic odor busters you've been searching for.

Chrysanthemum. This plant has everything. Besides being beautiful, it's used for health, cooking, and fighting pests. Chrysanthemum's flowers are highly fragrant and will quickly fill a room with their enticing aroma, overpowering obnoxious odors in your home.

Annual geranium. There is something timeless about geraniums' sweet fragrance, not to mention how they bring an air of elegance to any space they occupy. The early European perfume industry used scented geraniums for distinct and popular fragrances.

Different geraniums give off different aromas, such as peppermint, lemon, rose, nutmeg, coconut, pineapple, almond, old spice, and strawberry. Place a pot anywhere you need a natural odor fighter, and it will take care of even the strongest smells — even fish or smoke.

Jasmine. Jasmine is in the same family as olive plants and contains over 200 species. These beautiful plants adorn the outdoor spaces of many tropical regions.

When you bring this beauty indoors, sweet things happen to the air you breathe. Its tiny white flowers emit a rich and full scent that quickly pushes away unpleasant odors.

The flowers release most of their fragrance at night when they go to work to remove any lingering odors, leaving a trail of natural perfume behind.

Gardenia. Gardenias are spectacular flowering plants that are native to southern Asia and tropical regions of Africa. They have pale yellow or white, highly scented flowers and stunning shiny green foliage.

When you introduce a gardenia plant to your indoor air, even the foulest odor is no match for its alluring aroma. Gardenias are highly efficient at removing unpleasant scents while leaving behind an unmatched sweetness.

5 natural — and cheap — ways to make leaves shine

Shiny leaves are healthy leaves. If you want to keep them at their best, say no to commercial waxes that clog the leaf's pores. They prevent the leaves from releasing moisture and absorbing toxins from the air.

Instead, use natural, safe methods with products found in your kitchen cupboard to keep your plants shiny and dust-free.

Wipe with a damp cloth. Wet a soft cloth and rub it over the leaves. Add a little dish soap to clean off any stubborn dust.

Houseplants can warn you of deadly, silent gas leaks. If your indoor plants are super healthy and doing great but suddenly begin to turn brown, wilt, and die, that could mean danger. Check your gas lines or call your gas company immediately.

Wash with vinegar and water. Mix 1 teaspoon of vinegar with 1 gallon of water, and use it to wipe down the leaves' top and underside on your houseplants and break up residue from mineral deposits. As a bonus, it will help deter pests.

Shine with banana peels. When finished eating a banana, use the inside of the peel to shine houseplant leaves before you toss it into your compost bin.

Give them a milk bath. Combine equal parts milk and water in a dish, and gently rub it onto your houseplants. This is one of the best methods for increasing shine.

Slap on some mayo. Although it may seem strange, mayonnaise is highly effective for cleaning and protecting plant leaves. It also helps create a natural dust barrier.

Clean up mold and reduce allergies effortlessly

Nothing is more annoying than itchy eyes, a runny nose, and constant sneezing. Millions of people struggle with allergy symptoms like these. Many of these allergies are caused by indoor irritants such as mold and dust.

Houseplants can significantly help those who suffer from allergies. But you have to choose the right ones for the job as some plants can make your symptoms even worse.

Here are the top plants that help keep your indoor air fresh and clean, reducing allergy symptoms.

Peace lily. Peace lilies are elegant plants that can boost indoor air quality by up to 60%. This plant can decrease mold spores, absorbing them through their leaves and pushing them to their roots where they are used as foods. This plant loves dappled sunlight and consistent moisture.

Spider plant. People with allergies and asthma will enjoy the relief that spider plants bring. These plants have long, thin, beautifully striped leaves in green and white. Popular in hanging baskets, spider plants also look great in a pretty pot on the floor.

Toxins that cause allergies and asthma are no match for spider plants, which are also known to suck formaldehyde out of the air. According to a NASA study, spider plants are top of the list when it comes to their air-cleaning ability, with a 95% removal rate.

Spider plants are easy to maintain and super tough to kill, making them perfect for everyone.

Aloe vera. The aloe plant is well-known for its ability to remedy burns and cuts. It can also keep allergies at bay by absorbing indoor air pollutants. This popular succulent clears out benzene and formaldehyde.

Like most succulents, aloe vera prefers soil that is on the dry side. Water only when completely dry and drench the soil, allowing the water to drain out freely. Plant aloe in light-weight cacti potting mix for best results.

Beware — not every plant cleans the air

It is important for people with respiratory issues, allergies, asthma, or other sensitivities to pick houseplants wisely. Beware of these three common houseplants that can contaminate your home.

- Weeping fig. Although weeping figs are super easy to care for, they are top on the list for indoor sources of allergens, second only to dust mites and pets. Small particles that come from the leaves, trunk, and sap of weeping figs cause symptoms similar to a latex allergy.

- Male palm trees. While female palm trees can rid the air of irritants, male trees shed masses of pollen that can cause annoying allergy symptoms to spiral out of control.

- African violets. These little beauties look great in your window, but they can be a nightmare if you are sensitive. Violets do a perfect job of collecting dust on their foliage, which can aggravate symptoms in a dust mite allergy.

Try these easy-to-grow pest-fighting plants

Are you sick and tired of fighting off aphids, whiteflies, and spider mites? Do you know the formula for insecticidal soap by heart? Take heart — these pest-resistant houseplants will allow you to set down your spray bottle, sit back, and enjoy your bug-free home.

Dracena. With long, leathery, spear-shaped leaves, the dracena is an incredibly popular house-plant due to its hardy nature and the many colors and varieties. Give it a little filtered light, keep the soil moist, and this plant will thrive for years.

Beware — some of these plants are toxic to kids and pets. If you have any curious critters or toddlers running around, you might want to avoid having these houseplants in your home.

Jade plant. If you like the look of succulents, then this fast-growing plant is for you. The thick, juicy leaves produce a distasteful and toxic sap that keeps bugs at bay. It can easily be propagated from cuttings, making it a great plant to share with friends.

Snake plant. This intimidating plant is a sight to behold, with tall, striking leaves that shoot upward in various patterns and colors ranging from green to yellow. It is virtually indestructible, and the upright growth pattern doesn't allow many hiding places for any pesky bugs.

Herbs. Indoor herb gardens are all the rage these days and for good reason. Herbs are easy to grow indoors and convenient to have on hand when you're cooking up a storm. Plus they naturally produce insect-repellent oils and carry strong scents that deter most pests.

Tackle the top indoor houseplant pests

These pesky pests can turn your indoor jungle into a living — and slowly dying — nightmare, infecting your precious houseplants and making your house a plant graveyard.

Many of these pests hide out under leaves and in the soil. This is just one of the reasons that careful and regular inspection of your plants is necessary.

Here's what you need to know about the most common indoor plant pests and how you can get rid of them.

Pest	Looks like	Symptoms	What to do
aphids	small green, brown, or black bugs that are born wingless	curled, discolored leaves and stunted plant growth	Take plant outside and spray with a hose to remove aphids from leaves. Repeat as needed until bugs are gone.
spider mites	small, whitish-colored spiders barely visible to the naked eye	webbing at the base of the plant or in the leaves; yellowed foliage	Rinse off the webbing and keep the plant slightly moist by leaving a humidifier on nearby or misting daily. Mites thrive in dry environments.
fungus gnats	similar to fruit flies; will circle lazily around a plant when it is disturbed	more of an annoyance than a danger; larvae may eat plant material	Use sticky traps to catch flying adults, and sprinkle the bacteria *Bacillus thuringiensis* in soil to kill larvae.

Pest	Looks like	Symptoms	What to do
mealy-bugs	scale insect with white, cotton-like appearance	hides on the undersides of leaves or in the elbow of plant joints; spreads easily to other plants and stunts plant growth	Use an insecticidal soap or neem oil and keep infested plants away from other houseplants until infestation is under control.
scale	brown insects with a round or oval body	may stunt plant growth and leave stems dried out	Spray with insecticidal soap and use fingers or toothbrush to remove scale from leaves. Rinse plant off in the sink or shower.
thrips	tiny brown or tan insects with long bodies	holes in leaves and silvery discoloration	Release thrips predators and minute pirate bugs. They will feed on thrips without damaging your plant.
whitefly	similar to a gnat but white in color	leaves turn yellow or white and may fall off prematurely	Set out yellow sticky traps around the plants, and blast the leaves with a strong spurt of water from a hose.

Perk up your plants with special tonics

Sometimes houseplants need a little pick-me-up. Here are some easy-to-make tonics and elixirs to keep your plants looking their best.

Yogurt fixer. Treat your yellowing houseplants to this common dessert food and watch them green-up. Yogurt contains beneficial microbes that plants love. Mix 1 tablespoon of plain unsweetened yogurt in a cup of water and pour it in a spray bottle. Spray houseplants weekly with this special solution.

Tea bath. If you have your houseplants outdoors for the warm season and are ready to bring them in, a tea bath is a great way to prepare them for the transition.

Steep a tea bag in a quart of warm water, and add 3 teaspoons of liquid dish soap. Pour the solution into a spray bottle, and spray your houseplants daily for a week before moving them indoors.

The tannic acid in the tea helps the plants make more sugar and starch, and the dish soap opens up pores so plants can take in nutrients.

Molasses elixir. This unique mixture protects plants from pests, diseases, and heat stress.

Houseplants like to get outside every once in a while. Set your plants out in early spring to soak in April showers. The rain will wash off dust and debris collected on foliage and breathe new life into your plant. Be sure the temperatures are warm enough, and keep them out of direct sunlight.

- Pour 1 gallon of water into a 2-gallon bucket and let it sit for 24 hours.

- Take out 1 quart of water and heat it until warm. Add 1 tablespoon of blackstrap molasses to the water. Pour this molasses solution into the bigger bucket and stir well.

- Add 1/4 cup liquid seaweed, 1/4 cup fish emulsion, and 1 tablespoon of apple cider vinegar. Mix and let cool. Use the elixir to water plants every two weeks.

Recycle wine corks into mini planters

If you are looking for the perfect gift for your special friend or just something to decorate your refrigerator, this project is for you. Mini plants are cute and fun to display, and these easy-to-make magnetic corks are a great way to enjoy them.

What you need:

- wine corks

- magnets, small and round

- lightweight potting soil

- succulent cuttings

- glue gun

- sharp knife

- measuring spoon

How to make it:

1. Use the knife to hollow out the center of the cork. Turn the knife in a circular motion, being careful not to go all the way through the cork. Stop about three-quarters of the way through.

2. Secure a couple of magnets to the backside of the cork using hot glue.

3. Fill the cork about halfway with potting mix.

4. Place your succulent cutting in the soil, and fill the rest of the cork with potting mix. Tap down lightly using the back of a measuring spoon.

5. Drizzle with water.

Landscaping projects that won't break the bank — or your back

'C' your way to an inviting outdoor living space

It's easy to transform your backyard into a peaceful paradise, where you can entertain friends and family or relax and enjoy the serenity. Although the sky's the limit when it comes to outdoor living spaces, here are five essential elements to keep in mind when you start planning.

Climate. Where do you live? Climate plays a significant role in creating an outdoor living space. If you live in a cool area, you may opt for an outdoor living room with a fireplace or patio heaters. If you live in a more tropical climate, a pool might be the center of your landscape.

Covering. Your space will feel cozier with a cover overhead. It can be as elaborate as a pergola or deck roof or as simple as a shade cloth hung between two poles. The covering you choose should complement your theme and purpose.

Comfort. Of course, no matter what you intend to do with your outdoor space, it should be comfortable. This comfort comes from the type of furniture you choose and various elements like cushions and even outdoor heaters or fans.

Color. Pick a color scheme and work with it as you add various design elements like throw pillows, plants, and other decor items. Don't be afraid to use bright and bold colors. It will help create a fun and inviting space.

Coziness. Your outdoor living space is an extension of your home so you want to make it cozy, warm, and inviting. To achieve a relaxed feel, use warm lighting, outdoor candles, flowy curtains, flowers, rugs, and even a water feature or outdoor fireplace.

Cheap landscape ideas that make a huge impact

Many people think landscape projects are hugely expensive and will drain their bank accounts. The good news is that many budget-friendly projects make a significant impact on your outdoor space. Here are a few to consider.

Create a pallet walkway. No need to drop thousands of dollars on pavers when you can create a simple wooden walkway from pallet boards. Many stores will willingly part with pallets or allow you to purchase them cheap.

Be careful when disassembling the pallets. Once you have the pallet boards off the frame, cut them to size. Lay out your pathway, drill holes in either side of each pallet board, and use landscape spikes to nail them into the ground.

Divide your plants. Dividing plants and spreading them out around your landscape is a cost-effective way to bring bursts of color to different areas. Identify which perennial plants are ready to be separated, and divide them between fall and early spring.

Add window boxes. These cute additions to your house are super easy to make on your own. Or you can buy them and fill with your favorite seasonal beauties. You can even change the flowers out each season to add a new look to your landscape.

Play up natural elements. Every landscape offers unique natural elements. Perhaps you have some water on your property, or large boulders, beautiful shade trees, or hilly terrain.

Take advantage of these elements that are already in place, and develop a beautiful landscape around them. For instance, if you have a stream, build or buy some simple benches and add wildlife feeders to create a quiet place to enjoy nature.

Before landscaping your mailbox area, make sure the plants won't block the view of oncoming traffic when you back out of your driveway. If your mailbox is attached to your neighbor's box, share your plans and get their approval before moving forward.

Large boulders make excellent focal points in gardens, and shade trees are the perfect covering for an outdoor dining or resting area.

Dress up your mailbox. Mailboxes offer a unique opportunity to create a warm and welcome front landscape. Create a small bed with your favorite plants and outdoor decor items around your box. This fun weekend project won't cost a fortune but has a huge impact on your curb appeal.

4 creative ways to use the rocks you've got

If you have a landscape filled with rocks, you may not be too happy about it. But take heart. Natural stone is highly versatile, and landscaping with rocks allows you to add color, texture, and contrast.

Many landscape projects use rocks in a variety of creative ways. Here are just a few ideas on how to use them to add beauty and interest to your outdoor space.

Make a rock garden. If you have a space with rocks of different shapes, sizes, and colors, surround them with beautiful plantings to accentuate their striking features.

You can also plant around large boulders that naturally appear in your landscape. Choose sprawling and colorful plants to create a beautiful boulder bed.

Construct a fire pit. A stone fire pit provides a place to gather and entertain. Using your rocks to create a fire pit will give you a cheap, safe, and attractive site to build a cozy fire. For stability, stack rocks and use mortar to hold them together.

Build a fairy ring. Medium-sized landscape rocks are perfect for creating a unique fairy ring, a popular landscape feature. A fairy ring is a "magical" spot where you can relax and enjoy your garden. Your grandchildren will love it, too.

Stack landscape rocks several layers high, on grass, creating a circle with a 3 to 4 foot opening. Place beautiful flowers and plants around the outside wall. Add a decorative chair or bench inside the circle, and you'll have a special place where you can relax, imagine, and dream.

Use tiny stones for mulch. Small stones make an excellent, low-maintenance mulch for established garden areas. Rocks provide a striking contrast against plants and grass, which adds beauty and interest. You can easily set apart your favorite trees or bushes by surrounding them with beautiful stones.

Using small stones or rocks for mulch will provide you with durable lifetime coverage. And since you don't need to replace it every year, you'll save money, too.

Burglarproof landscape ideas that work

Did you know that 70% of burglars are amateurs — but smart enough to know when going into a particular house just isn't worth the trouble? Here's how to be that house.

Give burglars no place to hide. Trim all bushes and trees within 6 feet of your doors and windows regularly. Any neighbors must have a clear view of your home to spot trouble if you are away.

Don't skimp on lights. There is nothing more distracting to burglars than lights. Install plenty of motion sensors around your home in addition to landscape lighting.

Use view fencing. A solid fence may make you feel protected and safe, but if it is easy for a robber to climb, it is the perfect cover. Once inside your fence, they are no longer in plain view from the street or neighbors. When possible, use view fencing that surrounds your property but still lets people see into your yard.

> Burglarproof your home with these plants that encourage thieves to steer clear of your property. Thorny berries, cacti, roses, or any other plant with a prickly disposition are perfect for under windows. Anyone trying to get into your home will think twice about being attacked by your vegetative watchdog.

Eliminate stepping stones. Move any large boulders or stones located outside of windows that could be used as a stepping stone for burglars to climb in.

Choose gravel for walkways. Using gravel on your walkways will make it more difficult for someone to approach your home quietly.

Easy shade project that will cut your summer cooling bills

To quickly cut utility bills you can plant shade trees, but they take decades to grow. Instead, try one quick weekend project that will pay off this summer, and every year after.

Sometime during the spring, plant a fast-growing annual climber, like moonflower, morning glory, or scarlet runner bean, under windows that face south and west. Give your plants a trellis or other structure to climb. As they grow and spread, they'll block the intense summer rays that heat your home.

If you live in an apartment or condo, plant the fast-growing vines in window boxes, instead. Come autumn, cut them back or let them die back from the cold to let in warming winter light.

How can I create privacy on my condo balcony without spending a fortune?

Living in a condo, apartment, or townhome means you need to make an extra effort to create privacy in your outdoor space. Here are some things you can do that will make you forget you even have neighbors.

Install a lattice. With a nice coat of green or brown paint, a sheet of inexpensive plastic lattice transforms into a modern privacy screen. Set some of your favorite climbers in front of the lattice, and you will have a dramatic display as well as privacy.

Invest in curtains. Hanging curtains around your patio gives you the option of privacy or a more open feel. Choose curtains for outdoor use only, and be sure your rod is sturdy and allows you to open and close them easily.

Hang some planters. A variety of hanging planters hung at various heights can provide quite a bit of privacy. Choose baskets full of trailing plants that will do their part in creating a natural screen.

Plant bamboo in pots. This exotic plant can grow up to 3 feet in one day. Plant young bamboo in containers, and before you know it you will have a lovely natural wind-break and privacy screen.

Build a privacy screen. A cedar-slat privacy screen is easy to make and provides the perfect solution for too-close neighbors. Create a frame first, then lay out cedar boards at your desired width, and attach with nails or deck screws.

5 tips for foolproof transplanting

As your beautiful landscape evolves, you will have opportunities to move plants, introduce new ones, and relocate others. Most mature plants adapt well to transplanting as long as you pay careful attention to a few key things.

Here are some terrific tips for transplanting, whether you're moving a tiny seedling or an overgrown shrub.

Acclimatize young plants. When it's time to introduce an indoor seedling to the great outdoors, you need to harden the plant. Otherwise the shock may kill it. It takes about a week to properly harden off tender baby plants.

On day one, place the young plant outdoors for one hour protected from the wind with only dappled light. On day two, do the same thing, only for two hours. On day three, the plant can stay out for three hours and receive a little more sunlight.

Continue this schedule daily until you reach day seven, and your plant will be ready to remain outdoors in its new home.

Transplant on a cloudy day. Whether you are planting new seedlings or dividing and moving plants, do it on an overcast and cooler day. Transplanting under a hot sun puts more stress on plants.

Give it plenty of water. Watering before a transplant is as essential as watering after. If you are moving a larger plant, give it a good soak with the hose before digging it up. Likewise, fill your planting hole with plenty of water before setting the plant inside, and water the soil around the plant after planting.

Pick up the plant carefully. Handling plants is like handling young children. Just as you wouldn't pull a child by his arm or leg, you don't want to pull up a plant up by its stem, or carry it that way. That can crush cells within the stem that transport water and nutrients. Always have a hand on the plant's bottom — the rootball.

Eliminate air pockets. Once you have your transplant in its new home, gently press the soil around the plant to eliminate any air pockets around the roots. Don't stomp or tamp it. Roots will not grow through air pockets, and air will also interfere with water circulation.

Feed well a few days after planting. Diluted fish fertilizer works well for transplants. Place 2 tablespoons of fish fertilizer in a gallon of water, and pour the mixture around the plant. Use less solution for smaller plants and more for larger ones.

Sun or shade? Find out what to plant where

Perennial flowers and shrubs form a solid anchor in any landscape, and knowing which ones need sun and which need shade helps you plan. Give plants the amount of light they prefer, and you'll be rewarded with their best performance.

Perennials for sun		
Plant	**Zones**	**About**
bee balm	5-9	adds a stunning pop of color and attracts pollinators including butterflies, birds, and bees
tropical milkweed	3-9	brings color and height to the garden; use in the back of beds or to create a beautiful focal display
Russian sage	5-9	spiky purple flower and feathery foliage make this upright shrub a perfect landscape accent plant; tolerates a wide range of soil types
columbine	3-9	graceful and elegant plant that blooms from late spring into summer; lasts only a few years but drops seeds for new plants
hardy geranium	3-9	sturdy mounding plant with a sweet and spicy aroma; doubles in size each season and blooms in early summer
daylily	4-9	large blooms open in midsummer; plant quickly multiplies
lavender	5-9	spreading foliage coupled with beautiful purple flowers and a sweet aroma; perfect for outdoor living spaces and front entrances
cosmos	3-10	delicate plant loves dry soil and heat; thrives on neglect, making it the perfect plant for busy people
salvia	3-11	one of the prettiest, long-lasting perennials that comes in a multitude of colors; blooms from fall through summer
lantana	3-11	attractive clusters of flowers in yellow, purple, pink, white, and red; great for filling empty spaces

Perennials for shade		
Plant	**Zones**	**About**
hosta	3-10	known for their beautiful foliage, hostas also have tall spikes of flowers in the summer; come in a variety of colors, shapes, and textures, and may reach up to 2 feet in diameter
astilbe	3-8	fern-like foliage showcases impressive plumes of pink, red, lavender, white and salmon; perfect as a shady border plant or planted in containers
hydrangea	4-9	large round clusters of flowers in blue, white, and pink can be as large as a dinner plate; perfect for brightening up lightly shaded spots in the landscape
bleeding heart	3-9	arching stems showcase heart-shaped pink and white flowers; at home in any woodland shady garden
Christmas fern	3-9	perfect for hillside planting as it helps control erosion; beautifully green all year long
Ritak sausage vine	6-10	works well with tall trees in shady spots; gently clings to bark and puts on a spectacular display of purplish, cinnamon-scented flowers followed up by large lavender-colored fleshy fruit
caladium	8-11	fast-growing tropical plants have lush multicolored leaves; use in hanging baskets, containers, borders, or as a mass focal planting

Simple way to get rid of stumps for good

Get rid of an unsightly tree stump — without digging it up. This no-fuss method works wonders and saves you a boat-load of cash.

Let's face it, hiring a company to grind your stump can be costly. And other methods that involve chemicals or power tools may be dangerous and unpredictable.

Burying a stump in soil and leaving it alone is an easy and effective way to get rid of it. But it can take years to break down. To speed up the natural decaying process, you must create a favorable environment for fungi.

Here's how to do it. Bury the stump with rich compost and keep it moist. Turn the compost every two weeks to encourage airflow. That will promote the growth of fungi. Within 10 weeks, your stump should be soft enough to remove with a shovel.

Top 5 tricks for a low-maintenance landscape

If you love a beautiful outdoor living space but are short on time or energy, here are some tricks to keep your landscape appealing and low maintenance at the same time.

Choose to xeriscape. Xeriscaping is a great way to reduce or eliminate the need for watering your yard. This design is popular in primarily dry regions of the western United States.

Many trees, shrubs, and flowering plants do well in this type of landscape where the only water comes from nature. Check out the chapter *Xeriscape and other low-maintenance gardens* for more details.

Install an irrigation system. To reduce water, time, and cost, install an irrigation system, and set it on a timer. By providing just the right amount of water at the right time, an irrigation system allows you to enjoy your landscape without the worry of watering.

Create an outdoor dining area. Using space in your landscape for an outdoor dining area creates an extension of your home and shrinks your yard. Build an outdoor dining space on a gravel or paver foundation, which is much lower maintenance than grass.

Make rock gardens. By nature, rock gardens are low maintenance due to the type of plants used, which are usually drought tolerant. The rocks surrounding the garden need nothing and will remain forever.

Mulch as much as possible. You can't go wrong with mulch. Not only does it help retain moisture, but it is also an expert weed suppressor. Mulch comes in a variety of shapes and textures, and you can even make your own organic mulch, which will enrich the soil around your plants.

7 do's for fabulous outdoor lighting

Outdoor lighting can be the pièce de résistance in beautifying your yard. It's a wonderful way to create ambiance in your outdoor living areas or highlight a special planting or water feature. Plus it's a great safety feature on stairs, around pools, and for dark walkways.

Here are some tips on how to best use landscape lighting, including what you should and should not do.

Do light up your house first. The most valued possession in your landscape is your home. So light this up first before you work on other outdoor areas. The right lighting fixtures on and around your home will provide safety and security.

But don't stop there. Think about how you can use landscape lighting to bring attention to your home's unique architectural features.

Do focus on the vision before fixtures. What is the big picture, the impact you wish to accomplish with landscape lighting? Once you have determined this, you can focus on the type of fixtures that will achieve your goals.

Do draw attention to what you want to illuminate. It is easy to overdo landscape lighting. The first rule is to keep it simple, focusing only on what you wish to light up. Don't overdo it with too many lights. A streamlined lighting plan always outshines a cluttered plan.

Do get creative with path lighting. Placing landscape lights along a straight-line path looks more like a runway than an inviting walkway. Instead, stagger the path lights, or shine lights down upon the path so those on the walkway can still see where they are going.

Do choose the right bulbs. Incandescent bulbs with a high voltage can undermine the ambiance you want to achieve. Not to mention they gobble up tremendous amounts of energy. Choose warm LED lights for the best bang for your buck, and skip the unwanted glare.

Do light up small spaces. Adding accent lights to small, out-of-the-way spaces creates a sense of depth and beauty to your landscape and helps to keep all areas of your yard safe.

Do choose solar. If you have plenty of sunshine where you live, choose solar lighting. Not only will solar lighting save you money, it is good for the environment and easy to install.

Light up the night with cute solar lanterns

Mason jar solar lights are perfect for outdoor entertaining or even to light up pathways. Here is how you can make your very own solar lights.

What you need:

- mason jar with lid

- small solar garden light

- electrical tape

- scissors

- garden twine, 16 inches long

How to make it:

1. Wrap the solar light with electrical tape up near the top. The tape creates a buffer between the light and the jar. You will be wedging the light at the top of the jar to keep it from moving. If your jar and light are small, try about 15 wraps of tape.

2. Once you have wrapped the light, pull the tab on the solar light and push it into the jar's top. It should fit snugly.

3. Make a large loop with the garden twine. Hold the ring piece of the jar lid up, and place both ends of the twine between the ring and the circular lid piece. Screw the lid to the jar tightly and you have a handle.

4. Hang your light up outside, and enjoy it.

How do I easily beautify my hilly backyard?

Hilly lots can be quite beautiful but also challenging when it comes to landscape design and execution. But don't let this scare you. Many landscape solutions embrace the hills and give you an eye-catching and tidy landscape requiring little upkeep.

Incorporate stairs. If your hills eventually lead to a flatter piece of land, embrace the journey with a set of stairs.

That allows you to cross the hills quickly and safely and gives an anchor to your landscape. Choose wooden or concrete stairs, and accent them with your favorite plantings and some pretty landscape light.

Create a retaining wall. Cut out a portion of a hill and create a retaining wall to hold the soil back. A beautiful retaining wall provides a lovely landscape accent and gives you a dedicated planting spot behind the wall. Choose trailing plants that will fall gracefully over the wall and upright flowers and plants for color and height.

Install tiered raised beds. If your slope is only slight and catches the sun, don't let it go to waste. Create tiered raised beds to host your favorite veggies, herbs, and even fruit. Be sure you can navigate the hill to care for your garden. Create a path before installing the beds to make it easier.

Go native. Native plantings offer the most bang for their buck as far as durability goes. Not only are native plants accustomed to the climate in your area, but they will thrive and spread over your hills with little to no maintenance. Try grouping native plants by color for an eye-catching display.

Best poolside plantings for a sensational outdoor area

A pool is the perfect place for relaxation, exercise, and of course, fun. But if you really want to enjoy beautiful pool days with friends and family, you need to consider the overall look of the area.

Choosing the right poolside plantings will help integrate your pool into the entire landscape. Consider both perimeter plants such as trees and shrubs, and pots that look pretty sitting on your pool deck.

Remember to keep it low maintenance, and choose plants that won't drop fruit or leaves into your pool. These landscape plants are just the ticket.

Mediterranean fan palm. This beautiful palm is one of the toughest and most durable of all palms. It tolerates a wide variety of soil conditions and temperatures as cold as 10 degrees and as hot as 115 degrees. Numerous trunks of varying heights spring from its base and grow up to 20 feet tall.

Citrus trees. A citrus tree planted near a pool instantly gives off a tropical vibe while adding a splash of color when fruiting. Plant dwarf citrus in containers in the landscape around your pool, or choose larger ground planting varieties if your climate allows. Great choices include lemon, tangerine, lime, grapefruit, and orange.

Japanese maple. These beautiful plants are native to Japan and Korea and often considered a large bush rather than a tree. Suitable in growing zones 5-9, Japanese maples like the sun or part sun and well-draining soil. They grow very slowly and often reach 20 feet at maturity.

Fruitless olive. Because this tree lacks fruit, it is an excellent option around pools. These slow growers reach 20 to 25 feet at maturity and display attractive soft gray-green willow-like foliage. They prefer hot and dry summers and full sun. Plant this beautiful fruitless tree in growing zones 8-11.

Aged metal pipes create a great barrier between garden beds and other parts of your landscape. Stand the pipes upright along your border, and fill with attractive pebbles, shells, or even small plants. Stagger the heights for a unique look.

Here are some plants that are happy in poolside pots.

Lantana. Depending on where you live, lantana will be an annual or a perennial. Round and brightly colored clusters of flowers spill out over container edges, making lantana a poolside favorite.

Tufted evening primrose. Don't let this dainty little plant fool you. This evening primrose is drought tolerant, cold tolerant, and even deer resistant. Once planted, a little weekly water will keep this beauty blooming all summer long.

Salvia. This plant is very much at home as a focal point in a lovely container garden. Salvia has heart-shaped leaves in various colors, including blue, red, purple, orange, pink, yellow, white, green, and brown.

Verbena. Both upright and trailing varieties of verbena fill and spill in containers to create a dramatic display. You can find verbena in a rainbow of colors to suit any container theme. Verbena tolerates the midsummer heat well and will keep blooming as long as you give it a haircut now and then.

Unique fencing ideas that wow

Fencing is an excellent way to separate your space from your neighbor's space, contain children or pets, and create a boundary around your property to keep unwanted animal visitors out.

Depending on your objective, here are some unique fence materials that will have people stopping to take a second look.

Recycled lumber. Don't waste that leftover wood. Paint boards your favorite color to protect them, and create an attractive jagged fence. When installing this type of fence, it is useful to lay out your design first before digging it in.

Woven twigs. Some of the first settlers in America practiced the ancient art of twig woven fences. Made from flexible, long, and narrow green twigs, a woven twig fence is a practical work of art.

Pallets. Pallets are all the rage and are used to make everything from chicken coops to furniture. So it's not surprising they are popular as fencing material. Pallets joined together can easily create a perfect fence for your veggie patch or small dog's play yard.

Corrugated metal and rough lumber. Using corrugated metal pieces to break up a rough lumber fence creates an attractive marriage between rustic and modern. Wear gloves and use caution when building this fence as the metal can be sharp, and rough lumber tends to throw splinters.

Chicken wire. If you want to take advantage of a great view but still have the benefit of a fence, a contemporary view fence is for you. Adding a thin layer of chicken wire fencing to the back of a wide board split fence allows for privacy and the ability to see beyond your fence. To make your view fence ultramodern, consider painting your panels black.

Dog lover? Create a pooch-friendly yard

If you have pets, you want them to enjoy your outdoor living space with you safely. Here are some smart tips to keep your pet happy and healthy.

Put safety first. When considering landscape design, always ask yourself if what you are planning is safe for your dog. Eliminate any known hazards.

Think like a dog. You know your dog better than anyone else. What does he like to do outdoors? Perhaps he's an older, relaxed pooch who loves to lay in the lush grass. Or maybe he's a high-energy breed who would appreciate an obstacle course to keep him busy. Always include shady spots in the landscape to keep Fido cool.

Watch out for toxins. Many common landscape plants are toxic to dogs. A list of plants that dogs should stay clear of is available from the American Society for the Prevention of Cruelty to Animals (ASPCA). Just search for "toxic plants" on their website at aspca.org. Also, avoid using chemicals on your lawn and garden that could cause your dog to become ill.

Clean water is a must. If your dog will spend a lot of time outdoors, access to clean water is critical. Consider a splash fountain or a small dog-friendly water feature. Always keep the water source filled and free of debris.

Consider footing. The pads of a dog's feet are sensitive. Materials used underfoot should be easy for your pet to walk on. Good choices include flat rocks, pavers, and bricks.

If you want to have some pebbles and rocks, be sure they are big enough not to get caught in your dog's paws. Of course, all dogs love turf, even pet-friendly synthetic turf.

Use safe mulch. Although most mulch material is safe for dogs, avoid using rubber mulch or mulch made from cocoa bean shells. Stick to traditional organic mulch for flower beds and pathways.

Mulch magic: a natural layer to protect and beautify

9 key ways mulch saves you time and money

Want to protect your soil? Keep it nice and moist? Mulch is your answer. You can use both organic and inorganic materials to layer over your soil, depending on the area to be mulched. But whatever you use, your soil will benefit. Here are some key reasons to include mulch in your landscape.

Adds organic matter to the soil. Healthy, organic-rich soil breeds healthy plants that are more resistant to pests and disease. Extra benefit — saves money on pesticides and herbicides.

Supplies valuable slow-release nutrients. As the mulch decomposes, it offers plenty of nutrients and prevents vitamin loss in plants. Extra benefit — saves money on plant food.

Helps retain moisture. Mulch keeps moisture in the soil by protecting it from the sun. It also decreases water run-off during rain showers or watering. Extra benefit — reduces the amount of water needed, which saves money.

Provides a natural weed barrier. By blocking sunlight, mulch reduces the number of weeds that can grow and makes those that grow easier to pull out. Extra benefit — saves you time and energy.

Regulates temperature. Mulch does a fantastic job keeping the soil cool, which lowers the stress on plants and reduces the risk that your plants will get sick or die. Extra benefit — saves you money on new plants.

Increases biological activity. Beneficial microorganisms and earthworms feed on decomposing mulch. Extra benefit — enriches the soil.

Improves soil conditions. Mulching is a great way to improve soil conditions. It helps to bind sandy soils and aerate clay soils. Extra benefit — reduces the time and money needed to amend soil for planting.

> Mulched soil contains up to 70% more moisture than soil without a protective layer of mulch. So don't neglect this easy way to keep your ground hydrated.

Stops nutrients from leaching out. Adding a top layer of mulch prevents nutrients from leaching out of the soil. Extra benefit — less money and time spent enriching the soil.

Provides a clean surface for fruit and nuts to fall. Mulching under fruit and nut trees provides a softer and cleaner landing for your harvest to fall. Extra benefit — less-damaged fruit.

Handy chart to figure out mulching needs

You can buy mulch by the bag or by the cubic foot depending on how much you need. If you have a truck, you can often find mulch processors that will sell it to you for reasonable prices as long as you can haul it home.

Calculate the volume of mulch you need by multiplying the area (in square feet) by the depth (fraction of foot, not inches), then dividing by 27. Apply finer mulches (1/2 inch or smaller) 2 inches deep, and coarser mulch such as large bark chips, 4 inches deep.

Here is a handy table to help determine the cubic yards needed per desired depth.

Area size (square feet)	Cubic yards needed		
	2 inch	3 inch	4 inch
200	1	2	2.5
500	3	5	6
1,000	6	9	12
1,500	9	14	19
2,000	12	19	25

Mulching rules to garden by

Follow the mulching rules below for the healthiest plants and most attractive gardens and landscapes.

Create a good plan. Like anything you do in your garden, you need to define your mulching objectives. Know which areas need mulch in your garden, what type is best, and when you should spread it.

If possible, give mulching a page or two in your garden planner so you can stay on top of what you've done in the past, where you sourced your mulch, what types you used, and any issues you might have had.

Keep quality in mind. When shopping for mulch, always purchase from a reputable location. Remember, the higher the quality mulch, the healthier your plants will be.

Spread your mulch correctly. Piling up mulch too close to a plant or tree is a big no-no. It's a popular practice, but it can result in what is known as a mulching volcano.

When mulch is piled close to the stem or trunk, it keeps it wet, encouraging a shallow root system and even killing the plant. Effective mulching requires even spreading, not mounding.

Keep rock mulch looking clean and neat

Gravel, crushed gravel, pea gravel, and river rock are inorganic mulches used around established plantings or walkways, patios, or other outdoor living spaces.

Although it's highly attractive and durable, rock mulch can sometimes be a bit tricky to keep clean. Use these suggestions to keep your rock mulch looking great all year long.

- Combine it with landscape fabric. When applying rock mulch to established garden areas, always use heavy-duty landscape fabric underneath. It will help suppress any weeds that want to grow.

- Smooth it out with a rake. Use an appropriately sized rake to remove debris and level out rock after hard rains or winter weather.

- Blow off debris. Use a garden blower on heavier rock mulch to clear off any unwanted debris.

- Pick out larger scraps. If your rock mulch is below trees, sticks and limbs may fall into the mulch. The best way to remove this larger debris is to spend time hand-picking it out.

- Give it a refreshing shower. If you live in a dry climate without much rain, gravel and rock mulch can lose its luster. To keep your mulch looking great, spray it off with a strong bast of water at least once a week.

- Replace as needed. Depending on your climate, it may be necessary to top up your gravel mulch from time to time with a fresh supply.

Penny pinching ideas that work

Mulch, mulch, and more mulch. There's no better way to keep weeds out and moisture in. Don't waste money on store-bought mulch, though. Use these free mulch ideas instead.

Grass clippings. Toss extra grass clippings, even your neighbor's clippings (if you ask), in a big pile and let them break down. By next season they will do wonders to keep weeds away and moisture locked in. Don't use them before they break down as the nitrogen can burn plants.

Leaves. Simply run them over a few times with your mower and scatter them throughout your garden beds. This wonder material holds moisture, prevents weeds from sprouting, and helps improve the soil, giving you lush gardens, trees, and flower beds.

Shredded paper. If you are an avid newspaper reader or know others who have lots of old papers, consider shredding the paper for mulch. You can also shred junk mail, store flyers, and old bills for free mulch. Don't use glossy paper as it may contain toxic ink.

DIY wood chips. After you do your spring trimming and have a pile of limbs, why not rent a chipper? Check with neighbors who may want to share the cost of a chipper and make free wood chip mulch.

If you have local tree companies close by, you can also check to see if they'll let you have wood chips free or at a reduced rate.

What is the slimy, bright pink stuff in my mulch?

If you live in the eastern United States, you have likely seen some strange, colorful, and slimy-looking structures popping up through your mulch.

Slime mulch is not anything to be afraid of but is just fungi feeding on bacteria in the mulch.

Also called "dog vomit" fungus, these fungi are generally bright orange, pink, or yellow and appear in slimy masses that can range from 1 inch wide to more than a foot across.

They usually last for a short period and are confined to a small space. You can leave them to decompose or discard them in a compost pile, garbage can, or a location away from the mulch. They are not harmful to plants or humans unless eaten.

Top 3 types to improve and enrich soil

One of the great benefits of mulching is that, as it breaks down, it actually feeds the soil and provides food for beneficial organisms. These three types of mulch in particular will help you build rich soil loaded with nutrients.

Recycled plants. The absolute best kind of mulch to use no matter what kind of soil you have is recycled plant material. This includes leaves, spent plants, buds, bark, flowers, twigs, and other plant debris.

When you use recycled plant material in your garden beds as mulch, it breaks down much like it does in nature, providing rich and diverse organic matter for the soil and its inhabitants.

Native cedar. The second best choice, if you have to buy mulch, is shredded native cedar. Most folks don't know that cedar is the one mulch that repels bad bugs naturally, with no chemical additives.

The fragrant oil in fresh cedar drives away insects, allowing the rich soil to flourish. So you get an added bonus when you use this mulch.

Triple-hammered hardwood. This is another great type of mulching material for soil enrichment. Triple-hammered means that hardwood bark and lumber-processing scraps undergo a hammering process where they break down three times until they are almost a fine, sawdust consistency.

Organic and dye-free hardwood mulch processed this way adds vital nutrients, including nitrogen, as it decomposes and integrates into the soil.

Pros and cons of using rubber

With the introduction of rubber mulch into the landscape world, a whole new door opened. The question is, do you want to step through it?

Rubber mulch is made from recycled rubber tires and offers several benefits to gardeners, starting with a reduction in carbon footprint. But there are some important cautions you need to consider. Review the pros and cons before deciding if it's right for you.

Pro. Rubber mulch does a superior job of insulating plants against heat, much better than wood chips and other organic materials.

Con. Rubber mulch does not decompose because it is not organic. Therefore, it does not supply the soil or plants with beneficial nutrients.

> To make the most of rubber mulch, use it for hardscaping projects such as paths, around fountains, outdoor dining areas, and play structures. Avoid using rubber mulch for ornamental or edible plants, as well as around trees and shrubs.

Pro. Using rubber mulch on indoor gardens such as sunrooms or solariums is an excellent idea because it doesn't break down and emit a rotting smell.

Con. Rubber mulches do contain a chemical residue that can be harmful to plants. However, wood mulch can have residue, so it is crucial to find a good, chemical-free source for your wood mulch.

Pro. Rubber mulch does not attract insects. Some homeowners even use rubber mulch as a protective layer around their homes' foundation to discourage pests.

Con. Although rubber mulch may look attractive at a distance, many people are put off by it upon closer inspection because it does not look or feel organic.

Interested? Here are some other benefits that may help make up your mind.

- Rubber mulch will last forever and stay in one place, making it an excellent option for people short on time.

- You can choose from a wide range of colors so your design options are endless. And rubber mulch, unlike colored wood mulch, holds its color for up to 10 years.

- Rubber mulch goes twice as far as organic material as it only requires a 1.5-inch depth compared to 3-inch depth of organic mulch. The initial cost will be higher, but the long-term savings will make up for it.

Is it true wood chips steal nitrogen from my plants?

You may have heard that using wood chips as mulch will rob nitrogen from your plants. There's some truth to it, but any nitrogen loss will only be temporary. Here's why.

When you mulch, your soil will get an influx of bacteria to break down the wood chips. As they work, the bacteria hold on to some of the nitrogen to survive. Once the wood chips decompose, nitrogen releases into the soil, and the bacteria die off.

Keep in mind that the benefits of mulching far outweigh the short-lived nitrogen borrowing. But if you're concerned, here are some things you can do to lessen the impact.

- Avoid turning wood chips under the soil as that's mainly when the nitrogen gets tied up. In annual beds, rake away old mulch before planting, and re-mulch after you are finished. That will ensure the mulch does not get too heavily mixed into the soil.

- Apply wood chips in the early spring before the plants start to take off. If you are mulching a new garden area, apply the mulch several months before planting to give it time to break down and enrich the soil.

- If your plants begin to show signs of nitrogen defi-
  ciency, provide a nitrogen-rich, natural fertilizer
  such as well-aged manure tea. This rich elixir will
  keep your plants healthy until the bacteria decomposition work finishes.

Make your very own rubber mulch patio

Rubber mulch provides an attractive and long-lasting foundation for the perfect outdoor living space.

Creating a rubber mulch patio does not require any special
skills and can be a fun weekend project. As a bonus, your
rubber mulch patio will look fabulous for years to come.

- You first need to find a good location for your patio
  and determine how big you want it to be. The best spot
  is an area with no grass and not many weeds. Outline
  the patio area using some spray chalk.

- Lay some weed barrier fabric down, and overlap the
  edges by 6 inches all the way around. Use landscape
  pins to hold the material in place. To keep the rubber
  mulch contained, place timbers or another type of
  border material on top of the landscape fabric.

- Place a 4-inch layer of rubber mulch on top of the weed
  fabric, keeping it as even as possible. Rake the surface
  smooth using a bow rake.

- Water the mulch using the mist sprayer on your garden
  hose to help it settle. After it is wet, walk on it to further
  compact the mulch.

That's all there is to it. The only upkeep with your patio is to
spray and rake it from time to time to keep it looking great.

Best organic mulch for vegetable beds

Vegetables require excellent mulching practices. Here are the best mulches to consider for your food garden.

Type	Description	Depth	Benefits	Notes
corn stalks and cobs	shredded stalks and ground-up cobs	2"	no weed seeds and can be turned directly under the soil in spring	may blow away unless mixed with straw
cotton burrs	leftover parts from cotton harvest including seeds, stems, and leaves	1-2"	no weed seeds and can be turned directly under the soil in spring	do not use burrs from chemically treated plants
cover crops	includes rye-grass, winter rye, buck-wheat, barley oats, and annual clover	planted on top of the soil	can be cut and used as mulch before going to seed or turned under the soil before going to seed	attracts beneficial insects when flowering
shredded leaves	all leaves but those from beech, holly, sweet chestnut, eucalyptus, and walnut trees	2"	no weed seeds and can be turned directly under the soil in spring	use during cold months as an insulator to keep worms warm and happy
pine straw	also known as pine needles	2-3"	offers good winter protec-tion for fall veggies	weed suppression is not as good as other mulch and can't be turned under
straw	dry stalks of cereal plants	2-3"	can be turned under at end of the season	can easily blow around and may contain weed seeds; pre-sprout bales by wetting

Time your mulching for best results

Like many things in gardening, timing is essential when it comes to mulching. If you mulch too early or too late, it can cause problems.

Traditionally, mulching is done in mid to late spring as the soil warms up and the air temperature rises. If you put mulch down before that, it will hinder the warming process that is necessary for healthy soil.

Mulching late in the fall can also be a problem as it slows plant dormancy, which is needed for plants to survive the cold season. Here are some tips that will help you decide the best time to spread your mulch.

Mulch in spring if:

- you want to suppress weeds.

- you want a clean and fresh look.

- you can be patient and wait until mid to late spring to avoid trapping any cold moisture.

Mulch in fall if:

- you are busy or won't be home in the spring.

- aesthetics aren't a big deal since fall mulch will fade by spring.

- you live in an area with a harsh winter, or you have just added some new plants to your garden. Just be sure to wait until after a few freezes to mulch. Many people do this around Thanksgiving time.

Mulch in winter if:

- you have an abundance of perennials. As soil freezes and thaws, it can push plants out of the ground. Adding a protective layer of mulch can help keep this from happening by moderating the soil temperature.

- you have lots of evergreens. Evergreens get dry and often turn brown in the winter. A layer of mulch encourages them to retain moisture.

Recycling secret earthworms love

Do you order a lot of things online? If so, you most likely have a ton of cardboard boxes going out in your recycling bin. Why not repurpose all that cardboard as beneficial mulch?

Using cardboard as a base layer is known as sheet mulching. In a garden it helps retain moisture, suppress weeds, and also attract earthworms that feast on the cardboard and excrete nutrient-rich worm castings.

Here is how to sheet mulch for healthy soil and happy plants.

- Soak the area of soil where you plan to sheet mulch. Remove all tape from your cardboard and lay down pieces over the soil. Overlap the cardboard pieces by at least 6 inches so weeds don't slip through the cracks.

- Soak the cardboard using a water hose until it becomes saturated. Add 2 inches of composted manure on top of the cardboard. Add 2 inches of mulch on top of the manure. Repeat this process for another layer.

If you are planting perennials, including edible plants and trees, lay the sheet mulch and let it heat up for a few weeks.

When you are ready to plant, brush away the organic material, and cut a hole in the cardboard. Let the sheet mulch decompose for a year before planting annual crops.

No. 1 best thing you can do for your trees

Is it a good idea to mulch around your trees? The answer is yes, most definitely. Mulching is the single best thing you can do for a tree after you get it in the ground.

- According to U.S. Forest Service data, mulch speeds up the growth rate of walnut trees by 89%. Other hardwood trees like oak, maple, birch, beech, and cherry grow 79% faster with mulch.

- Mulching around trees also prevents weed seeds from germinating. One study found that mulch reduced weed growth by 45% in the first year and 85% in the second year. Use coarse organic mulch, not finer compost mulch, for the best weed suppression.

- Organic mulch will reduce water evaporation by 35% compared to bare soil. That means water is more readily available for your trees. Plus you won't have to water as much.

> The most important thing to remember when mulching a tree is to start about 3 to 6 inches away from the trunk and continue outwards in all directions at least 3 feet. Six feet is even better. Under no circumstances should the mulch ever touch the trunk. A properly mulched tree will appear to be encircled by a raised ring.

- Happy roots make happy trees. Mulch provides the perfect insulation for tree roots, keeping them warm in the winter and cool in the summer.

Taking the time to mulch around trees helps the soil accumulate valuable nutrients such as nitrogen, phosphorus, and calcium. Don't overdo it though — too much mulch can damage trees. For best results, stick with 2 to 3 inches.

If you choose not to mulch, you will have issues, especially with new trees. These include increased weeds, slow root growth, and pest problems, as weak and dehydrated trees lack the energy to protect themselves.

7 clever ways to use recycled glass in the garden

Glass mulch is a unique recycled product created from tumbled glass. Like gravel or stones in the landscape, it adds a decorative touch in hardscaping projects. Plus, recycling glass this way helps keep it out of the landfill.

The intense colors of glass mulch remain bold and bright for a long time. It's usually available in various amber, green, and blue shades from 2 to 6 inches in size.

Because tumbled glass has no sharp corners, it is useful for many garden projects, including:

- paths and walkways.

- as a top cover for container plants.

- around ponds and other water features.

- in rock gardens.

- around fire pits.

- surrounding garden art.

- as an embellishment in handmade stepping stones.

As a general rule, use 7 pounds of glass mulch to cover 1 square foot. Check local garden stores for this recycled wonder, or hit up city recycling centers.

Put a quick stop to your carpenter ant problem

Garden sheds, decks, and mulch are favorite places for carpenter ants to build their nests. If you're an avid gardener, you know what a severe nuisance these ants can be. Although they don't eat wood mulch, they chew and make tunnels in the wood to create their nests.

Carpenter ants don't bite, but they can make quick work of any wooden structures, and if left untreated can even damage your home.

Here are some tried and true ways to get a handle on the ant infestation in your mulch.

Thin out your mulch. Reducing the amount of wood mulch in your gardens makes it harder for ants to build a nest. If they don't have enough material to work with, they will find another spot to nest.

Stir it regularly. Take the time to stir up the mulch a few times a week using a garden hoe. This effort discourages ants from building a nest and destroys any nests already constructed.

Watch where you put it. Keep the mulch at least 3 inches away from tree trunks and use an inorganic mulch only around wooden structures like decks and sheds.

Douse them with an ant-be-gone elixir. Mix up this special brew and use it wherever you see ant activity.

- 1/4 cup powdered sugar

- 1 1/2 tablespoons borax powder

- 2 cups of water

- empty jar with lid

- cotton balls

- tinfoil

Boil the water and pour it into the jar. Add the sugar and borax and stir until it dissolves completely. Soak cotton balls in the mixture. Set the cotton balls on small pieces of tinfoil. Place a few cotton balls on top of the mulch in areas of activity.

The ants will take the mixture to their nest. When ants eat the sugary drink, the borax mixes with the formic acid inside the ants where it explodes, killing the ants.

Ornamental gardens that wow

7 design tips for balance and beauty in your front yard

When you create a garden in your front yard, have a vision in mind. What is your landscape's overall theme, and what works best with your home style or other existing natural features?

Keep in mind that a front-yard garden is highly visible. A well-done garden adds value to your home while a haphazard and unruly garden can detract from its value.

Use these design tips to help you achieve balance and beauty in your front garden. They will help guide you as you move from paper to placement.

Use what nature has provided. Before designing your garden space, take inventory of what nature has already provided. It might be a collection of boulders, a magnificent towering oak, or beautiful Saguaro cactus.

These elements make fantastic anchor points to build out your garden space. It's important to integrate new planting and design with what already exists for a smooth and flowing space.

Define your space softly. Hardscape elements like fences define and welcome at the same time. Of course, if you build a 6-foot wall around your home, it would not be overly welcoming. But a short, wide picket or wrought-iron fence allows those who pass by to enjoy your garden and feel welcome while softly defining boundaries and adding charm to your property.

Plant some evergreens. Adding a few exciting evergreen plants, shrubs, or trees gives a garden space some year-round structure and cuts down on garden maintenance. Along with the evergreen, add some other plants that have all-year interest or color.

Take advantage of vertical surfaces. Walls offer unlimited planting potential for your favorite climbers. Roses, clematis, and wisteria are some great options that add color and fragrance to any space while drawing the eye upward. Virginia creeper or Boston ivy adds seasonal color interest as well.

> Ornamental gardens are designed for aesthetic pleasure and incorporate one or more types of living plants, including flowering plants, bulbs, foliage plants, vines, ornamental grasses, shrubs, and trees. The three common design styles include formal gardens, marked by symmetrical or geometrical patterns; informal gardens, with flowing curves and natural shapes; and wild gardens, which are designed to mimic nature.

Mix in container plantings. Never underestimate the value of a well-placed container in a front garden area. Container plants do a great job transitioning garden space to indoor space.

Consider using baskets, boxes, and other fun containers stuffed with fragrant herbs, flowers, and trailing plants. Place your potted prizes where they will be most enjoyed — generally on your front steps, porch, or along a path leading to your front door.

Choose the perfect palette. Will you go with soft and subtle colors or bold and dramatic? A lot of this depends on your home's size and style and the garden vibe you want to achieve.

Subtle colors work well with smaller structures as they don't overpower. Bolder, more dramatic colors pair exceptionally well with more extensive and modern structures. The key is to keep color simple and not introduce too many colors in one space as it can become distracting.

Bring in more color with annuals. Annual plants allow for flexibility in front gardens. For instance, you can change out annuals a few different times in the growing season to reflect a new color pattern or simply to refresh your garden.

Top foliage plants for unique garden interest

Formal, informal, and wild gardens all benefit from plants with stunning foliage. Select plants that add fine texture, brilliant color, and bold shapes.

Some foliage plants are excellent for adding interest in shady spots. Some even change color with the season, adding additional visual appeal. Here are some popular foliage plants to include in your landscape.

Coleus. At one point in history, shade-loving coleus was the only type available. Today sun-loving coleus plants have found the hearts of gardeners far and wide.

These pretty plants are popular in containers and even indoors as houseplants. Splashes of bright green, pinks, and reds in exciting patterns make this plant a winner.

Caladium. Also called "angel wings," these plants have stunning, large arrowhead-shaped leaves present in various color combinations, including green, red, pink, and white.

Caladiums like partial shade, where they shine brightly. Grow these plants as perennials in zone 9 and as annuals in colder climates where you can bring them indoors for the winter.

Hosta. No ornamental garden would be complete without some hosta plants. These dramatic foliage beauties come in shades of green, gold, and blue in addition to variegated leaves.

> Slugs will happily munch on your hostas if given the chance. To keep them away, place a ring of table salt around your hosta about 5 inches from the center of the plant. Slugs will stay clear of this salty defense ring, and your beautiful hostas will be safe.

Hostas prefer partial shade, although several varieties thrive in full sun, which opens up loads of opportunities to enjoy this plant.

Dusty miller. This plant is often grown as an annual filler plant in containers. Its soft, powdery foliage and short habit make it a great companion to brightly colored flowers such as yellow coreopsis and hot pink petunias. Dusty miller is a drought-tolerant plant that makes it great for low-water areas in the garden.

Elephant ear. Grown from tuberous rhizomes, these plants can reach up to 6 feet tall at maturity and have huge, 3-foot, heart-shaped leaves in black, yellow, emerald green, purple, or a mix of colors. Use elephant ears as a focal point or for height in the back of your garden beds.

How to create the perfect cottage garden

A cottage garden is a type of informal ornamental garden that softens the landscape and draws your eye inward to a place of romance, warmth, and beauty. There is something truly magical about a well-designed cottage garden that everyone can enjoy.

Here are some design tips to help you get started planning and creating the perfect cottage garden.

- Bring on the romance by using a pastel color template and fragrant flowers.

- Enclose the garden with a picket fence or lattices that are short enough to catch a peek of this magical space.

- Create informal crowding by placing plants close together. Use annuals, perennials, foliage plants, and vegetables for interest.

- Insert curving pathways. Use brick, gravel, flagstone, colored stone, or mulch to create flowing paths throughout the garden.

- Add whimsical elements. Old wheelbarrows, bathtubs, sinks, vintage barrels, old tools, hypertufa planters, or fairy lights can inject a sense of whimsy into the garden.

- Try unique color combinations like purple and red or orange and pink.

- Don't forget water. A bubbling water feature or quaint pond provides interest and enhances the peaceful setting.

- Make sure you include a stone bench or other seating. Your cottage garden is the perfect place to sit and reflect.

- Attract birds and other pollinators with a variety of feeders and houses.

- Be a rule breaker. The sky is the limit with a cottage garden. Let your imagination soar.

Tricks for bigger, better roses every time

The timeless beauty of roses remains an anchor in gardens around the globe. Commonly seen in formal gardens, roses are also popular in informal landscape designs as well. Roses are by far the most popular garden center plant.

Roses are divided into two main classes — bush roses and climbing roses — based on their growth habits. Each of these categories further divides into several different types.

Want to grow the best roses ever? Here are some timeless tips for creating bigger and better roses every time.

Before you plant a bare-root rose bush, soak it in this head-start elixir for eight to 12 hours. Combine 1 table-spoon each of vegetable and flower food (5-8-5), shampoo, and corn syrup with 1 gallon of water. When you finish soaking your new rose bushes, use the mixture to water established bushes for a great treat.

Protect them from harsh weather. If you live where winters are harsh, help your springtime bush roses bounce into action by protecting them from extreme winter weather.

After the first killing frost, while the soil is still workable, pile 10 inches of new soil around the canes. Tie canes together to keep them from blowing around.

If your temperatures drop below zero, pile some straw around the canes, and toss a few shovels of dirt on top to keep it in place. As soon as all danger of frost passes, remove the protection, and watch your roses come to life.

Give them a midsummer pick-me-up. Make your roses bloom bigger and prettier this summer without slaving hours in the hot sun. The secret? Tea leaves.

It may sound strange, but giving your roses a midsummer pick-me-up will help them finish the season strong. Place used tea bags on the soil underneath your rose bushes. The tannic acid in the bags creates slightly acidic soil conditions that roses love.

Try a simple weed-killing trick. Rose roots grow close to the soil surface, and it's easy to injure them if you're not careful when removing weeds.

For healthy roses that are easier to maintain, use newspaper to smother weeds instead. Newspaper kills weeds instantly and keeps them from coming back for an entire season.

Insects eating your roses? Place two cloves of garlic under each rose bush. They will never have an issue with aphids or other potentially destructive insects again.

In early spring, before weeds start to spread, spray your rose garden bed well. Cover weeds with newspaper and spray them with water. Top the wet paper with 3 inches of shredded leaves or other mulching material.

Along with managing weeds, the newspaper will provide valuable food for beneficial soil organisms as it breaks down.

Snip roses right with this handy hint

Before you snip that gorgeous rose, be sure to cut at the right spot. If you don't, you'll get spindly little shoots instead of a strong stem full of new blossoms.

How do you know exactly where to cut? Here's a hint — the number of leaves will tell you. If you prune during the growing season, find a mature leaflet of five to seven leaves that face out from the center of the plant.

Cut at a 45-degree angle about 1/4 inch above the leaflet. This will encourage outward growth and keep the inside of the plant open for good air circulation.

When pruning roses with sharp thorns, avoid being poked by using a clothespin to hang onto the stems while you cut.

It also allows rainwater to run down behind a bud eye and not over it, causing a moisture buildup. Always remember to use clean and sharp pruning shears.

Enjoy fresh cut flowers for longer

Nothing is quite as beautiful as a bouquet of fresh-cut flowers on your dining table. And clipping them from your own garden allows you to bring a little bit of nature into your home.

The only sad thing about cut flowers is that they fade fast. Follow these tips to keep your cut flowers looking great so you can enjoy them as long as possible.

Cut the stems. Use clean garden shears to trim cut flower stems about 1 inch on an angle. This allows them to take up water easily. Retrim every few days.

Use the right water. Place cut flowers in cold water, and be sure to dump out and replace the water every other day.

Remove bottom leaves. Snip all leaves below the water line to prevent bacterial growth. Check your bouquet every few days, and remove floating leaves.

Display them wisely. Keep your fresh flowers out of direct sun, high heat, and drafts. Do not place your bouquet near appliances that generate heat, or open windows or ceiling fans that dry flowers out.

Also, don't put your fresh-cut flowers near ripening fruit like bananas that give off ethylene gas. It can reduce your flowers' beauty and life.

Keep them cool. Nighttime is fridge time. Place your bouquet in the refrigerator before bed for eight hours. Cut flowers love cooler temperatures that help stall aging.

Feed them with a special elixir. Most people have apple cider vinegar and sugar in their pantry. Retain the beauty of cut flowers by combining two tablespoons each of these two popular pantry items in a quart of water.

The sugar acts as food, while vinegar is an antibacterial agent that helps keep your flowers fresh. Add a little to your vase each day to keep your bouquet looking great.

> To remove built-up hard water stains in your glass flower vases, soak them in a solution of one part white vinegar to four parts water for at least two hours. Rinse with warm water and let dry.

Easy perennials brighten your garden from spring to fall

Perennials are a boon to your landscape. They come in every shape, color, and texture imaginable and can fit in virtually any spot in any ornamental garden. Plus they come back year after year — a value that can't be beat.

You can easily achieve all-season color, from spring to fall, with the right collection of long-blooming perennials. Here are some top easy-growers that definitely won't let you down.

Russian sage. This reliable long-bloomer has beautiful sky blue flowers that show up in midsummer and last for over 10 weeks. Hardy in zones 5 to 9, Russian sage is perfect for low-water areas and can reach a height of 4 feet. Place this beauty in the back of your garden for a spectacular pop of color.

Coneflower. A member of the daisy family, the coneflower adds vibrant color and interest to any garden all season long starting in midsummer. It has bright flowers that attract pollinators to the garden, such as butterflies and hummingbirds. Hardy in zones 4 to 8, coneflowers are durable and drought-tolerant once established.

Dahlia. This tuberous plant is a relative of the sunflower, daisy, zinnia, and chrysanthemum. It will give your garden beautiful color from late summer through autumn.

Dahlias' pom-pom flowers range from 2 inches in diameter to plate size and reach up to 5 feet tall. Choose from a wide variety of colors, including yellow, white, red, peach, lavender, pink, and bicolor.

These plants are hardy in zones 8 to 11. In other zones they need to be dug up in the fall and replanted in the spring.

Keep your new perennials happy all season long with this strange but successful flower-boosting blend. In a 5-gallon pail, mix together 2 pounds dry oatmeal, 2 pounds crushed dry dog food, 1 handful human hair, and 1/2 cup sugar. Place a handful in each planting hole.

Hellebore. This beautiful plant is one of the first perennials to bloom in the season. It has large saucer-shaped flowers that bloom white with striking pink, yellow, or maroon markings. Hellebore is deer-resistant and does best in light shade and in growing zones 4 to 9.

Peony. Nothing is quite as striking as a mature peony bush in the springtime. Cloud-like fragrant blooms welcome the garden season in a wide range of colors, including yellow, white, salmon, pink, and rose. It grows well in zones 3 to 8.

> ## *Show gardener's secret to spectacular flowers*
>
> Jordan has been growing show flowers for over 20 years. Her specialty is plants with large, vibrant flowers like peonies, dahlias, and sunflowers. She has spent countless hours perfecting the art of creating spectacular, awe-inspiring flowers.
>
> Here are just a few of her favorite, time-tested tips. Grow the biggest, most beautiful blooms ever with these easy secrets.
>
> **Start with healthy soil.** Soil that is rich in organic matter, light, and well-draining provides a constant supply of nutrients for plants. Add plenty of composted manure to the soil when planting, and add it during the season to keep bacterial activity high and plants well-fed.
>
> **Make deadheading a regular habit.** Stroll through your garden daily and spend the time to pinch or pop off spent blooms. Energy will no longer be diverted to the spent flowers, which can lead to healthy new buds.
>
> If you want to grow show-quality blooms, Jordan says, remove all the buds on a stem, leaving just one at the tip. This is called dis-budding, and it forces the plant to devote all its energy into growing a single spectacular flower.
>
> **Feed throughout the blooming season.** Blooming plants require a healthy dose of all-purpose organic feed with a higher amount of phosphorus than nitrogen. It is phosphorus that promotes more flower buds.
>
> **Watch your watering.** Too much water can cause foliage to develop in the absence of flowers. A lack of water can cause plants to drop flower buds. Moderate watering is best.

Quick trick for amazing flower displays

By late season, it is likely that many of your annual flowers are losing their luster. You won't believe how easy it is to perk them up and make them go wild with blooms.

Bring back their flower power with this easy-to-make tonic. Add the following ingredients to a gallon of water and give your plants a nice long drink.

- 1/4 cup beer

- 1 tablespoon corn syrup

- 1 tablespoon baby shampoo

- 1 tablespoon 15-30-15 fertilizer

Savings bonanza: Grow free flowers from cuttings

Growing flowers from cuttings allows you to multiply the beauty in your landscape for free. And by propagating cuttings, your new plants will be genetically identical to the parent plant that you love.

To be successful, take the cuttings during the parent plant's active growing season. The best plants to divide by cuttings are those that have new growth and are healthy and vibrant.

What you need:

- scissors

- razorblade

- pencil

- parent plant

- plastic wrap

- soilless potting mix

- rooting hormone

- containers

- alcohol

How to do it:

1. Select a clean container for the cutting, and fill it with fresh, new soilless potting mix.

2. Locate a green stem that has a node on the parent plant. This is where new roots will grow.

3. Sterilize your scissors in alcohol. Cut just below the node, including at least two leaves. A 4- to 6-inch piece is long enough.

4. Lay newspaper on a hard and level surface, and set the cutting down. Use the razor blade to make a cut through the middle of the node to improve the likelihood that roots will form.

5. Remove all but one or two leaves.

6. Add a little rooting hormone to a container and a little water to another container.

7. Dip the node end of the cutting into water and then into the rooting hormone. Shake any excess hormone off, and throw away any extra hormone in the container.

8. Use the pencil to make a small hole in the soil a bit larger in diameter than the cutting.

9. Place the cutting into the hole, and gently pat the soil around the cutting. If you have more than one cutting, be sure their leaves don't touch each other.

10. Put plastic around the container to trap humidity, but don't seal the plastic as it will interfere with airflow.

11. Place the container in a warm spot where it will get indirect light. Move to direct light after you see new

leaves form on the stem. Check the soil daily — it needs to stay moist but not saturated.

After two to three weeks, check the plant to see if roots have developed. Gently tug on the plant, and if you feel resistance, roots have formed. Transplant the plant to a larger pot or directly into the ground.

Why are my ornamental grasses dying in the middle?

Ornamental grasses are fabulous, trouble-free plants that add texture and motion to the landscape. Tall grasses make an excellent privacy screen, and when used as a focal point, they bring stability to a formal landscape.

If you notice the centers dying in ornamental grass, it just means the plant is getting older and a little tired. As grasses age, they can die in the center, leaving them looking less than vibrant.

To prevent this, it is essential to divide them every two or three years. The best time to divide an ornamental grass is in the early spring before new growth emerges. Here's what to do.

- Water the grass to be divided a few days thoroughly before splitting. This will keep the plant healthy and make it easier to dig.

- Cut the grass to a height of 8 inches, and insert a sharp spade into the soil a few inches from the clump. Work around the grass in a circle digging deeply to cut the roots.

- Lift out the section carefully and split in half. Discard or compost the dead center.

Prepare new planting holes before you divide the grass so you can transplant immediately. If you can't get them into the ground right away, be sure to keep them cool and moist.

Need quick coverage? Flowering vines to the rescue

When you plan your ornamental garden, don't forget to look up. Are there spots you can add vertical climbing plants for a little pizzazz?

One of the best ways to add a pop of upward color is to use climbing vines. They come in all shapes, sizes, and hues. For the price of a pack of seeds, you get fast-growing plants with eye-catching color.

Because they snowball quickly, you can use annual vines to cover an eyesore such as a chain link fence. Climbing annual vines also offer quick coverage and shade for your outdoor living space.

You can count on these three top-performing annual vines for stellar performance in your garden.

Morning glory. This elegant vine opens its trumpet-shaped blooms in the early morning and closes them at the end of each day. Morning glories grow easily from seed and even reseed themselves, giving you more bang for your buck.

You can find these popular vines in purple flowers with a white throat as well as pale blue, white, brown, pink, and magenta. Morning glories perform well in dappled, full sun to light shade and will reach 6 to 15 feet at maturity with a spreading habit.

Cup and saucer vine. Sometimes called "missionary bells," this beautiful vine makes its way upwards using foot-long tendrils ending in small, sharp hooks. A long-lasting bloom of large, creamy green, bell-shaped flowers dangles down.

When it matures, it becomes violet and then a stunning purple color with a sweet honey aroma. This fast-growing vine likes full sun and some afternoon shade in hot climates and will reach 10 to 20 feet tall with a spreading habit. Start seeds indoors eight to 10 weeks before the last frost date.

Black-eyed Susan. This vintage favorite has golden, open-faced petals that surround a dark eye. Some newer varieties bloom in shades of white, blue, and salmon. It grows quickly and flowers nonstop as it winds around anything in its path.

Black-eyed Susan prefers full sun to part shade and will grow 3 to 8 feet tall with a spreading habit. Sow directly into the soil after all threats of frost have passed.

Secret to overwintering your favorite flowers

When the chill of late summer, early fall begins to creep into your garden, you know it's time to rescue tender plants from the onslaught of winter.

The good news is you can have gorgeous geraniums that keep coming back — along with many other favorite flowers — by following a few simple overwintering rules for success. No greenhouse needed.

Many flowers are quite happy to spend the winter in a bright room or window of your home. Plants you can move in for the winter include the beloved geranium, sweet potato vine, coleus, hibiscus, caladium, Boston fern, begonias, and rosemary.

Follow these tips to keep your favorite outdoor plants happy indoors all winter.

- Bring plants in before the first frost, and place them near a window with eastern, southern, or western exposure.

- Cut large plants back by half or two-thirds to reduce their size and slow their growth a bit.

- Use grow lights if natural light is insufficient.

- Provide a humidifier if the air is quite dry.

- Water whenever the soil gets dry.

- Turn plants each week so that all sides get exposed to the light.

- When reintroducing plants back outdoors in the spring, don't rush. Set plants out on cloudy days before replanting or repotting so they're not shocked by too much sun.

Cold-hardy perennials that are practically indestructible

Why plant anything else? Perennials are dependable, beautiful, and cost-effective. While all perennials are great, hardy perennials are even better. And cold-hardy perennials are the best because they come back even after extreme winter weather.

Here are some of the top cold-hardy perennials to consider if you live in areas where winter weather brings freezing temperatures and loads of snow.

Bee balm. Pollinators love this favorite hardy perennial that grows up to 4 feet in height and bears happy flowers in pink, red, orange, blue, white, or purple depending on the variety. This plant is a member of the mint family and requires lots of room to spread out. Cold hardy to zone 4.

Siberian iris. This northern Turkey and Russian native does not shy away from subzero temperatures. When the weather starts to break in the spring, this reliable plant puts on a dazzling show with purple, yellow, white, blue, or lilac flowers.

These plants grow up to 3- to 4-feet tall and produce thick clumps of dark green, strap-like leaves. For best results, plant this iris in rich and slightly moist soil. Cold hardy to zone 3.

Catmint. This plant with gorgeous purple flowers and fragrant foliage is one of the first perennials to bust through the cold ground after winter. If you clip the plant back after the first flower show, you may be lucky enough to get a second bloom in late summer.

Clip catmint back in the fall to encourage snow to pile up on the crown. This will provide it with excellent insulation all winter long. Cold hardy to zone 3.

Coreopsis. "Moonbeam" coreopsis is an incredibly hardy variety of this garden favorite. Winter is no match for this rugged plant that boasts stunning yellow flowers on short stalks. They bring sunshine to the garden continuously from early summer into fall.

To keep this plant looking its best, divide it every three years and spread the love elsewhere in your garden. Cold hardy to zone 4.

Keep your hardy perennials in great shape heading into winter, and they'll come back robust and healthy in the spring. A little extra attention during the season to keep them well-watered, fed, and weed-free will do the trick.

Pesky pests and easy homemade solutions

Amazing tricks to banish pests from your garden forever

Sometimes the best ways to fight off pests are the old-fashioned, tried-and-true methods your grandpa used. Here's what worked for him, and they can work for you, too.

Pick them off. Although this may seem like a slow and arduous process, it works well early in the season. When you remove adult pests before they get a chance to lay eggs, you stop the cycle and minimize damage.

The best types of pests for picking include those that move slowly like caterpillars, slugs, snails, and Colorado potato beetles. After you handpick, dispose of the pests in a container of soapy water.

Prune away. When handpicking is not quite enough, combine it with selective pruning. Taking off leaves and branches where you find eggs will prevent or lessen damage.

Cut away water sprouts and root suckers from woody plants, which reduces plant growth that attracts insects. You can control aphids, garden webworms, tent caterpillars, and leafminers with this pruning technique.

Remember to sterilize garden tools before and after using them to prevent the spread of disease or pests.

Shake them down. Farmers have long used shaking to get pests to fall to the ground so they can monitor their population. In small home gardens, shaking pests may remove enough of them to keep damage low.

Shaking dislodges bugs that crawl on plants, such as Japanese beetles, earwigs, cucumber beetles, and Colorado potato beetles. Shake pests from plants early in the morning when they have not yet woken up. You can also capture night-feeding insects just after the sun sets when the temperature begins to drop.

For trees and shrubs, spread a cloth underneath and shake with your hands, or tap limbs with a stick. When finished, turn over the fabric and dispose of the pests.

Spray them off. Aphids, leafhoppers, spider mites, and thrips easily fall from plants when hit with a strong spray of water. Adjust the nozzle on your garden sprayer to the fan setting so it covers a large area.

> If slugs are destroying your plants, try this common household remedy. Crush up leftover eggshells, and put them around plants for protection. As a bonus, the eggshells release valuable calcium into the soil when they break down.

Keep in mind that hard streams of water directed at one spot can damage foliage and flowers. Move the water spray back and forth among your plants, and don't forget the undersides of leaves where many insects hide.

Minimize disease risk by spraying in the early morning, and refrain from spraying in hot and humid weather.

2 practically perfect ways to protect your harvest

Nothing is more frustrating than discovering something other than you has been munching on your veggies. Many pests will move in and gobble up your garden plants if given a chance.

The good news is you have multiple natural options for both prevention and treatment to protect your harvest.

Rotate your crops. Rotating crops is an age-old practice to fool pests that like to come back and eat the same plant year after year. Soil pests such as root-knot nematode round-worms hang out in the soil unless predators invade.

Planting the same crop or even something in the same family each season means the pest will quickly locate its target again. So change it up every few years. To guarantee success, keep a garden planting diary to track what works and what you have planted each year.

> Keeping hungry pests away from your vegetable garden will get a whole lot easier when you know one sneaky trick. Super easy, super cheap. Tear up some tinfoil into small pieces, and mix them in with your garden mulch. The light will reflect off the foil and onto your plants, driving pests away.

Bring in some ladybugs. Not only are they cute, but they are also a great secret weapon against vegetable pests. Ladybugs are true garden warriors that can quickly devour up to 60 aphids each per day, along with other pests.

To attract ladybugs, try planting sunflowers, yarrow, fennel, marigolds, cosmos, dill, and angelica. They'll return the favor by gobbling up aphids, thrips, scale, mites, and lots of other destructive pests.

If you don't want to wait for ladybugs to show up, you can buy them at your local garden shop or even online.

Is it OK to use chemicals for pest control?

Chemical pesticides are the go-to for many home gardeners as well as in agricultural and commercial settings. But their use has consequences — some of them quite severe. Here's why you should avoid them at all costs and replace them with natural and organic controls.

Health issues. Adverse effects range from dizziness and nausea to more severe issues like reproductive problems and neurological challenges. Glyphosate, known as Roundup, damages genes and causes congenital disabilities, yet almost 200 million pounds are used annually in the United States.

Food contamination. About 60% of produce still contains one or more pesticides even after washing and peeling, says the U.S. Department of Agriculture. This tainted food is not something you want to eat or feed your family.

Harmful to pets. Using pesticides in areas where pets roam can cause significant harm to your furry friends. Every year the American Association of Poison Control Centers receives thousands of calls regarding poisoned pets. Symptoms include skin rashes, vomiting, nausea, eye irritations, and respiratory problems.

Threat to environment. A national study revealed that 90% of our nation's urban streams are contaminated with pesticides, which poses a tremendous threat to wildlife, including fish and birds.

Snag pesky pests with easy handmade traps

Trapping troublesome pests is one way to protect your favorite plants. Here are some easy-to-make traps that offer excellent pest protection where it matters most.

Leaf-eater slug trap. Slugs come out at night to nibble on leaves, their favorite delicacy. Chop up a few strawberries and place them in a shallow container. Pour an inch of beer over the strawberries, and set the dish in your garden. Slugs are drawn to the sweet treat and will get caught in the trap and be unable to climb out.

Sticky trap for small pests. Aphids, flies, flea beetles, and whiteflies are easily caught using this homemade sticky trap. Staple or glue a popsicle stick to a playing card, coat the card in petroleum jelly, and place it among your garden plants. You will be surprised at how many tiny pests this sticky card snags.

Yellow pan trap. Many insects are attracted to the color yellow. Set a yellow Frisbee filled with water between your garden plants, and watch the small pests jump in and get caught.

To attract more significant bugs like the squash vine borer moth, use a deeper yellow pan with at least 2 inches of water. To keep from snagging beneficial insects, place a lid on your trap, and cut holes to the exact size of the insect you wish to catch.

Annoying ants? 10 tip-top natural ways to get rid of them

Ants start showing up in your garden as the weather warms up in mid-to-late spring. The best way to deal with them is to eliminate their nest. Each ant colony may contain thousands of ants. If you leave them alone, they quickly multiply, and what started as a small annoyance can soon turn into your worst nightmare.

You may be tempted to turn to commercial ant applications, but they contain toxic substances that are not safe for children or pets. The good news is, there are many safe and effective natural alternatives available. Here are some to try.

Remove rotting wood and tree stumps. A favorite place for ants to develop colonies is in rotting wood or old tree stumps. Keep your garden and landscape clean and remove any stumps.

Drown the nest with boiling water. If you come upon an ant nest, rake it open and pour boiling water down inside. You can also add some dish soap for extra killing power.

Use a white vinegar mixture. Mix equal parts vinegar and tap water. Add a few drops of liquid soap. Rake open nests, and pour the solution inside. Be careful not to get any of this mixture on lawns or foliage as it will burn vegetation.

Take advantage of a natural pesticide. Orange peel contains a natural pesticide known as D-Limonene. You can destroy anthills with a tiny bit of this fruit's peel. Place the peels from one orange in a blender along with one cup of water. Puree the solution. Rake anthills and pour the solution into the colony.

Snuff them out with cinnamon. When an ant inhales cinnamon, it suffocates and dies. Use cinnamon around an anthill opening and along their trails. You can also use cinnamon essential oil. Mix a few drops of cinnamon oil with water and spray along ant trails, at the opening of colonies, and around doors, windows, and cracks in your home.

Surround their home with pepper. Ants hate pepper. Both black and cayenne pepper work well to abolish ants. Sprinkle a generous amount of pepper around a colony entrance and anywhere else where ants are a problem. You can also mix pepper in water to make a spray deterrent.

Spray lemon juice. Ants are not a fan of this tart treat. Make a solution using one part lemon juice and three parts water in a spray bottle. Spray around anthills, along ant paths, and around the perimeter of your home and garden to keep them out.

Lure them in with cornmeal. Cornmeal is an ant attracter rather than repeller, but it's still effective at getting rid of them. Spread it across ant paths and in the landscape. The ants readily nibble on the cornmeal but they can't digest it. When they drink water, it swells inside of them, and they die.

Use oranges and lemons together to make a powerful recipe that will send ants scurrying out of your yard for good. Blend one part orange juice, one part lemon juice, and three parts water with the peels from one orange and one lemon. Pour it into a bottle, and spray the mixture inside anthills and around the edges.

Spread cedar mulch. The sweet aroma of cedar repulses ants, along with other pesky pests. Spread cedar mulch around plants and in landscape areas to deter ants from setting up house. Refresh mulch annually for continued protection.

Sprinkle a special food. Food-grade diatomaceous earth (DE) is the fossilized remains of marine phytoplankton. It has razor-sharp edges that easily cut through the exoskeleton of an ant, which makes the ant's body dry out. To use DE, gently sprinkle in and around anthills, along trails, and anywhere else ants are an issue.

Simple solutions to make fleas flee

An infestation of fleas spells trouble not only for your pet but also the other members of your household. You can bring in the heavy-duty chemical team, but who wants to breathe in all those toxins?

Enjoy a flea-free yard without using harmful chemicals. Don't miss this list of easy flea-away home remedies.

- Clean it up. It's critical to keep your lawn and gardens cleaned up and neat at all times. The more debris, the more fleas. Keep your lawn mowed short. Prune foliage regularly, and pick up and dispose of all clippings and yard waste.

- Spray them away. Make a bubbly flea spray for your garden using dish soap and water. Fill a garden sprayer with water, and add an ounce of dish soap. Spray all over your garden in the evening.

- Put lime to good use. Lime dehydrates fleas and kills them. Sprinkle it over your lawn and gardens, and soak it well with water. Be sure to use agricultural-grade lime only as any other type can burn your grass.

- Repurpose Epsom salts. Like lime, Epsom salts dehydrate fleas. Sprinkle these moisture-sucking salts around flowers and shrubs and in shady places where fleas congregate. Repeat every few weeks. Not only will fleas flee, but your flowers will bloom bigger and brighter.

End mosquito mayhem in your outdoor spaces

Nothing can ruin outdoor fun quicker than mosquito party crashers. They buzz and bite and send people running. Even worse, they carry diseases.

Try these expert tips to put an end to mosquito mayhem so you can enjoy your outdoor spaces once again.

Repel with fragrance. Some pretty plants smell pretty bad to mosquitoes. Plant them near your patio for a pest-free zone.

Try marigolds, basil, lavender, chives, and scented geraniums around the perimeter of your outdoor living spaces. They'll give you a beautiful garden display as well as a living mosquito-repelling border.

These plants look stunning, are easy to care for, and help create a mosquito-free zone. You can set them out in containers on balconies, decks, and patios for protection in these spaces as well.

> Tackle mosquitoes from the inside out by eating the right foods. Mosquitoes tend to stay clear if you eat garlic, apple cider vinegar, beans, tomatoes, lentils, lemongrass, and chili peppers. Beware of foods with a lot of sugar, salt, or alcohol, as they'll turn you into a mosquito magnet.

Dress for success. Wear the right clothes and you can turn off mosquitoes. Choose light colors such as tan, light gray, or white to make them less interested in you. Wear black or bright colors, on the other hand, and the mosquitoes will come flying right to you.

Long sleeves and pants are best, and a hat with a neck guard is a must if you are going into a woodsy and damp area where mosquitoes swarm.

Get rid of standing water. Don't waste money on an expensive bug zapper to keep mosquitoes out of your yard. Do this for free instead. Take the time to pick up any debris or junk on your property, and look for items that have filled with water.

Standing water is a favorite of mosquitoes, as that's where they like to lay their eggs. Turn over anything that can collect and hold water.

How to create a dragonfly paradise — and why you should

Did you know that dragonflies eat mosquitoes, houseflies, and gnats? They're one insect you definitely want to keep around. Here's how to attract these beauties to your yard.

Set up a water feature. Dragonflies are aquatic insects that spend most of their time in and around water. They lay their eggs there and like to perch on surrounding vegetation.

Depending on the species, some dragonflies prefer flowing water while others are attracted to standing water. Once you determine which species inhabits your area, you can create a just-right water feature to draw them into your landscape.

Make your water source at least 2 feet deep with shallow sides. This will deter mosquitoes whose larvae survive best in shallow water. Including a bubble or fountain feature will also help ward off mosquitoes.

Place vegetation in and around the water. While a water source is an excellent start to your dragonfly paradise, adding some greenery is crucial if you want to keep the dragonflies around. Here's why.

- Plants submerged in water protect eggs and nymphs.

- Partially emerged vegetation allows baby dragonflies on the edge of adulthood a way to get out of the water.

- Floating plants are natural perches for adults to rest and lay eggs.

- Plants positioned around the water's perimeter, also known as marginal vegetation, along with shrubs and trees, provide a resting and roosting spot for adult dragonflies.

Add some pollinator plants. A water source ensures that dragonflies get a continual supply of mosquitoes and gnats, but they also like other types of insects. To keep your dragonfly buffet in business, mix in some pollinator plants with the aquatic plants.

Good options that attract moths, bees, and even butterflies include irises, buttercups, yarrow, and lavender.

> While you wait for plants to grow, place some sticks or bamboo stakes around your water feature and in your garden. This will give dragonflies a place to land and rest.

How can I keep rabbits out of my garden?

Yes, they are cute and fluffy, but they can also wreak havoc on your garden. Rabbits have a massive appetite and can make quick work out of many garden plants. They love to munch on the leaves and stems of plants and are determined to get their lunch.

Here are a few ways to signal to the rabbits that your garden diner is closed for the season.

Surround it with chicken wire. Perhaps you have tried wire, and it has not worked. When done right, however, wire fencing can make a difference. A 2-foot high chicken-wire fence, buried 6 inches deep around the perimeter of your garden, works well to protect your precious plants.

Plant a living fence. You may not believe it, but rabbits don't like all plants. They actually find some plants disgusting, and these make the perfect living fence for your garden. You can also scatter them throughout your garden for a stronger defense.

Rabbits are easily offended by prickly plants as well as those with a powerful aroma. Perfect plants for your living fence include onions, lavender, thyme, sage, bee balm, yarrow, Japanese maple, Virginia creeper, English ivy, and rosemary.

Distract them with their favorite foods. Although it may sound a little crazy, planting a few crops that rabbits love — but far away from your vegetable patch — can keep them from destroying your garden.

Plant a small patch of clover or alfalfa to satisfy their desire to munch. It's the perfect way for your garden and those rascally rabbits to coexist.

Entice purple martins for powerful pest control

You may not be familiar with the purple martin, but this is one beautiful bird you want in your yard. In fact you want a lot of them. These hungry flyers gobble up thousands of insects each day.

To attract these large swallows to your yard and keep them happy, you need to give them four simple things.

- Food. You don't have to set up any special bird feeders for purple martins. As long as you don't spray pesticides, they will find plenty to eat. Martins benefit from some fine gravel or crushed eggshells as a calcium supplement.

- Water. Instead of birdbaths, martins like large natural water sources like lakes, ponds, or streams. If you don't have a natural water source nearby, create a large, elongated pond so these helpful birds can swoop down and scoop up water on the fly.

- Shelter. Purple martins shelter in artificial houses. They prefer open areas where they have a clear line of sight. They will also use scattered perches where they can scan for threats, watch for food, and roost. Tall poles with antenna-like structures are best.

- Nesting area. These birds nest in colonies and require large houses with lots of compartments. They are attracted to white nesting boxes that reflect heat. Place birdhouses 30 to 120 feet away from large trees and other structures so they can easily feed on passing pests. Provide nesting materials like small piles of grass, twigs, and leaves along with some mud that the birds use to keep their nests together.

7 secret weapons to fight irritating insects

Natural pest control is never easier or more beautiful than when you do it with living plants. When you landscape with pest-fighting plants, they do double duty by beautifying your outdoor living spaces and keeping them bug-free so you can enjoy being outside.

Take marigolds for example. These delightful flowers actually deter harmful bugs from your tomatoes, roses, peas, and more. That's why they were probably in your grandmother's garden.

Birds, bees, and butterflies will flock to your yard when you add these pest-repellant plants to your garden. They will attract the insects you want and repel the ones you don't.

Plant	Growing conditions	Pest-fighting tips
lemon thyme	prefers rocky and shallow soil	bruise leaves to ignite pest-repelling properties; cut a few stems and rub between your hands and wipe over clothing for pest protection
lavender	needs full sun and well-drained, sandy, loamy soil	plant in sunny areas, including entryways, to keep them pest-free; apply oil extracted from flowers to your skin for pest protection

Plant	Growing conditions	Pest-fighting tips
sage	needs medium to full sun and well-drained, sandy, loamy soil	throw a little sage into your outdoor fire before lighting to help repel mosquitoes
rosemary	needs at least eight hours of sunlight and well-drained, sandy soil	place in vases on your outdoor dining table for a pest-free meal
petunias	need bright, indirect light, and well-drained, sandy soil	plant near vegetables and herbs and close to outdoor living spaces in containers to repel aphids, tomato worms, and other pests
marigolds	need bright light and well-drained, sandy, loamy soil	scatter throughout veggie gardens to keep your harvest safe from nematodes and other pests
geraniums	need four to six hours of direct sunlight and a well-drained potting mixture for containers	place containers around your outdoor living spaces for beauty and pest protection

Homemade pest-away elixirs that work

It is easier than you think to make toxin-free, natural pest-away elixirs that keep you, your family, and your pets safe while keeping annoying pests at bay. Here are some time-tested recipes to try.

All-pest potion. Chase away pests big and small. Repel everything from insects to deer with a potion made from dishwashing liquid and two simple household ingredients.

Combine 2 teaspoons dish soap, 1 quart distilled water, and 30 drops peppermint essential oil. Pour into a spray bottle, and spray areas where you want to ward off pests. Reapply after rain.

Rabbit repeller. This natural repellent contains ingredients that rabbits detest. It will send them hopping away without causing any harm.

Blend three chili peppers, three large onions, and one large bunch of garlic. Place the mixture in a glass bowl, and cover it with water. Let it sit overnight.

Add enough water to the mixture to make a gallon. Pour into a spray bottle, and spray on plants you want to protect. Reapply after rain.

Squirrel scram. Sending squirrels packing is a breeze — make that a sneeze. This black pepper trick sends them high-tailing away in an instant.

Boil 1 1/2 quarts of water and add:

- 1 tablespoon black pepper

- 1 teaspoon cayenne pepper

- 1 chopped jalapeno pepper

- 2 chopped onions

Turn down the heat and simmer for about 30 minutes, then stir. Turn off the stove and let the mixture cool. Strain the mixture into a spray bottle. Spray on surfaces and in areas where you want to fend off pesky squirrels.

5 old-timey tips to keep cats out of your garden

Do you have a problem with neighborhood cats that spray your plants, use your gardens as a litter box, and even dig up your beds? More than likely, they make a huge mess and damage your beautiful plants.

Here are some helpful tips to make unwelcome cats turn up their noses at your yard and keep away permanently. These natural deterrents won't hurt the cats, your kids, or other pets.

Scatter citrus peels. Cats detest the aroma of citrus. Simply scatter orange or lemon peels around your garden and raised beds to keep felines at bay. Be sure to refresh the peels often, placing old peels in your compost pile.

Spray essential oils. Cats have 80 million smell receptors compared to humans lowly 5 million. So heavily concentrated essential oils overwhelm their senses. In fact, cats find them downright offensive.

Some of the best "cat away" oils include rosemary, orange, and citronella. Add 10 drops of oil to 2 cups of water in a spray bottle. Spray the areas of concern with the mixture every two weeks and after rain. Unwelcome kitties will soon find another garden to pester.

Install a motion-activated sprinkler. If you know anything about cats, you know they detest water. Have you ever tried bathing a cat?

Motion-activated sprinklers use infrared technology to sense an animal's heat and movement up to 35 feet away. When it detects something, the sprinkler lets off an intense burst of water along with noise and motion, which are enough to send any cat scurrying.

Cover the soil. Make things prickly for wandering cats. Cover the soil in your garden beds with pine cones. Cats can't dig to do their business when the cones are in the way.

You can also try covering the soil with rocks or gravel, making it incredibly difficult for cats to use your garden as their outdoor litter box.

Put Fido to work. If you own a dog, he will likely do a good job patrolling your garden. But a safer method — for the cat at least — is to use your dog's hair as a deterrent instead.

Scatter handfuls of dog hair throughout your garden. If you don't have a dog, stop by your local dog grooming shop, and ask if they have some hair they will share.

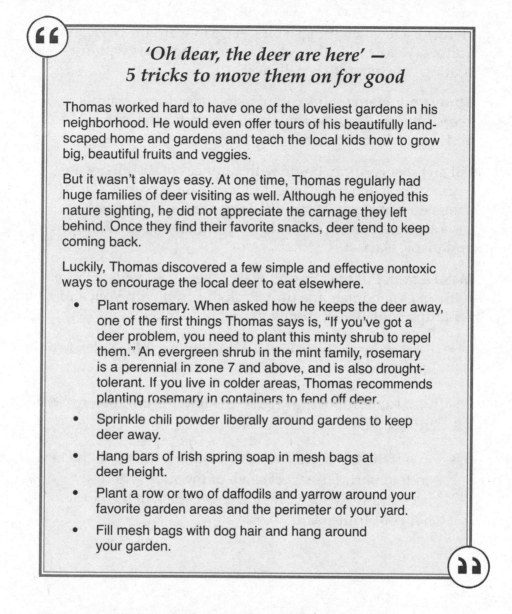

> ## 'Oh dear, the deer are here' —
> ## 5 tricks to move them on for good
>
> Thomas worked hard to have one of the loveliest gardens in his neighborhood. He would even offer tours of his beautifully landscaped home and gardens and teach the local kids how to grow big, beautiful fruits and veggies.
>
> But it wasn't always easy. At one time, Thomas regularly had huge families of deer visiting as well. Although he enjoyed this nature sighting, he did not appreciate the carnage they left behind. Once they find their favorite snacks, deer tend to keep coming back.
>
> Luckily, Thomas discovered a few simple and effective nontoxic ways to encourage the local deer to eat elsewhere.
>
> - Plant rosemary. When asked how he keeps the deer away, one of the first things Thomas says is, "If you've got a deer problem, you need to plant this minty shrub to repel them." An evergreen shrub in the mint family, rosemary is a perennial in zone 7 and above, and is also drought-tolerant. If you live in colder areas, Thomas recommends planting rosemary in containers to fend off deer.
>
> - Sprinkle chili powder liberally around gardens to keep deer away.
>
> - Hang bars of Irish spring soap in mesh bags at deer height.
>
> - Plant a row or two of daffodils and yarrow around your favorite garden areas and the perimeter of your yard.
>
> - Fill mesh bags with dog hair and hang around your garden.

How to have the perfect pest-free picnic

The weather is beautiful, and you have the perfect spot picked out for your picnic. But it just happens to be by a little stream where flying insects are hanging about waiting to make you miserable.

Here are a few key things you can do to ward off bugs, mosquitoes, yellow jackets, and other irritating pests without coating yourself with repellant.

Spray your blanket. Instead of using harmful chemicals to keep flying pests away from your lunch, try this natural body and fabric repellent spray instead.

Fill an 8-ounce spray bottle with 4 ounces of distilled water, 3 ounces of witch hazel, and 1/2 teaspoon glycerin. Add 10 drops each of clove, geranium, lemongrass, and rosemary essential oils. Shake the bottle well and mist your clothing and picnic blanket.

Make a trap. Put the sting on wasps, bees, and yellow jackets with an easy homemade trap. Pack this trap with you, and set it up about 10 feet from your picnic blanket.

- Cut the upper one-third off the top of a 2-liter plastic soda bottle.

- Put a handful of gravel into the bottom, and pour a little soda over it.

- Invert the top of the bottle so that it nests inside the bottom part. The sweet smell of the soda will draw bees and wasps, and they will get stuck in the bottle, not your fruit salad.

Repurposing projects for pennies

6 surprising reasons to repurpose rather than recycle

You may think repurposing and recycling are the same thing, but actually they're different. To reuse or repurpose is to take an item that is past its usefulness and use it again in a new way.

Upcycling is a variation of that where you take an object and change it into something else of more value. This is where the "turning trash into treasure" saying comes from.

In comparison, recycling is the process of taking a used product, melting the raw materials, and molding them into new products.

If taking care of the planet and saving money are on your agenda, repurposing is for you. Here are some excellent reasons to practice reusing and repurposing in your garden, a widespread practice before the "disposable" age.

Less expensive than recycling.
Recycling means you first buy
something new, which costs
more for you, the recycling
company, and the planet. By
saving and repurposing items,
you save the cost of buying
new things while reducing
your carbon footprint.

Plastic shopping
bags take anywhere from
20 to 1,000 years to
decompose in a landfill.
That's devastating for
the environment, but it
means these bags are
super sturdy. Take
advantage of this fea-
ture, and repurpose
those bags in your yard
to keep insects off trees
and shelter tender plants
from cold nights.

Uses less energy. Recycling is
energy-intensive because items
have to be heated up, melted,
and changed into something
else. This is especially true for
things like glass bottles and jars that can easily be used around
the home and in the garden.

Causes no pollution. Recycling requires energy, which creates
pollution. When you reuse or repurpose something, you use
the item as is and don't use a chemical process to convert it
into something new.

Encourages quality over quantity. If you have the mindset
that you will not just throw items away and buy replacements,
you're more likely to buy high-quality items that last. Reckless shopping is hard on the environment. Mindful shopping,
on the other hand, greatly benefits the planet.

It's more responsible. While recycled items avoid the landfill,
they still get rebirthed into the waste channel as something
new. By repurposing, you say no to overconsumption. It
makes you responsible for your own waste and encourages
you to think about the impact your decisions have on
other people.

Can be a lot of fun. Repurposing things offers an excellent opportunity to be creative. It can be very satisfying to turn something headed for the landfill into a garden treasure or a practical tool to solve a problem.

Uncommon ways to use common things in the garden

You would be surprised at the many items you have lying around that can be put to practical use in your garden. Here are some garden hacks that won't cost you a dime.

Coffee filter liner. Place a coffee filter in the bottom of a plant container to keep the soil from washing out the hole.

Diaper hydrator. Cut a diaper into small pieces, and place pieces in the bottom of a container. Fill with soil and plant as usual. The diaper will retain water and hydrate your plants when they need it most.

Coffee sleeve seed starter. Don't throw away those coffee sleeves from your favorite latte. Place the sleeves in a tray and fill with potting soil. The sleeves make the perfect seed starter and can be reused many times over.

Fruit protector hosiery. If you snag a hole in your panty-hose, don't throw them out. Cut the hose and use pieces to protect young fruit, such as melons, from pest infestation. Slip the fruit inside the hose and tie the ends loosely. As the fruit grows, it will expand within the protective cover.

Berry basket crocus protector. Turn plastic and cardboard berry baskets upside down on top of crocus bulbs to keep squirrels and other rodents from digging and stealing bulbs.

Coffee grounds pH fixer. Plants such as roses and hydrangeas will appreciate some spent coffee grounds to keep the soil on the acidic side.

Tinfoil pest fighter. Ball up small pieces of tinfoil, and place them in garden beds where aphids are an issue. When the sunlight reflects off the aluminum balls, it will scare them away.

Another excellent use for spent nylons in the garden is to help aerate the soil. Place pieces of pantyhose in the bottom of containers to keep the soil oxygenated and plants happy.

Serving spoon trowel. No need to buy a fancy garden trowel when a serving spoon will do the trick, especially for container planting. If you don't have an extra around the house, pick one up at your local thrift store.

Transform 7 throwaways into handy helpers

Sustainability sometimes means getting creative. Take a look at what else you toss out, and imagine some of those materials with a new life as a garden tool. Here are a few household throwaways that can be handy outdoors.

Shoeboxes. How many shoeboxes end up in landfills each year? The answer is millions upon millions. Instead of throwing away these boxes, keep a few for use around your garden.

Use a sturdy shoebox with a lid to organize small things in your garden shed. You can even store your hand tools in a shoebox over the winter months. After you plant young seedlings in your garden, use shoeboxes as a protective cover for chilly nights.

Egg cartons. Instead of throwing out egg cartons, use them to start seeds. The little compartments are just right for seedlings. If you use the paper cartons, cut them apart, and plant them in the soil with the transplants. The cartons will degrade naturally, adding nutrients to your soil.

Glass jars. Your empty glass jars — from pickles, jams, mustards, and more — are ideal storage containers for many garden items because they seal out moisture.

Store seeds, dried herbs from the garden, and metal parts for tools in these containers, where they will stay dry and safe.

Paring or putty knives. Don't throw out old paring or putty knives. You can transform them into useful garden tools to cut transplants from flats and harvest fruit from plants.

Plastic or metal cans. Wash and dry plastic or metal cans, and keep a few in your garden shed. These come in handy to support developing fruit such as melons, and large squash as they mature. As a bonus, the cans keep fruit off the soil and away from soil-borne pests and disease.

Newspaper. If you still get the daily newspaper or the free ones in the mail, consider giving them new life in the garden instead of dumping them in the recycling bin. Put old newspaper down between plant rows as a weed barrier, or shred it to use as mulch.

Old linens. When it's time to replace sheets, pillowcases, and tablecloths, find new uses for them in the garden. A simple solution is to cut them into rags for cleaning garden tools, but you can do so much more.

For instance, an old cotton sheet, especially in a dark color, is a great weed barrier. A lighter-colored sheet protects tender plants on frosty, transitional days. Use pillowcases as storage bags or to harvest and carry produce.

These and other throwaway items make great tools for the garden. Repurpose them to save money and save the earth at the same time.

Paint-can project your birds will love

It can take a paint can over 200 years to decompose in a landfill. Why not feed your feathered friends by giving an old paint can new life as a bird feeder?

What you need:

- small to medium-size paint can

- 3-inch dowel

- glue gun

- spray paint

- ribbon

- birdseed

How to make it:

1. Make sure the paint can is empty. Use a hose to spray it out so no paint residue remains. Let the can dry.

2. Spray paint the outside of the can any color and let it dry.

3. Turn the can on its side, and attach the dowel to the edge of the opening using hot glue. Let it dry completely. This creates a perch for birds to sit on while they eat.

4. Wrap a piece of broader ribbon around the can, and tie the feeder to a tree branch.

5. Fill with seed and watch your feathered friends arrive to eat.

How can I use old furniture in my garden?

You may not have a use for outdated or broken furniture in your home, but don't say goodbye just yet. You can find many practical ways to use it in your yard and garden. Here are some fun repurposing projects to try.

Broken chair planter. Do you have a chair that is missing a seat? Sit a planter bowl down inside the seat frame, and place your chair as a charming welcome on your porch by your front door.

Chest of drawers floral display. A small chest of drawers makes a quaint outdoor display for your favorite annuals.

Pull out the drawers and drill several drainage holes in the bottom of each one. Spray the drawers with an outdoor sealer, and fill with light potting soil and pretty flowers. Try some trailing varieties to add interest.

Coffee table raised-herb planter. Spray paint that old coffee table a fun color, and cut a center section to hold a rectangular planter or two. Drop the planters down inside the table, and plant your favorite herbs.

Buffet table drink cooler. Repurpose your old buffet table by turning it into a drink cooler. Paint the table in a color of your choice. Cut a hole in the top of the table so that your drink cooler will sit inside without slipping through the hole. No more bending down to get your drinks.

Cool things to do with leftover bricks

Do you keep staring at that pile of bricks behind your patio, wondering what you can do with them? Rather than letting moss grow over them, consider some really neat projects to use them up.

Succulent and candleholder. If you have the type of bricks with holes, plant a beautiful succulent in one hole and place a small glass votive candle holder in the other. These sweet decor items make an excellent gift or centerpiece for your outdoor table.

Tree ring. Consider edging your special trees with your left-over bricks. If you have enough, make your tree ring several layers high for an elegant effect.

Raised patio planters. Paint bricks in a color you like, and stack them to create a holder for rectangular or square containers. Make several different-sized raised planters for an eye-catching display.

Whimsical garden art. Engage the grandkids to make some fun and colorful yard art using bricks. Paint the bricks in fun colors, and strategically place them together to form flowers, fun designs, or even a stacked abstract work of art.

Edge garden bed. By digging a shallow trench and setting bricks on their sides, you can create an elegant border around your garden beds. You can also lay them flat for a seamless look.

7 clever ways to use broken clay pot pieces

Wait, don't throw out that broken terra cotta pot. Instead, breathe new life into it by finding creative and fun ways to use the pieces.

Mark your plants. The rims of small and medium broken clay pots make perfect pot markers. Use acrylic paint to write the names of plants you wish to mark. Carefully push the pot piece into the ground so the name can be seen.

Protect your container garden. Use pieces of broken pots to lay over the soil in your container garden pots. This will protect plants from squirrels, raccoons, and other critters.

Design a spilled pot display. A spill pot is a half pot turned on its side near low-growing plants. The idea is to partially bury the pot to create the illusion that the low-growing plants are spilling from it.

Drain and retain. A few terra cotta hunks placed inside another pot help keep water flowing around plant roots and draining correctly. This is an excellent way to use up shattered pot parts instead of throwing them out.

Make a toad home. A pot with a small chip or sliver on the pot's upper edge can leave it functional but not as attractive as you may like for your plants.

If you don't want to throw out your pot, put it to good use by making a whimsical toad house. Paint your pot with fun colors and designs, and turn it upside down. Toads can slip through the chipped space and call it home.

Embellish a rock garden path. If you have an existing rock path, have fun decorating it with colored terra cotta pieces. Grab a can of spray paint, and choose your favorite pieces for your path. Just be sure to sand sharp broken-pot edges first.

Create a candleholder. If your terra cotta pot breaks, leaving the bottom half of the pot still in one piece, create an amphitheater effect. Pots like this make a great outdoor candleholder.

Simply toss some pebbles into the bottom and set a few candles on top. You'll have a pretty garden-party accent that you can also use for citronella candles when the bugs get bad.

Inventive solutions to garden problems

Some common garden problems can easily be solved by
breathing new life into familiar objects.

Problem	The fix	How to use it
lost plant identification tags	key ring	place plant tags on the key ring to keep track of what you plant
seeds spilling from envelopes	binder clip	fold seed package over and use binder clip to hold shut
squirrels eating birdseed from feeder	ceiling light cover	thread chain from the bird feeder through hole in light cover so it blocks the feeder from the squirrels
critters eating the bottom of small tree	empty yogurt container	cut the bottom out of the container and make a slit up the side; slip the container around the young tree for protection
rip seed packages when opening	seam ripper	slide the seam ripper carefully into a top corner of the seed package and pull down for a clean opening
wildflowers drooping over	hair clip	position a plant stake next to the drooping flower and clip the flower to it using a hair clip
spilling birdseed when filling feeders	plastic soda bottle	cut the bottom quarter off the bottle and leave on the lid; fill bottle with seed and open lid to let seed pour neatly into the feeder
garden hose tangling	old tire rim	bolt tire rim to a solid surface and wrap garden hose around the outside of the rim
hummingbird feeder hanger broken	shower curtain hook	put the open shower curtain hook through the hanging hole; hang up and close the hook

Turn an old wheelbarrow into a spectacular fire pit

Have you replaced your old metal wheelbarrow with something more functional? Rather than turning the old one over and forgetting about it, why not upcycle it into something spectacular, like a fire pit?

What you need:

- deep metal wheelbarrow

- cement bricks

- gravel

- tools to disassemble the wheelbarrow

- shovel

- marking paint

- stones

How to make it:

1. Take the bucket off the frame. The average wheelbarrow is held together with four bolts.

2. Clean the bucket of any debris.

3. Select a fire pit location that is not close to power lines, trees, shrubbery, or anything flammable.

4. Turn the bucket over and trace the shape on the ground using marking paint.

5. Dig a hole a couple of inches wider than your marks and 2 inches deeper than the bucket.

6. Add 2 inches of gravel to the bottom of the hole.

7. Place your bucket in the hole, leaving a couple of inches sticking out of the ground.

To finish your fire pit, add a decorative ring of rocks around the pit. Add 2 inches of gravel to the bottom of the bucket and top with kindling. Light your fire and let it burn a couple of times to let any residue burn off. Then sit back and enjoy.

> Let your fire pit do double duty. Lay an old barbecue grill over the top of the wheelbarrow bucket so that you can cook your camp favorites. Burgers anyone?

Extra potting soil? Nifty ideas to give it new life

If container gardening is your thing, you're bound to have extra potting soil hanging around. Don't let this valuable resource go to waste.

You can use potting soil to solve some popular gardening problems. But before you reuse it, there are a few things you need to do. Follow these tips to get the most bang for your buck.

Let used soil dry out. Dump used soil on a tarp, and allow it to dry out in a sheltered location. The soil must be completely dry before storing it. Moisture will create the perfect conditions for unwanted microbes to multiply.

Store old soil correctly. Always store potting soil that supported flowers separate from soil used for growing vegetables. This limits the number of diseases that may carry over from one year to the next.

Store the soil in any container that will keep the soil dry, such as small garbage cans or even heavy-duty plastic bags. Exposing used soil to freezing temperatures is a great way to kill insects, including adult pupae or eggs.

Put old potting soil to good use. Once you've taken care of your soil, you can use the stored flower soil for vegetables next season and vice versa. Or you can be creative and come up with other ideas like these.

- Repurpose soil into a top dressing for newly planted seeds. It will hold in moisture and encourage germination.

- Stored potting soil comes in handy when moles, dogs, or other critters dig unwanted holes in your lawn that need to be filled.

- Cover any newly planted grass seed with a thin layer of stored garden soil to keep weeds down and protect young grass seedlings.

5 unique ways to upcycle a garden hose

Has your old garden hose sprung a leak? If so, it is probably time to retire it from its original job and find something else for it to do. Here are five unique and fun ways to keep your garden hose from ending up in the landfill.

Soaker hose. Turning your holey hose into a soaker hose doubles the benefit. Not only do you repurpose the hose, you create a way to water your garden cheaply and efficiently.

Use a drill and small drill bit to make evenly spaced holes along the length of the hose. Attach an end cap to one end, and attach the other end to a water source.

Swing chain covers. Your grandkids will thank you when you cover the chains on their swing with pieces of soft rubber hose. Protecting little fingers from getting caught in the chain is easy. All you have to do is measure, slice, and slide the hose over the chains.

In-pot watering system. Watering your houseplants and container plants is a snap with this type of system. You don't need to invest in expensive gadgets when you can easily create your own using small pieces of old garden hose.

Cut a section of hose to match your pot's depth, and drill several small holes along the length of hose. Dig a hole in your pot, and push the hose down until it touches the bottom. When it comes time to water, simply pour water down the hose, and it will seep out and gently water your plant.

Protective pot coil. To protect outdoor tables, decks, and porches from being damaged by plant pots, make a garden hose coil to sit underneath. Cut a piece of old hose to the desired length and coil it up. Tie the coil using some garden twine, and place under pots.

Fake snake bird deterrent. Cut a length of garden hose, and paint it the colors of one of your most popular regional garden snakes. Place the phony snake in your garden to keep birds from snacking on your valuable harvest.

Use landscape staples to keep your snake in a realistic pose. Move your snake around a few times a week to keep birds on their toes.

Jump on the wood pallet bandwagon — safely

Using wood for projects is all the rage. Let's face it, pallets provide a great free or super cheap source of lumber. Just think of all the fun things you can make with it — tables, couches, chairs, rabbit cages, planters, fences, and more.

But before you jump on the pallet bandwagon, you need to know the do's and don'ts of finding and preparing the pallets. Here are some tips to help you stay safe.

Check the IPPC code. Not all pallets are safe for home projects. You must check the treatment code to know what, if any, treatment is on the pallet. Look for this label stamped on the wood.

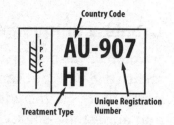

HT means the pallet has been heat treated and is safe to use. If you see DB, that means it's debarked and also safe to use. MB stands for methyl bromide, which makes a pallet unsafe for use.

You'll also see a country code and registration number. Domestic pallets may not have any codes, which leaves you guessing whether or not they are safe.

Inspect pallets thoroughly. Take the time to carefully scan your pallet choice. If it looks like something has spilled on the pallet or the wood is rotten, don't use it. If sharp nails or staples are sticking out of the pallet, pass on that as well.

Carefully remove boards. Set pallets on a flat surface, and use a nail bar and mallet to pry up the pallet frame boards. You want to remove the boards without pulling the nail heads through them. Be careful not to damage the boards.

Take out and dispose of nails. Push the nails back with a hammer, and pull them out with pliers. Dispose of nails carefully, and inspect all boards to ensure no nails or nail parts are left on the boards.

Clean and sand boards. Use a stiff wire brush to clean all boards of excess debris. Sand boards smooth so you don't get splinters.

Create a unique fence that wows

If you have a small space to fence in and are looking for a creative way to put some old doors to work, this project is perfect for you. Include all sorts of doors of varying sizes and appearances like church doors, school doors, interior doors, and cabinet doors. Here's how to do it.

1. Lay the doors on a solid surface, and take off any hardware, hinges, handles, latches, brackets, and nails. Sand any areas that need smoothing.

2. Arrange the doors in a pleasing pattern by height, color, or randomly. Do this in sections of four.

3. Attach one board 2 feet down from the top of the doors and another board 2 feet up from the bottom. Attach the boards using screws, and cut off any wood pieces hanging over the ends. Do this for every set of four boards.

4. Repeat steps two and three until you have the fence length you desire.

5. Mark a straight line for your fence. Dig holes for posts one-third as deep as the height of the post. Place a thin layer of gravel in the bottom of the hole, and set the post in place. Use concrete to secure the post.

6. Place posts every 4 to 6 feet along your fence line. Determine the exact distance for the posts based on the length of each door section.

7. Install the door sections to the fence posts. Make sure they are flush with the ground. Attach the doors to posts using outdoor screws about every 12 inches down the post.

8. Brighten up your fence if you wish by repainting, or attach plant holders or trellises.

Mason jar magic in your garden

Most people have at least a few extra mason jars hanging around. If not, they are easy to find at thrift stores or even garage sales. Mason jars are one of those timeless items that never seem to lose their value. And they can be used for all kinds of things in your garden.

Tool holder. Mason jars are super handy in the potting shed or greenhouse to hold all of your garden hand tools in one place.

Seed storage. A great way to keep seeds dry and contained is to put them in mason jars with tight-fitting lids. You can even attach a label to the jars so you know which seeds are in which jar.

Outdoor table centerpiece. Turn your mason jar into an attractive outdoor centerpiece. Spray paint it with lovely silver glass paint, pour a few inches of sand inside the jar, and set a votive inside. The pretty color on the outside of the jar will light up, creating a warm glow, perfect for that romantic outdoor dinner.

Diatomaceous earth shaker. Punch holes in a small mason jar lid. Fill the jar with diatomaceous earth, and shake over the garden as needed. You can also use this jar as an Epsom salts shaker.

Butterfly waterer. Fill a mason jar with pretty river stones. Place the pebble-filled jar in your garden topped with a pie pan full of fresh water. Watch butterflies, moths, and even hummingbirds come in for a drink. Keep the pan filled with water at all times.

Garden twine detangler. Place your garden twine inside a mason jar. Use a pretty lid with a straw hole, or punch a small hole in the lid's top. Thread the twine through the hole and screw on the lid. If you make the hole yourself, sand any sharp edges of metal so you don't cut your finger or damage the twine.

Can I use kitchen scraps in my garden without composting?

Composting kitchen scraps is a valuable way to repurpose old food. But what if you don't have a composting bin? Try trench gardening. It gives you all the benefits of composting without the need to keep up a bin.

To create a trench, dig 12 inches into your garden bed and fill it halfway with fruit and veggie scraps. Avoid putting bread products, oils, meat, dairy, human waste, rice, and sawdust into the trench. Cover the channel back up with soil, and let nature go to work breaking down the scraps and enriching it.

To keep the soil in your garden bed well-fed, relocate the scrap trench each year. You'll need to divide your garden bed into three zones. Use one zone for the compost trench and two zones for planting. Rotate which zone you use for the trench each growing season.

You can also place trenches between row crops or along shrub borders and flower or vegetable plants.

Light up a path without spending a fortune

Landscape lights range from the outrageously expensive to the almost free. Making your own lights out of repurposed materials is a nearly free option and a great way to create ambiance without spending a lot of money.

Wine bottle garden lights offer a versatile and attractive alternative to other more expensive options. Plus it gives you something to do with all your empty bottles. For the most impact, choose beautiful cobalt-blue bottles to line your garden path.

What you need:

- empty wine bottles

- 2 sets of outdoor solar string lights

- hand shovel

- sand

How to make it:

1. Use the shovel to dig a 6-inch deep trench on both sides of the walkway that is as wide as one bottle.

2. Spread an inch of sand evenly along the bottom of the trench.

3. Slide a short strand of lights into the bottle, and place it upside down in the trench.

4. Pour 4 inches of sand around the bottle for stabilization. The sand will also help keep moisture away from the lights.

5. Repeat this process for the entire path.

6. Once you have finished lining both sides of your path, add 2 inches of soil on top of the sand and around the bottles. Leave about 5 inches of the lower part of the bottles sticking up.

7. Place the solar light controllers in a good location, and bury any additional wiring.

Save the environment with easy tire projects

Tires are not biodegradable, so they take up valuable real estate in landfills. While many tires are recycled to create things like rubber mulch, mats, and automobile belts, you can also save the environment by repurposing them in your landscape. Here are a few ideas.

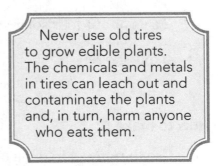

-   Retaining wall. Earth-filled tires rammed into the hillside can stop erosion in hilly terrain.

    Never use old tires to grow edible plants. The chemicals and metals in tires can leach out and contaminate the plants and, in turn, harm anyone who eats them.

-   Composting bin. Stack tires to make a neat and tidy compost bin. The tires hold heat, which helps with decomposition. If you live in a dry climate, be sure to keep your compost moist.

-   Vertical planters. Decorate a large wall or even a fence with vertical tire planters. Attach the tire first, fill with potting soil, and plant.

-   Decorative stacked planters. Paint used tires in fun colors and fill them with your favorite plants. Get creative and stack several tires on top of each other for a beautiful floral display.

- Dust bath for chickens. Place a tire in your chicken yard and fill with sand. Your chickens will love this little contained dust bath where they can dig and throw sand around.

- Garden seating. Turn tires into sweet and comfortable garden stools with a little help from some foam and outdoor fabric. For benches, stack tires to the desired height, and place sturdy boards between the two stacks.

- Tire swing. Who can resist the idyllic tire swing hanging from the massive tree just waiting for someone to have fun?

- Water feature. With a liner's help, you can quickly transform a tire into a small birdbath or even a neat water feature for your garden.

Seeding tricks to kick-start your growing season

7 must do's when starting seeds

Few gardening efforts are as rewarding as starting a plant from a tiny seed. Although it's not really difficult, you'll increase the chance of speedy germination and healthy seedlings if you follow these time-tested tips.

Pick the right container. Wide and shallow containers are best because they prevent overcrowding. If you are upcycling a container, choose one that is clean and free of any bacteria. You can sanitize it by soaking it in a 10% bleach solution for at least 15 minutes. Allow to air dry.

Be sure seeds make contact. In order to germinate, seeds must have direct contact with the potting mix. Tiny seeds and those that need light to germinate must lay directly on the potting mix.

Use a pestle or the bottom of a glass to tap seeds down into the mix gently. For other seeds, use a kitchen sieve to sprinkle potting mix over the top of seeds.

Focus on airflow and drainage. Too much moisture and poor air circulation can cause a fungal infection known as damping-off. To avoid this problem, spread a thin layer of 50% each sphagnum and chicken grit over top of the potting mix and around sprouting seeds.

> Your garden journal is a great place to record plant propagation history. Note where you bought seeds, planting dates, germination date and rate, and when the seedlings were ready to transplant. This will help you with future seed starts.

Place a small fan near your seedling trays to promote good air circulation. Set the fan on low speed, and allow it to blow across the containers at soil level to move trapped air along.

Help them get moisture. Place plastic wrap around seedlings to create a mini-greenhouse effect. This helps to keep moisture levels consistent.

Water properly. If seedlings need more moisture, water from the bottom only. Set seedling trays in another tray with water, and allow them to soak up the water for about 15 minutes before dumping it off.

Keep seeds warm. Most seeds require a temperature between 65 to 75 degrees to germinate. Place seedling containers near a heater or use a space heater to keep them warm.

Another option is to use a heating mat placed underneath the seed containers to encourage germination. If using a heater, be sure to check moisture levels often as the seedlings will dry out more quickly.

Provide enough light. Most seeds will not start without adequate light. A south-facing window may be enough, but if not, use supplemental grow lights for 12 to 16 hours until sprouted. Turn seedlings daily to keep the growth even, and rub your hand over the top of them to encourage strong growth.

Use recycled newspaper for earth-friendly pots

Crafting seed-starting pots from newspapers is thrifty, fun, and eco-friendly. The best part? When the time comes to transplant seedlings into their garden bed, you simply plop the biodegradable paper pot and seedling into the planting hole. The root stays intact, and transplanting is a breeze.

What you need:

- newspaper (do not use glossy or colored sheets)

- flour

- paintbrush

- water

- soup can

How to make it:

1. Lay a sheet of newspaper out on a flat surface. Fold in half lengthwise, and place soup can on the edge. (See graphic.)

2. Mix flour and water to make a paste.

3. Start at one end and roll the can in the paper one full turn.

4. Paint the strip of newspaper close to the can with glue.

5. Repeat the process of rolling and gluing until you get to the end of the sheet of paper.

6. After the glue dries, remove the can, and cut the paper tube into 3-inch sections.

7. Set the open-ended newspaper pots in a tray. Fill each pot with potting mix and plant your seeds.

Will the seeds in expired packages still grow?

Manufacturers put expiration dates on seed packages to let you know how likely it is the seeds will germinate and grow. Most vegetable and flower seeds remain viable for a few years when stored in low humidity and temperature.

What is the ideal humidity and temperature? According to the USDA, room temperature and relative humidity that add up to less than 100 is perfect.

Seeds in unopened packages will generally germinate quickly if they are only a year old or slightly older. On the other hand, seeds from open packages kept in less than ideal conditions need to go through a germination test.

- Place 10 sample seeds inside two moist paper towels, and put the towels in a plastic bag.

- Mark the type of seeds on the front, but don't seal the bag.

- Place the bag in the warmest room of your house. Check it on day five and every day after that. If the seeds are good, they should sprout within 10 days. If they don't sprout, or less than a third sprout, you should get new, fresh seed.

To prevent waste, store your seeds properly. A great way is in a glass jar with a few moisture-absorbing pouches.

Expert tips for thinning seedlings

Does the thought of thinning seedlings make you sigh? If so, you are not alone. This necessary task can be tedious, so much so that some gardeners just don't do it. The result is overcrowding and stunted growth as aging plants compete for limited resources.

Follow these expert tips to thin seedlings quickly and efficiently, which will allow plenty of room for plants to grow.

Spread just a few seeds. Don't seed too thickly as this can result in severe overcrowding. Plant two to three seeds only per seed-starting cup.

Get the timing right. After your seeds sprout, let them grow until they have two sets of "true" leaves.

Snip, don't rip. Use clean micro-pruning scissors to snip any weak or crowded seedlings carefully. Don't rip the seedling up from the planting medium. Doing this can easily disrupt the roots of the remaining plants. Clipping the weaker seedlings gives the remaining plants plenty of room to spread out.

If all the seedlings appear healthy, just pick a couple to thin out, giving one an excellent chance to grow strong and healthy.

Feed the remaining plants. Once you thin out seedlings, it is time to take care of the ones that are left. Seedlings do well at this time with a dose of fish emulsion.

Beautify your yard with wildflower seed balls

Do you have a barren area in your yard that could use some help? You may benefit from a seed ball — or maybe two or three. This concoction is simply a dried-out mix of seeds, clay, and compost that can bring color and interest to an area that otherwise lacks beauty.

The idea originated in Japan in the 1940s and was used extensively by "guerilla gardeners" in the 1970s who threw the balls, like grenades, into areas lacking vegetation and color. When conditions are right, the balls germinate and grow into plants.

Seed balls make great gifts for gardening friends, or you can use them yourself to bring color to a barren place in your landscape. Here's how to make your own.

What you need:

- wildflower seed for your growing zone

- potter's clay powder

- peat-free compost

- water

- bowl

- baking pan

How to make it:

1. Mix three handfuls of clay, five handfuls of compost, and one handful of seed together in a bowl.

2. Slowly add water and mix everything until you get a consistency that you can roll into truffle-sized balls.

3. Set the balls on a baking pan, and place them in a sunny windowsill for three hours minimum or until they are dry.

Seed selection — what you need to know

Picking the best seeds for your garden is crucial as it will determine what you grow and how. Seed type influences plant growth and health, resistance to pests and disease, yield, consistency, and more.

One critical decision is whether to plant open-pollinated or hybrid seeds. Which type of seed you choose depends on your needs and preferences, but there's no reason you can't use both. Here's a guide to help you decide the right choice for you.

Open-pollinated seeds. These are plants that either pollinate themselves or other plants of the same species. As long as you keep different varieties separate to avoid cross-pollination, they grow true to type. In other words, they grow into plants identical to the parents. You know what you'll get.

Here are some pros to using these types of seeds.

> Want a cheap and easy way to vary your seed collection? Get together with a few of your gardening friends, and throw a saved-seed swap party. You can share your favorite seeds with others and gather some new seeds to try.

- You can save your seeds because you know what you will get when planting them next year.

- You'll save money, as hybrids are usually more expensive than open-pollinated seeds and can't carry over from one year to the next.

- You'll enjoy better flavor in your vegetables and fruits than most hybrid varieties.

Hybrid seeds. When two varieties of an open-pollinated species cross, they produce a hybrid. The seeds from the hybrid may not grow true to type. You'll know hybrid seeds when you buy them because the packet is labeled either "hybrid" or "F1."

Hybrids are deliberately created for certain desirable traits, like fast growth and high yields. But some things get lost in the process, such as flavor.

The benefits of using hybrid seeds include:

- better disease and pest resistance than most open-pollinated varieties.

- improved uniformity and consistency in growing vegetables and fruits.

- greater crop yield and more vigorous, healthy plants.

Harden off seedlings in 8 easy steps

Once your seedlings have spent enough time in their incubator and are ready for the real world — the big outdoors — there are a few things to consider before making the transplant.

Yes, you may be anxious to get your new babies into their garden home, but rushing the transition can result in disaster. Seedlings are tender and require some special handling before they are ready for their final home. This is called "hardening off." Follow these steps to ensure your young plants have the best start possible.

Check the frost date. While some plants are OK to harden off while still a risk of frost, others are not as hardy. Make sure you know when it is safe to transplant, and don't do it a day too soon. Even if the weather seems promising, it can turn on a dime and freeze.

Suspend feeding. One week before you plan to transplant your seedlings, stop all supplemental watering and feeding.

Choose a sheltered location. Select a place outdoors that is protected from pests, animals, wind, and sun. Good options include a shady spot up against your home, a table under a tree, or in a cold frame.

Give them some preliminary outside time. Place your seedlings outside for a couple of hours in mid to late afternoon. Bring them back inside after their first exposure to the great outdoors. If you have plants in a cold frame, be sure to close the lid.

Lengthen the time outdoors. Leave your seedlings outside for an hour more than the previous day, giving them a little more time in the sunlight each day. You can also move the seedlings a little farther away from their sheltered location.

Be prepared to protect them. Temperatures may dip during the hardening-off period. Be ready to bring seedlings indoors or close the cover on your cold frame. If it is just a small cold snap, row covers may also be useful.

Extend the nighttime hardening-off time. Once seedlings have had several days of acclimation to daytime conditions, it is time to adapt them to nighttime hours. Leave them outside for longer and longer periods until they are ready to spend all night outdoors.

Keep up with watering. If your seedlings start to wilt, provide some water, and they should perk up pretty quickly.

These simple steps are enough to harden off your seedlings, but don't forget to keep timing in mind. Know the frost tolerance of each plant and your area's average last frost. This will help you decide the appropriate week for hardening off.

9 common seed-starting problems fixed

Seed starting is not always smooth sailing. The first few weeks after planting can sometimes be touch and go. Here are the top common seed problems and how to take quick action to fix them.

Problem	Reason	Fix
seeds don't come up	too long in storage or soil mixture too dry	plant fresh seeds and soak them 30 minutes in water before planting in dampened soil
seed coat stuck	planted seeds too shallow or the soil is too dry	plant seeds three times deeper than size of the seed; spritz seed casing and rub off with your fingers; keep soil damp
leggy stems and tiny leaves	light source too far away causes sprouts to reach upwards	fluorescent and LED lights should be 4" from top of plants and adjusted as plants grow; keep high-intensity lights 18" from tops of plants
droopy stems and leaves	overwatering drowns the roots; happens often with a small plant in a big pot	start seeds in a potting mix, not garden soil that holds too much moisture; plant seeds in small containers no bigger than 4"
curly and crumbly leaves	hot grow lights and dry air can easily dry out seedlings	use a potting mix that includes perlite or vermiculite as both hold water; keep mix damp but not soggy
yellow or brown leaf tips	warm temps are great for germinating, but seedlings easily overheat from high-intensity lighting or poor ventilation	keep room temperature at 65 degrees while seedlings are establishing; use a fan to keep small plants cool and improve circulation
purplish and red leaves	lack of phosphorus stops growth and brings out red in veins of leaves	feed with an organic phosphorus-rich solution after leaves appear
growth stopped; pale or yellow streaked leaves	lack of nitrogen after the plant gets true leaves	begin feeding after plant gets its two embryonic leaves; follow directions and provide an organic nitrogen-rich solution
yellow spots or black mold	whiteflies suck sap from plants and cause yellow spots; flies leave excrement on leaves, which is a breeding ground for black mold	use sticky traps or tape to catch whiteflies before they kill seedlings

Secret to the perfect soilless starter mix

Starting seeds inside is a great way to jump-start the gardening season in late winter or early spring. All you need to do is fill a starter tray with dirt from your garden, and you're ready to go, right?

Not so fast. Gardening soil is compact, heavy, and does not drain well. Plus it doesn't provide enough air flow to the roots, and they can't push through the heavy soil to grow. Not to mention it may include pests or disease-causing fungus.

The best way to give seeds what they need is to use a soilless potting mix. Although you can buy this type of mix, you can also make your own, which gives you control over what goes into the blend. Plus it saves you money.

Many soilless mixes contain peat moss, but the environmental cost of peat moss is huge. Harvesting is unsustainable, destroying animal habitats in the process. This do-it-yourself soilless seed-starting mix uses the perfect alternative to peat moss and is easy to make.

The secret to the perfect starter mix is a balance between water retention and drainage. You need just a few basic materials from the local garden center to make the right blend.

- Coconut coir is an alternative to peat moss. It's made from coconut fibers, has a neutral pH, and holds moisture well.

- Perlite is a mineral that looks and feels a bit like Styrofoam. It adds drainage to a mix and improves airflow. Be careful not to breathe in perlite when working with it.

- Vermiculite is also a mineral, similar to mica. It's the shiny pieces you see in mixes. Vermiculite balances perlite by adding water retention to the mix.

Making the mix takes a bit of trial and error, but fearless gardeners who have gone before have come up with a pretty good recipe. Simply mix one part each coconut coir, perlite, and vermiculite.

The recipe works well for most seeds, but you can always change it for better results. For instance, sand adds more drainage to a mix and opens up air flow. For specific plants picky about pH, amend the mix with gypsum or limestone.

" 5 seed-saving tips for success

Melanie knows that saving seeds is a thrifty way to make the most of her garden. She likes to share them with friends, do seed exchanges, and carry plants over from one year to the next. Plus it's a great way to keep the plants she loves most. Here's what she recommends to make the most of your favorite plants and their seeds.

Don't save seeds from hybrid varieties. Hybrids will not be true to type when you replant their seeds. Most plants sold at garden centers are hybrids. Look for hybrid or F1 on the label.

Start simple if you're a beginner. If you have not saved seeds before, start with plants that are easy to harvest and use, like peas, beans, lettuce, or tomatoes. For flowers, try zinnia, foxglove, four o'clock, and nasturtium.

Space plants for seed collection. Cross-pollination can mess up your true-to-type plants. Follow spacing guidelines between different varieties of the same species to reduce that possibility.

Harvest at the right time. Watch the maturing seed pods for signs of when to harvest them. Research each plant type, so you know when the time is right for seeds you can use next year.

Dry seeds and store properly. For some plants, like flowers, the seeds dry on the plant. Shake them out and store them. Others, like tomato seeds, need extra drying. Soak in water to remove the pulp, and let them dry thoroughly before storage. Keep seeds in a cool, dry, and dark spot.

"

Super sprouting idea you need to try

Sowing seeds directly in the garden is fast and easy, but it can also be tricky. You have to consider wind, rain, frost, and critters. Starting seeds indoors allows for more control, and every gardener has a unique method for doing it.

One idea you may not have tried yet is a simple plastic bag. It works because the bag acts as a mini-greenhouse, keeping seeds moist, warm, and protected as they germinate and sprout. Here's how to do it.

> All sorts of cheap products work as seed starters. You can reuse plastic trays from garden centers. Fold in the ends of empty toilet paper rolls to make biodegradable planters. Egg cartons work, but so do eggshells, which are also biodegradable. And used citrus peels make great seed cups that can be planted directly into the ground.

- Moisten a couple of sheets of paper towel. They should be thoroughly damp but not dripping wet.

- Fold each paper towel over so that the seeds are covered and touching both sides of the damp towel.

- Slide it into a sealable plastic bag and leave it in a warm area. The top of the refrigerator is a good spot.

- If the seeds need some light to germinate, place the bag in a sunny window. The paper towel will let in enough sunlight.

- Check on your seeds every day or two, and sow them as they begin to sprout.

- Every five to seven days, release some of the moisture from the bag by leaving it open for a few minutes. This will prevent damping off.

Cheap and easy DIY seed starter tape

Seed tape is a fantastic way to keep your garden rows and small seeds organized and evenly spaced. There is no need to purchase costly seed tape when you can easily make your own.

What you need:

- ruler

- marker

- 2 tablespoons white flour

- single-ply toilet paper

- seeds

- toothpicks

How to make it:

1. Create a glue by mixing the white flour with one table-spoon of water. The adhesive should not be runny but relatively thick.

2. Unroll the toilet paper to the desired length for your seed tape.

3. Fold the paper over horizontally and unfold to create a crease.

4. Check your seed package for instructions on how far apart to plant the seeds.

5. Measure and mark the distance between each seed by placing a dot along the crease. Start about 1 inch from the end of the paper.

6. Spread some seeds out in a shallow tray.

7. Dip the tip of the toothpick into the glue and pick up one seed.

8. Place it on the first dot on the toilet paper. Continue until you have a seed on each dot.

9. Place dots of glue around the toilet paper's perimeter and fold it up to create a seal. Let it sit until dry.

10. Roll up the seed tape and store it in a cool and dry location until you are ready to plant.

How and when to direct sow

Starting plants from seeds is so rewarding. Yes, there are good reasons to use transplants, like being able to control the environment for seed starting. But certain plants, like melons, don't transplant well. And others, like beans, actually prefer to be sown directly in the soil.

Direct sowing is easier, requires fewer materials, and costs less. Use these guidelines to have a successful experience each and every time.

Follow seed directions. The seed packet provides important information collected from years, even centuries, of experience. Sow the seeds as described on the packet for the best results.

Know your last frost date. Look up the average last frost date for your location before direct sowing, and again, consult the seed packet. Some seeds can go outside before this date, but others must go out after the danger of frost. Check the weather regularly, too. If a surprise frost comes along late, use row covers to protect seedlings.

Time sowing according to time to maturity. In addition to the weather and frost date, check the seed packet for time to maturity. This will tell you the time, usually in days, from when you plant the seeds to when the vegetable will be mature and ready to harvest. Use the information to help you decide when to sow, and stagger crops for more constant harvests.

Keep the soil moist. Seeds directly sown outdoors are at the mercy of the weather to some degree. Keep the soil constantly moist as they germinate and sprout. Do not soak the ground. A good rule of thumb is that larger seeds need more water.

Try a row cover. Even without a frost risk, a row cover over seeds protects them from excessive rain, wind, and hot sun that easily turns the soil into a thick crust. While it is not strictly necessary, a row cover offers protection from extreme elements and may increase germination success and rate.

Storage secrets for future success

Good seed storage is crucial to starting next year's garden. Letting seeds get too wet or warm interferes with germination success and rate. Storage also requires organization, so you don't lose track of what seeds you have. Be smart about storing seeds for an easier start to the next gardening season.

Get organized. Before devising the ideal storage solution, make a plan for your seeds. Collect seeds from the best plants in your garden and dry them thoroughly. Make notes on how you want to use them next year so you won't forget.

Create an inventory. Knowing what seeds you have will help you plan for next year and determine if you need to buy or borrow anything. If you have old seeds, test them for germination to see if they are worth storing.

Store seeds correctly. Above all else, your seeds must be kept dry. Keep the seeds in a cool, dry place, so they remain usable for next year. Here are some smart and easy solutions.

- Envelopes are the classic way to store seeds. Because they are vulnerable to moisture, be sure you find a dry spot for storage. Keep labeled envelopes organized and easy to see and access by tucking them into the pockets of a photo album or in the folders of a filing cabinet.

- If a dry spot is hard to find, protect seed envelopes by sealing them in a large jar or sealable plastic bags.

- Place your seeds directly into sealable glass jars. Moisture can't get in, so where you store the jars will be less critical. Put the jars in a box with dividers to keep them organized.

- A pillbox is a handy way to store seeds, too. Label the top of each box in the container, and snap shut to store seeds securely.

Tool time tuneup: thrifty tips to make them last

Choose the best tool for the job

Gardening can be challenging work with all the bending, crouching, pulling, and lifting. You can make any garden chore a little easier, not to mention less painful, by choosing the right tool for the job and using it correctly.

For protection. No gardener should be without a good pair of gloves to protect from scratches, bug bites, and cuts. Invest in a high-quality pair — thick and durable, but thin enough to do more delicate tasks, like picking up seeds. Wear them for all chores out in the garden.

For digging. You need two tools to cover digging jobs. A sturdy shovel will help you dig holes for large transplants, like shrugs, while a good trowel makes smaller jobs easy and fast. Choose these tools for sturdiness but also a comfortable grip as you will use them often.

For trimming and pruning. A good pair of pruning shears is essential for trimming unruly plants and maintaining others. Use bypass pruners, which are like scissors, for cutting live plants. Anvil pruners, with a flat edge, are best for clipping deadwood. Keep all shears sharp for best results and easier cuts.

For weeding. Pulling weeds can be backbreaking work. The right tool won't magically remove weeds at the root, but it will make the job easier. With a Cape Cod weeder, you can hack through the soil and slice weeds. A fork-style weeder allows you to get under roots and leverage them out of the soil.

Gardening can be hard on your hands, even if you wear gloves. This hand elixir restores moisture and eases tired hands. Mix 2 cups warm water with 1 cup apple cider vinegar, 3 tablespoons olive oil, and 10 drops tea tree essential oil in a shallow bowl. Soak your hands for 10 to 15 minutes and pat dry. Follow up with your favorite moisturizer.

For moving heavy things. Life in the garden is much easier if you have a wheelbarrow to move soil, mulch, new trees and shrubs, rocks, and other heavy materials. You'll save time, and your back, with a wheelbarrow. You don't need anything fancy. Choose one that is durable and that will last for many loads.

Save money by keeping your gear in great shape

Gardening can get expensive if you let it. These budget-friendly tips will help you enjoy your hobby without breaking the bank.

One of the most important tips to remember is to use sturdy, long-lasting tools and keep them in good condition. With regular maintenance, your tools will stay in great shape for many years, saving you tons of money in replacement costs.

Clean tools every time. Clean the tools you use after every day in the garden. This is one of the most important things you can do to make tools last. In most cases, a quick hose down is adequate. For more stubborn, caked dirt, use a screwdriver or drywall knife to pry out the last bits. Always dry your tools after cleaning to prevent rust.

Oil tools regularly. Rust and other buildups will ruin your metal tools after a while, especially hinged tools like loppers and pruning shears. Rub these down when clean with an oily rag, or spray them with a lubricant. Use linseed oil on wooden handles to prevent them from deteriorating over time.

Keep tools sharp. A dull set of shears is no use to you and could cause an accident. You also need to sharpen shovels and trowels. A flat file will sharpen edges, but you can also take your tools to a hardware store for professional sharpening. If you don't have experience sharpening your tools, this is a good idea.

Store them correctly. Just throwing your tools inside a box or in the corner of your garden shed may cause damage that shortens the life of the tool. Instead, create an organized system for storing tools. This will lengthen your tool's life and make it much easier to find the right tool when you need it.

> Need an easy cleaner? Soak your handheld tools in cold black tea for one hour to remove caked-on dirt and debris. Rinse in cold water and dry well before storing.

How can I restore old, rusty garden tools?

Maybe it has been some time since you've gardened, and you're ready to pick up this fabulous hobby once again. But when you wrangle up your garden tools, you find them rusty and seemingly unusable.

Don't fret. Just grab a few common household products, and you'll quickly bring your rusty garden tools back to life.

Soak them in vinegar. Add one part vinegar to two parts water, and soak your rusty garden tools overnight. Rinse the tools in the morning, and use a stiff brush to remove leftover rust. Once the rust is gone, wash your tools in soapy water and let them dry. Apply coconut oil to metal parts using a soft cloth.

Sprinkle salt and lemon juice. Sprinkle a little salt onto the rust, and pour some lemon juice on top. Allow the solution to sit on the tools for two hours. The lemon juice dissolves the rust, and the salt is like a gentle abrasive.

After soaking, rub the lemon rind in a circular motion to remove loose rust. Repeat as necessary to get off all of the rust. Wash with soapy water and allow tools to dry before using.

Treat with tomato sauce. Tools that only have a few spots of rust benefit from a tomato sauce treatment. Dot some tomato sauce on rusty spots, and allow tools to sit overnight. The acid in the tomato sauce will eat away at the rust. Wash tools with soapy water and allow them to dry before using.

Rub with a potato. Although it seems odd, potatoes can help renew garden tools because they contain oxalic acid — a rust-eating compound.

Cut a potato in half and sprinkle some salt on the smooth side. Rub this on your tools to remove rust. Wash tools with soapy water and allow them to dry before you get to work.

Clean and sharpen with 1 easy-to-make solution

Keep your garden tools sharp and clean to make them last and ensure they do the job right. A dull, rusty spade just won't cut it — literally. But cleaning and sharpening chores are time-consuming and can even be dangerous if you get distracted while using a file.

What can you do? With just a few simple materials, you can make a tool-cleaning pot that also doubles as a sharpening and storage solution.

What you need:

- medium or large terra cotta flower pot

- large bucket

- mineral or baby oil

- clean sand

- decorative materials for the pot if desired

How to make it:

1. If you want a pretty tool storage pot, decorate it first with craft paints. Or leave it rustic.

2. Fill a large bucket with clean sand and 20 to 30 ounces of mineral oil. Mix it up until the oil is evenly distributed throughout the sand.

3. Seal up the drainage holes in the pot, and then add the oil and sand mixture.

4. Pack the sand down into the pot until you have it filled up to about an inch or two from the top edge.

5. Stick your tools into the sand for storage at the end of the day, handles up.

The abrasive sand in the mixture helps keep your tools sharp. Every time you put them in and pull them out, the sand files the edges slightly. The sand also removes some remaining dirt, although you will still want to rinse or scrub off big chunks of debris before storage.

The mineral oil in the mixture also helps keep the tools clean. It lubricates the metal, preventing both rust accumulation and dirt buildup.

This easy project takes just minutes to make, and it will save you a lot of time in the future.

Keep your power tools looking good as new

Electric tools such as drills and chainsaws need regular attention to keep them in peak working condition.

- Woodworking tools can collect dust over time. Clear it out using a compressed air duster before cleaning.

- Wipe down power tools using a cleaning solution and rag. Be sure to stay clear of power cables and motors when cleaning. A cotton swab or toothbrush works well to clean around buttons and toggles.

When finished cleaning, wipe down all tools with a clean, dry rag. Use steel wool to clean away any rust.

5 household items that double up in the yard

Why buy a tool twice? Save money by repurposing common household items and even trash to get chores done in the garden. Many things around the house can do double duty. It just requires a little creative thinking on your part.

5-gallon bucket. You can toss these sturdy plastic buckets when they outlive their usefulness, but why not give one a second life instead? With the lid firmly in place, a bucket makes a great garden stool. Put the tools you need inside, sit on top, and save your knees as you work in your garden beds.

Laundry basket. Picking up leaves each fall can be quite a chore. It's really not all that easy to hold a bag open and get the leaves inside before it collapses. Thankfully, there is a common household item that can help.

Before you throw out that old laundry basket, cut the bottom out, and use it as a leaf funnel. Set it inside a yard waste bag to keep it open as you shovel in leaves.

Don't ever pay for garden plant markers again. You can find these simple tools everywhere. Some great ideas include paint stirrers, plastic utensils, old wooden spoons, and ice pop sticks. Use a permanent marker to write on your upcycled plant signs.

Plastic food container. How many used containers have you tossed into the trash? The good news is these containers make a perfect greenhouse for starting your favorite seeds.

Clean them out well, then punch some holes in the bottom. Fill the container with lightweight growing medium and add seeds. Keep the lid closed until the seeds sprout, then open it up for air and light.

Wire hanger. The cheap wire hangers you get from the cleaners can find new life as garden stakes. Twist them into straight stakes or cut them into the right size to stake some of your plants. They also make great holders for plant labels, or to attach hanging plants to a frame or fence.

Plastic jug. Use something you would typically toss out to make a useful garden tool like a watering can. Fill the jug with water, and screw on the lid. Use an awl to randomly make holes in the top.

To water plants, shake the jug up and down over your plants. If you'd like a more traditional watering can, make the holes bigger to improve the flow.

Tips to organize your tool shed on a dime

A messy, disorganized tool shed can cause a lot of problems and frustration. Without a sound organizational system, you waste time looking for the right tool for a job or even lose tools. They are more likely to get dirty and rusty. Perhaps most importantly, disorganized storage is a dangerous trip hazard.

Keeping your tools organized, stored, and cleaned is possible even on a budget. Get creative with your ideas, or try these inexpensive hacks and upcycle whenever possible.

Hang up a wood pallet. You can pick up versatile free pallets from companies that will otherwise throw them away. Hang one or two on the wall of your shed for a DIY organizer. Hammer in a few strategically placed nails to hang tools.

Make a handy pegboard. A pegboard with dowels is another good tool organizer. Pegboard is inexpensive, but you can also make your own. Grab some extra plywood, drill holes and add dowels, and voila — your very own homemade board.

Find the perfect place for small parts. Small garden items are easily lost without proper storage. Old plastic cups hung on nails or dowels are perfect for holding pencils, row markers, plant labels, and more.

Likewise, vertical hanging shoe organizers are ideal for gloves, small tools, garden twine, and even seed packets.

Organize tall tools with PVC pipe. Cut PVC pipe into small sections to create a simple organizing system for rakes, shovels, hoes, and similar long-handled tools.

For each tool, attach a piece of pipe to the wall at floor level and another piece a few feet higher. Slot the handle into both pieces of pipe to secure the tool. Never again worry about getting dinged on the head by a falling rake.

Use the internet as a tool to obtain free stuff

The internet has a bajillion websites, and many will lead you to free plants, pots, tools, and more. It's certainly one "tool" you should take advantage of. And it won't cost you a cent if you have a computer or access to one.

Some websites will offer free items in exchange for your email address. Just make sure you understand all the terms before you type in your address. Many sites will also pro-vide great products in exchange for a review or paying only shipping and handling.

Here are some popular gardening websites where you can score a lot of pretty cool garden stuff.

Site name	Web address	What you can get
Local Tools	localtools.org	locations of tool-lending libraries where you can borrow tools
Burgess Seed & Plant Company	eburgess.com	a variety of free gifts when you place an order
Annies Annuals	anniesannuals.com	free online instructional videos
The Spruce	thespruce.com	free garden planner to download
Spring Hill Nursery	springhillnursery.com/ catalog_request	sign up to get a catalog and get a $25 coupon
Arbor Day Foundation	shop.arborday.org	get 10 free trees when you join
World Plant Exchange	worldplantexchange.com	people from all over the world share plants, seeds, and a passion for gardening
Proven Winners	nwf.org/Butterfly-Heroes/ Pledge.aspx	free garden idea book

Learn how to grow anything, inside or out, with the help of these great gardening sites. Be sure you bookmark them so you can easily find them again.

Site name	Web address	Information
Frugal Gardening	frugalgardening.com	tips on finding free plants, mulch, and containers
Gardening Know How	gardeningknowhow.com	get all your tough garden questions answered by seasoned gardeners
National Gardening Association	garden.org	free gardening downloads, plant database, and a large community of plant lovers
Dave's Garden	davesgarden.com	daily informative garden blog, plant database, and a beautiful plant and landscape picture gallery
Birds and Blooms	birdsandblooms.com	backyard projects, birding, and gardening information
Gardening Guides	gardenguides.com	garden planner and a large volume of "how to" articles on everything gardening

Make a no-sew garden apron from old jeans

Old jeans have a lot of uses. You can transform them into quilts and rugs — even purses or baskets. When your favorite pair of denim is out of style or a little too worn, how about turning them into something for the garden?

An apron is perfect. It keeps your clothes clean and provides pockets to hold tools as you work. Sure, you can buy an apron, but this project will save you money.

The best part? It's so simple it takes just five minutes and you don't even have to know how to sew. Here's what to do.

- Cut off the legs of the jeans about an inch below the bottom edge of the back pockets.

- On the front of the jeans, open the zipper. You need to cut just below the waistband. Start at the zipper and cut to the side seam. Repeat on the other side.

- Cut down the side seam on each side to the end of the leg. Remove the front part of the jeans and discard.

That's all there is to it. You now have a handy apron you can use for all your gardening chores.

Place the back pockets in front, reach the waistband around your waist toward your back. Fasten the button behind you. It should fit just as if you were wearing a pair of jeans.

You can use the pockets in front to store seeds and tools. If you like to sew, attach a piece of denim at the waistband with strings to tie around your neck. Add a pocket to this part for even more storage.

Upkeep to keep your garden looking its best

10 terrific nontoxic ways to kill weeds

Some people refer to weeds as plants out of place. If you are a gardener, you may think of them as the bane of your existence. Weeds are a constant battle, but they must be dealt with if you want to keep your yard and garden healthy and beautiful.

It may be tempting to pour or spray heavy chemicals on weeds for a quick result. The truth is, many chemicals don't work and do way more harm than good. But don't worry — you have many nontoxic options for getting rid of obstinate weeds.

- Goat power. When you have large areas overgrown with weeds, goats are an unusual, but effective, remedy. These natural weed whackers can munch through a large patch of weeds and overgrown brush in no time, killing weeds to the root. Rent a goat for a daily rate, or buy one of your own for a fairly cheap way to get the job done.

- Layering. Two of the biggest obstacles in starting a garden are eliminating weeds and building rich and organic soil. The solution is a type of organic gardening called layering. It's a way to turn hard soil into rich topsoil in one season and get rid of weeds — all without tilling.

  The basic system involves layering brown material like shredded newspaper, peat, and pine needles with green materials, including vegetable scraps, grass, and garden clippings. The brown material needs to be twice as deep as the green material. Lay down heavy sheets of toxic-free plastic for the base layer, and they'll immediately go to work smothering weeds.

- Pickle juice. Weed-proof your lawn without toxic chemicals. This kitchen item does the trick. Pickle brine contains vinegar and salt, which makes it a weed-busting superstar. Just apply to problem plants and watch them fade fast.

In addition to the natural weed-killing methods above, try these when persistent weeds drive you crazy.

- Pull by hand early in the season. Use a claw to get the entire weed.

- Smother them with newspaper.

- Pour boiling water on weeds between patio and walkway stones.

- Use a weed torch.

- Sprinkle salt in driveway cracks or between walkway stones. Don't use salt in areas you'll be replanting.

- Mulch early in the growing season.

- Cover a weedy area with a heavy black plastic sheet, and let the sun heat problem plants out of existence in about eight weeks.

Weed-be-gone tonic your pets will appreciate

A pet-safe weed killer is easy to make. Combine vinegar plus these household ingredients for a spray that won't harm pets but is lethal to weeds.

This easy weed-stopping solution for your yard will actually save you money because it uses inexpensive household items.

- 1 gallon of vinegar

- 1 cup of salt

- 1 tablespoon of dish soap

Leave out the salt for areas you want to replant. Spray the mixture directly onto leaves, avoiding other plants, when there is no chance of rain.

Kill poison ivy without expensive chemicals

You love the natural wooded areas in your backyard but not the poison ivy that runs rampant. If this irritating plant has invaded your space, you may wonder if chemical herbicides are your only option.

If you worry about their safety and the harm they cause the natural environment and nearby plants, here are some great alternatives. Try more than one if the first effort fails to do the job.

Pull them out at the root. You can remove any weed with a little elbow grease, but poison ivy presents a special problem because touching it can irritate your skin. Still, it's doable.

Wear long pants tucked into socks, long sleeves, and gloves. Wait until after a rain when the soil is soft and moist, and pull the poison ivy out, root and all. Dispose of the plant carefully, and immediately wash your clothing and any tools you use.

Smother the plants. If you have a small, manageable infestation of poison ivy, you can smother it with cardboard or a tarp. Cover plants until they die. Watch out for any roots that run out beyond the edges of the tarp. Pull those out.

Make a salt spray. An effective natural herbicide can take out poison ivy with a few applications. Dissolve a cup of salt in a gallon of water, and add a tablespoon of dish soap.

Spray the leaves, avoiding other plants as best you can. Apply on a sunny day with no chance of rain. Spray regularly until the pesky plants are gone.

Once you have removed the poison ivy, take steps to prevent its return. The best way to do it is to replace it with other plants. Look for those that will thrive in a wooded environment, like native, shade-loving groundcovers or berry canes and shrubs.

> This all-natural poison ivy balm stops the itch fast. Mix 2 tablespoons each of bentonite clay, baking soda, and Dead Sea salt with 20 drops lavender essential oil, and keep in a glass jar with a lid in a cool place. When needed, combine 1 tablespoon of the mixture with enough water to make a paste, and apply.

Select plants for their weed-defeating superpowers

Weeding is one of the most labor-intensive chores for gardeners, but these unwanted plants cannot stay. They compete with other plants for water and nutrients, and they just don't look nice. A weedy bed is a messy bed.

What if you could plan your beds for weed prevention, and minimize the time spent on your knees pulling weeds out by the roots? A few careful design choices and plant selections can help do the trick.

Here are three categories of beautiful plants that are proven to suppress weeds.

Dense, colony-forming plants. Try growing groundcovers where weeds are difficult to control and tend to take over. These are low-growing, densely packed plants that spread out to fill the space. They tend to grow aggressively, not giving weeds a chance to take root.

Try these great groundcovers for shady spots.

- lily-of-the-valley
- yellow archangel
- bugle
- pachysandra
- sweet woodruff

Here are some good choices to fill your sunny spots.

- creeping phlox
- red creeping thyme
- stonecrop
- yarrow
- lamb's ear
- ice plant

Small plants to fill out beds. Another strategy for choking out weeds is to fill in gaps in your beds with smaller plants. Groundcovers may not be the best choice here because they tend to take over beds.

Use small annual or perennial flowers that do not spread readily that you can tuck into corners and between larger perennials. These are some good options.

- dwarf hostas
- coral bells
- heuchera
- impatiens
- marigolds
- petunias

Native plants. This category of plants has science backing up its weed-conquering abilities. Researchers have found that native plantings excel at controlling weeds.

Because they evolve to thrive in the local environment, native plants out-compete many types of weeds. Check with your local extension office or garden center to find out which plant species are native to your area.

Soda bottle trick saves the plants you love

One of the big problems with weed killers — both chemical and natural — is they often destroy not only the weeds but also the surrounding vegetation.

With the help of a 2-liter plastic soda bottle, you can easily protect surrounding plants and hone in on the weeds you want to kill. Just one bottle is all you need for your entire yard.

- Clean out the soda bottle and remove the lid.

- Cut off the bottom portion of the bottle.

- Cover the weed in question with the top half of the bottle.

- Spray your solution through the open top, and wait a bit for the weed to show signs of wilting.

That's all there is to it. This upcycled plastic shield is great in garden areas where you want to protect plants you love. Use it over and over again.

3 reasons to prune a tree — and the right way to do it

A tree-trimming company could come up with 20 reasons to keep your trees pruned, but it boils down to three main factors — safety, health, and beauty.

Safety. Safety is a big factor in pruning trees. Unlike small shrubs, loose, dead, or broken branches can cause serious harm. Trim out broken or diseased branches at risk of falling.

It's also important to prune back branches that block sidewalks and driving views and those that threaten to take out power lines.

Health. The next most important factor is the health of the tree. Overgrowth is bad for a tree and can weaken it over time as healthy branches compete for resources. Pruning also takes out diseased or infested branches to slow or stop the spread.

Beauty. Finally, a well-trimmed tree looks better. Regular pruning keeps a tree looking tidy and also allows you to create a pleasing shape. You will have less debris on the lawn, too, as you remove dead and weak branches.

If you want to take on tree-pruning jobs yourself, follow these three rules for cutting based on the diameter of the branches.

- Trim away branches with V-shaped, narrow angles. Those that are U-shaped and wider are stronger and should stay in place.

- When removing branches, cut them back to a lateral branch that is about one-third the diameter. This allows the remaining portion to remain a strong branch.

- Pruning cuts should be no more than 2 inches for trees that don't seal well such as birches, poplars, crab apples, and maples. For other trees, you can make cuts that are up to 4 inches in diameter.

Pruning can make a significant positive impact, but it can also be harmful to a tree if you do it wrong. If in doubt about what to do, call in the pros.

Expert tips to prune plants perfectly

It takes some skill and knowledge to prune correctly and safely. One of the most important things to keep in mind is timing.

Knowing when you should never prune outdoor plants helps to keep your landscape plants healthy and thriving.

All plants have their ideal pruning times, but the general rule is to avoid pruning in fall. It's tempting to clean up shrubs and trees as you pick up leaves, but don't do it. The cuts stimulate new growth exactly when the plant is going dormant. The result is a weaker plant. Also, cuts can bring out sap that freezes overnight.

By learning simple rules-of-thumb for pruning every plant in your landscape, you'll make way for abundant blooms.

- Spring-flowering deciduous shrubs. Prune shrubs like forsythia and lilac soon after the flowers fade. This gives them time to grow and prepare for next year's buds. Prune an overgrown shrub in late winter. It will restore health and vigor but may reduce blooms for a couple of years.

- Summer-flowering shrubs. Shrubs that bloom in summer, like spirea, are best trimmed in late winter or even in early spring. Flowers will appear on the new growth.

- Non-flowering deciduous shrubs. Prune these in late winter or early spring.

- Evergreen shrubs. Prune juniper, yew, and other evergreen shrubs about mid-spring, before new growth comes in. Midsummer is also acceptable for light pruning.

- Deciduous trees. The best time to prune most deciduous trees is late winter and early spring. This timing allows you to see branches and gives the cuts time to heal. This includes fruit trees, which you should not prune after bud break.

- Evergreen trees. Pine, fir, spruce, and other evergreen trees don't need much pruning in general. Remove dead or diseased branches any time of year. Late winter is best for clearing out low branches if you want to raise the canopy. You can also cut back shoots to the next lateral bud in late spring for bushier, denser growth.

Easy month-to-month guide to garden maintenance

The maintenance chores you'll do each month depend on your location and climate, but a general checklist helps you stay organized no matter where your garden is. Follow this monthly calendar to help you remember essential chores so you can have your best yard and garden ever.

January

- In the coldest climates, plan for spring. Buy seeds, redesign beds, and pick out new shrubs or perennials.
- Where winters are milder, protect tender plants during cold snaps with tarps or a bedsheet.

February

- Prune shrubs and trees, especially spring bloomers.
- Take advantage of warmer days to make repairs to fences, sheds, or other garden infrastructure.

March

- Fertilize plants as they get ready for the growing season.
- Prepare beds by cleaning out any debris from last year, turning the soil, and adding compost.
- Get a head start on weeds by pulling them now.
- Clean out and prepare water features for spring.

April

- Work in cover crops if you use them.
- Deadhead flowering bulbs, but keep leaves intact.
- Start mowing the lawn as needed.
- Start planting vegetables outdoors.

May

- Plant new perennials.
- Plant annuals after the last freeze date.
- Use a natural pre-emergent weed killer and feed on your front and back lawn.
- Add new mulch to garden beds.

June

- Water plants regularly as the days heat up.
- Perform any needed maintenance on irrigation systems.
- Fertilize garden plants.

July

- Keep an eye on rainfall, and water plants as often as needed.
- Deadhead flowers.
- Check plants for pests and diseases.
- Cut the grass higher and less frequently.

August

- Keep watering and weeding daily if necessary.
- Cut annuals back to encourage new growth.
- Harvest vegetables.

September

- Keep harvesting vegetables.
- Water less often, but continue as needed.
- Clean leaves out of water features.
- Reseed bare patches of lawn.

October

- Plant spring bulbs.
- Rake leaves and compost or put out for pickup.
- Clean out beds of old plant debris.
- Compost spent annuals.

November

- Give lawn a final mow before the first snowfall.
- Bring tender potted perennials inside.

December

- Take a break and dream about next spring.

5 surprising things you need to spruce up your landscape

Certain aspects of creating a gorgeous garden will never change, such as designing beds, maintaining plants, and of course, weeding. But a little creativity can add beauty to your landscape in new ways. Try these tips and tricks to beautify your outdoor space and keep it looking great season after season.

Gravel. Yes, humble rock can make your garden look nicer and more finished. Defined walkways create order and structure in a garden, and using gravel is a cheap and easy way to do it. Outline paths between and around beds, grade the soil, and add a layer of gravel.

- Upkeep tip — top up gravel annually as needed.

Upcycled planters. Fancy planters add class and elegance to gardens, but they cost a lot. Get creative and make planters out of upcycled objects and materials. An old washtub, a wheelbarrow, tea tins, colanders, tires, and more can become pretty planters with a coat of paint and some creative placement.

- Upkeep tip — clean out and store planters in a shed or garage during the winter months to keep them looking their best.

Strategic lighting. Show off your garden after dark when shadows and night-blooming flowers play with light and create a completely different look from daytime. Lights don't have to be over the top or expensive to be effective. Use a few strings of fairy lights or solar-powered lights in beds and along paths.

- Upkeep tip — keep foliage trimmed and away from the solar window, and replace batteries as needed.

Attractive rug. Rugs aren't just for indoor spaces. A simple outdoor rug helps create a defined space for entertaining, relaxing, and enjoying your garden.

- Upkeep tip — clean outdoor rugs annually, and roll up and store in the garden shed if your winters are rough.

Good pruning shears. Invest in a sturdy pair of shears, and you'll never regret it. One of the best ways to keep your landscape looking gorgeous is to keep plants trimmed. The difference between a shaped shrub and a natural one is not subtle. It makes a big difference to the overall look of the space.

- Upkeep tip — clean and oil tools regularly, and keep them out of the weather.

How can I make my yard and garden easier to maintain?

Everyone loves a pretty garden, but not everyone enjoys the upkeep or has the time for it. If you fall into that category, you need to plan a low-maintenance outdoor space.

Reduce the lawn footprint. Mowing the lawn, fertilizing it, worrying about weeds and crabgrass — these are all reasons a grassy lawn can be the most time-consuming element of your landscape. It requires constant care and maintenance. For less work, replace areas of turf with a stone patio, mulched bed, or even a wildflower meadow.

Embrace mulch. Putting down mulch is a significant chore, but it will make the rest of the season so much easier. Mulching between plants in your beds holds water in the soil, suppresses weeds, and gives beds a tidy look with less effort.

Grow more shrubs. Perennial and annual flowers are popular in garden beds, but they also require maintenance weekly or even daily during the growing season. As you plan a garden, use attractive shrubs and even ornamental trees, and fewer perennials.

Choose native plants. Plants that have evolved to grow in your garden's natural environment will need the least maintenance. They thrive in local conditions, tolerate drought, and remain strong in the face of storms, pests, or competition from weeds.

Weed early. Weeding is one of the most time-consuming of all garden chores. You may not be able to avoid it entirely, but you can minimize it. Start with a good layer of mulch, and begin the chore early in the spring. The sooner you can pull out little weeds, the easier maintenance will be later.

Secret to keeping your outdoor living space looking great

Your patio or deck is the perfect spot to enjoy your garden, warm summer nights, chilly mornings with a cup of coffee, or time with friends. But building an entertaining and comfortable outdoor space is not the end of your job. To keep it looking nice year round, you need to do one critical thing — protect it.

Prevention is the best defense when it comes to almost anything, including your home and yard. Preventing damage, dirt, and decay in your outdoor living space is much easier — and cheaper — than treating it.

Here are a few areas where preventive maintenance will allow you to enjoy the outdoor space you built for years to come.

Protect your deck. If you have a deck in your outdoor space, give it a protective coating to seal it from rain and wind. If you have yet to build that deck, go for a composite material that will stand up to weather and needs no maintenance.

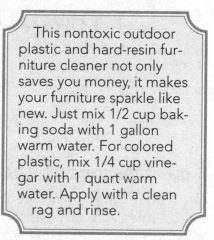

This nontoxic outdoor plastic and hard-resin furniture cleaner not only saves you money, it makes your furniture sparkle like new. Just mix 1/2 cup baking soda with 1 gallon warm water. For colored plastic, mix 1/4 cup vinegar with 1 quart warm water. Apply with a clean rag and rinse.

Keep furniture clean. Invest in good covers for your patio furniture, and it will last much longer. Furniture doesn't just get dirty — it can rust, rot, and eventually fall apart. Bring cushions indoors when not in use and for the duration of the winter. Clean and cover furniture that is too heavy to move indoors for the winter.

Prevent rust. Metal elements in your outdoor space can quickly rust and become unsightly and dangerous. To prevent rust, keep metal furniture and other objects clean. Give them a thorough cleaning at least twice a year.

Handle metal pieces carefully. Nicks and dings are spots where rust can take hold. Bring them indoors for winter or during rainy seasons, if possible.

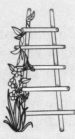

Vertical designs for spectacular upward interest

8 great reasons why you should grow vertically

Growing plants upwards is an innovative and beautiful way to add interest to any garden space. It's also practical. Here's why you should consider it.

Maximizes your space. Growing plants vertically maximizes space like nothing else. If you have a limited amount of garden space available but want to produce a big harvest or just a beautiful display of plants, growing upwards is the best answer.

It's more accessible. A vertical garden is an excellent idea for people with bad knees, backs, or other flexibility issues. Plants grown upward are easier to access than those sprawling along the ground. Gardening vertically makes everything from fertilizing to harvesting easier.

Plants are healthier. Healthy plants need plenty of air circulation, and growing upwards makes this possible. Plus there is less chance of pest infestation or disease. Any pests that visit vertically growing plants will be much easier to spot than they would in a conventional garden.

Increases your harvest. Many food crops are happy to take up vertical space. A great example is pumpkin. Pumpkins take up a lot of real estate in a garden. Dwarf varieties, however, are perfectly suited to an upward habit and will reward you with plenty of perfect little pumpkins.

Creates a living privacy screen. Vining, twining, and climbing plants are a perfect option for creating a stunning living privacy screen. Apartment or condo dwellers can efficiently use vertical space to make a private outdoor living space.

Grows in nontraditional spaces. One of the most significant advantages of growing vertically is having plants in unconventional areas such as walls or fences. And when you grow plants vertically in containers, you can place them anywhere for instant beauty and coverage.

Produces cleaner crops. Plants that are grown vertically produce cleaner crops that don't have direct contact with the soil. Trellising plants protects them from water splash, which can cause disease.

Makes weeding easier. With plants not directly on top of the soil, tending a garden is easy. You don't have to worry about digging in and compromising fruit or flowers when you pull up weeds.

Go up, up, up with these cool designs

The sky is the limit when it comes to vertical garden design and construction. Of course, like any other garden, planning is essential, as is budget, space, and time. Here are some common types of vertical gardens to consider.

Trellis garden. When you think of vertical gardens, a trellis garden is most likely the first garden that comes to mind.

These gardens come in all shapes and sizes, and trellis structures are easy to construct and add to existing raised beds or even containers.

An ancient type of trellis garden is a teepee garden. You can easily form a teepee using bamboo pieces together with garden twine or wire. A teepee trellis works great for vine crops such as cucumbers, tomatoes, and squash.

Green wall garden. A green wall is a classic and ageless design that adds beauty and mystery to any outdoor space. This design uses your home structure or a wall or section of your home for living plants.

Crawlers like ivy are a popular option for a green wall, but other plants, including flowering vines, also work for this design. Keep in mind, if you don't want your entire home covered with vines, you need to prune your vine to a constrained area.

Convert an old pallet or pallet-shaped box into a makeshift gutter garden by stapling landscape fabric to the box, filling the inside with lightweight potting soil, and planting beautiful hanging plants through the slats. Set it in one corner of your patio or balcony for eye-catching interest.

Pocket garden. There are many ways to create a pocket wall, which involves attaching pocket-shaped pots to walls or other structures. Pocket gardens are highly versatile and easy to mix up. They're also practical for growing herbs and small fruits and veggies.

Pipe garden. Strawberries and other bushy plants are incredibly happy in a pipe garden. These simple-to-make gardens look fantastic mounted on any solid surface.

Simply drill large holes into the pipe for the plants, fill with soil, and mount either horizontally or vertically. As the plant matures, it will sprout outward around the pipe, creating a pleasing appearance, sometimes covering the entire pipe.

Gutter garden. Rain gutters hold the perfect amount of soil for many hanging and even fruiting plants such as strawberries. Attach gutters to walls or fences, or hang several using a sturdy chain for a beautiful vertical display.

Arbors and arches garden. Growing plants on solidly constructed pieces creates the perfect space for heavy-duty climbers like roses, wisteria, bougainvillea, and climbing fruiting plants.

The more substantial the structure, the heartier plant it can accommodate. Along with arbors and arches, consider decorating your pergola or gazebo. Adding vining and climbing plants to these structures generates additional interest and also creates shade and privacy.

7 surprising materials that make excellent trellises

You can find many beautiful and practical trellis structures available to buy, but plants aren't picky about what they climb. You likely have plenty of trellis material just hanging around your home that won't require you to open your pocketbook. Here are a few examples.

Bicycle wheels. Attach bicycle wheels of various sizes to a post in your garden. Climbers will happily make their way upwards and fill in the spaces on the wheels. If you are looking for a conversation piece in your garden, this is it.

Bedspring. Secure an old bedspring to a fence or simply stake it into your landscape. The bedspring provides a rustic element that plants will love to wind and twine around.

Badminton net. Create an instant vertical garden by stringing an old badminton net between two poles and planting twining and vining plants at the base of the net. Fast-growing vines will quickly cover the net, creating the perfect living privacy fence.

Twigs. Don't throw out those twigs after pruning — use them in your veggie garden for supports. Screw various sized limbs together to make a trellis, and attach it to your raised bed planted with climbers like peas and beans.

Old door frames. Fasten chicken wire to an old door frame to create the perfect vertical space for your favorite climbing plants.

Vintage garden tools. Attach some old garden tools to a fence, or concrete them into your garden space. Shovels, rakes, and hoes add vintage charm and provide excellent support for twining and winding vines such as morning glories or Black-eyed Susans.

Old crib. The slats on a crib bottom are perfect for many plants to wind and climb around. Try attaching an old crib bottom to a raised bed, and use it as a trellis for beans, cucumbers, squash, and peas. Attach two old cribs for the ultimate teepee trellis for beans and other vigorous climbers.

Best veggie crops to grow vertically

Perhaps you want to grow more food in a smaller space, or you'd love to add an ornamental element to your garden using various forms of trellises. Look no further than your favorite vegetables. Many are exceptionally well-suited for growing vertically.

Here are some of the best veggies to consider for growing up, along with tips to keep them healthy.

Pole beans. These are not only easy to grow, they are incredibly zealous climbers that eagerly wind and twine their way towards the sun on any willing trellis, teepee, netting, or other support. Varieties in purple, yellow, and green are easy to find, plant, and harvest.

Peas. Numerous varieties of peas will exceed 3 feet when supported by a trellis. A net set between a couple of sturdy stakes works well as long as it can handle the weight of mature pea vines.

Pick peas every other day when pods are ready. Choose from sugar pea, snap pea, and shell pea varieties.

> Use old pieces of cut-up shirts to tie plants to a trellis structure. Fabric is soft and easy on plants and adds a nice decorative touch to your garden. You can also cut up old nylon stockings.

Cucumbers. You can choose between two broad groups of cucumbers — bush and vining. Select vining types for your vertical garden, and be sure to provide a sturdy and tall trellis — at least 4- to 6-feet tall.

Although cucumber vines are lightweight, they become heavy with mature fruit. Cucumbers do well on fan-like trellises as well as arch-style trellises. Use sturdy garden twine to train and support the vine, but keep the twine loose so as not to choke the vine.

Summer squash. Summer squash is known as a garden hog, so vertically growing these plants saves valuable garden space. Squash plants are not natural climbers, so they need quite a bit of help to get going and stay on course.

The easiest way to keep squash on the support is to weave the branches through wire or nylon mesh or use heavy-duty wire to attach vines loosely to a sturdy trellis structure.

Indeterminate tomatoes. These are also known as vining tomatoes and are natural climbers that are happy to twine and climb. Use twine to hold branches in place. It allows you to position the plant to receive more light and air, thus keeping disease at bay.

How to make an arched cucumber trellis

Growing cucumbers on an arched trellis is a great way to promote healthy plants and create an impressive vertical display in your garden. The design of this trellis also makes harvesting a breeze — no bending required. Place this arched trellis next to two raised beds or directly in your garden bed.

What you need:

- 16x4-foot welded wire cattle panel
- 4 metal stakes each 3-feet tall
- rubber mallet
- wire clippers
- hog rings
- bailing wire
- pliers

How to make it:

1. Hammer two metal stakes 4 feet apart using a rubber mallet. Push the stakes 12 inches into the ground.

2. Hammer two more metal stakes in the same manner, 3 feet from the first stakes and facing them.

3. Use pliers to cut the metal panel in half to make two 8-foot pieces. Trim off the loose ends.

4. Place the panels on top of each other, and attach the top of the 4-foot edges using hog rings. Bend the rings around the panels until they overlap and make a loop.

5. Stand the attached panels up. They should easily arch. Make sure the bound edge is at the top. Set the bottom edges up against the metal stakes.

6. Use bailing wire to secure the panel to the stakes.

Now you can plant your cucumbers and train them to climb up, up, up on the trellis.

Top 3 must do's for vertical gardens

Although maintaining a vertical garden is easier than a conventional garden, it does not entirely erase all care. Here are the top three tips to help you keep your garden looking great.

Water deeply. As with any type of garden, it is best to water at the base of plants and be careful not to splash water on the foliage. Watering plants deeply encourages them to develop robust root systems. Fewer deeper waterings are better than more shallow waterings.

Vertical gardens such as those in pockets, buckets, or other containers require proper drainage. Use mulch to help with moisture retention. Using a soaker hose or drip system in your vertical garden saves money and time while providing consistent moisture.

Don't forget to weed. Vertical container gardens all but eliminate weed issues. But gardens in the ground are another story. They are subject to weeds just like any conventional garden and require regular weeding to do their best.

Applying a thick layer of mulch is one of the best ways to suppress weed growth. Because of the plants' upward training, mulch application is easy. Use 3 to 4 inches in each bed. If weeds are a severe issue, lay down a weed barrier such as a thick piece of cardboard, newspaper, or weed barrier fabric.

When you water, don't spray the entire garden space because that will encourage weeds to grow, too. Water just at the base of each plant instead.

Train plants to climb. Many plants are excellent climbers and will quickly adhere to and cover surfaces without any additional help. However, some need training and may need to be tied to something to encourage a skyward habit.

Once plants begin their upward ascent and establish themselves, tying is usually not necessary. But some plants may need to remain tied to stay neat and orderly. Use twine, flexible plant ties, or pieces of scrap fabric to keep those plants in place.

I'm having issues with fungus — what should I do?

Vertically grown plants often have fewer issues with soil-borne disease or fungus, but that does not mean it won't happen. Fungal pathogens hide in the soil and strike weak plants, leaving them at higher risk for diseases and pest invasion.

One of the best ways to stay ahead of serious issues is to inspect plants regularly. This allows you to spot trouble before it becomes a huge issue. Here are some other ways to control fungus and disease in your garden.

Fight back with a natural remedy. Homemade fungicide is easy to make and offers a natural way to combat fungus issues in the garden. Mix 4 teaspoons of baking soda with a gallon of water, and put it into a spray bottle. Spray plants with fungus issues early in the morning, before the sun gets too hot.

Keep up with pruning. Vining plants can become thick, and regular pruning helps improve circulation and prevent disease and fungus. Always sterilize pruners before and after pruning.

Mulch for protection. Mulching around the base of plants protects the rest of the plant from water splash that contributes to disease and fungus.

Water at the right time. Watering plants in the morning allows leaves to dry out during the day. This helps prevent or stop the spread of fungus and other problems.

Feed plants regularly. Healthy plants are more resistant to pests, diseases, and fungi. Feed plants a well-balanced organic fertilizer regularly during the growing season to keep them in top shape.

Use fresh potting soil. If your vertical garden is in containers, never reuse the potting soil. Always use new, sterile soil when planting in any container.

Dispose of diseased plants properly. Never put diseased plants into your compost pile. Instead, put them in the trash or burn them if you can.

Stunning flowered climbers supply the wow factor

Vertically growing plants can easily create a stunning focal point in any garden. Whether they are scrambling across a wall or fence, or positioned perfectly on a trellis, these beautiful plants help break up garden space, create interest, and draw the eye upward.

Passion vines. Over 400 species of passion flowers exist, most of which are tendril bearing vines with large, vibrant blooms. The curly tendrils of this tropical beauty make it a robust climber.

- The plant's tops die in the winter, but a few plant species will emerge in the spring in growing zones as cold as zone 5. Most passion vines grow in zones 7 to 10.

- Passion vines can reach up to 20 feet in height and do best with two feedings during the year — once in spring and once in midsummer.

- Best climbing structures are arbors, fences, and pergolas.

Mandevilla. Although Mandevilla plants are cold hardy only in the warmest regions — zones 10 to 11 — they are sold in pots elsewhere and bear beautiful flowers in pink shades.

- These vining beauties need some shade each day as they can burn in direct sunlight.

- To have the best blooms possible, feed your plant a high phosphorus, water-soluble fertilizer twice a month. Pinch the tops of each stem for a fuller, bushier appearance.

- Best climbing structures are a sturdy fan trellis, lattice, or chain link fence.

Trumpet vine. Striking, trumpet-shaped, red, orange, or yellow flowers on this vine draw pollinators from far and wide.

- Although easy to grow, this woody vine can sometimes be hard to restrain. Annual maintenance helps to keep it under control as it happily spreads in growing zones 4 to 9.

- Provide moist soil and plenty of mulch for the most rewarding results.

- Best climbing structures are fences, arbors, pergolas, and decks.

Honeysuckle. Nothing is quite so sweet as the enticing aroma of honeysuckle and its delicious nectar. Add a honeysuckle plant to your landscape in growing zones 4 to 9. It will draw a large number of pollinators with its stunning yellow to bright-red blossoms.

- Honeysuckle prefers full sun but can tolerate some shade and does best in rich, well-draining soil.

- As the plant grows, it is vital to keep the top half thinned out, so it does not shade the lower half of the plant. Thin out the plants in the dormant season only.

- Best climbing structures are a sturdy trellis, arbor, pergola, fence, or arch.

Cheap — but effective — way to support your fruiting plants

If you have fruiting plants in your vertical garden, try this creative trick to keep them off the ground. Use old panty-hose or a piece of an old T-shirt to make a handy sling.

Cut the material to a size that matches the estimated mature fruit size. Tie one end to the plant support structure, and gently spread the fabric so that the fruit hangs just slightly above the sling.

Tie the other end of the material to the support structure. Spread out the fabric in the shape of a small hammock. As the fruit matures, it will drop down into your homemade support sling.

Recycle your bottles in a funky hanging garden

Rather than contribute to landfill waste, put those plastic beverage bottles to work for you in a vertical garden. This simple hanging recycled bottle garden is perfect for herbs, flowers, or veggies.

What you need:

- empty 2-liter plastic bottle

- permanent marker

- craft knife

- paracord

- small rocks, gravel

- lightweight potting soil

How to make it:

1. Position the bottle upright, and outline a window on each side using the permanent marker.

2. Use the craft knife to cut out both windows.

3. Make four holes near the mouth of the bottle. Pass the paracord through the holes to make two loops, which will hang the planter.

4. Place about a half inch of rocks at the bottom of the bottle.

5. Fill the bottle with lightweight potting soil, and plant it with your favorite plant. Trailing plants look great in these bottles.

6. Make several of these bottles, and hang them at varying heights for an eye-catching display.

Water features
that make
a splash

5-star reasons to add a water focal point

A water feature is a valuable addition to any outdoor space. If you've been thinking about introducing a bubbling fountain, peaceful pond, or other water element to your landscape but need a little convincing, check out these five reasons why you should go for it.

Water is therapeutic. It's a hectic world, and sometimes it's easy to get caught up in the stress of daily life. Evidence shows that water is highly therapeutic, and moving water even more so.

A water feature in your landscape can relieve stress and promote a sense of relaxation — something everyone could use.

It draws beautiful wildlife. Every living thing needs water to survive, and once you install a water feature, nature will quickly hone in. Depending on the size and nature of your special attraction, a wide variety of wildlife will show up for your enjoyment.

If you are lucky enough, your water feature will even draw interesting birds along their migratory journey.

It's more low-maintenance than you think. Many water devices are easy to care for, especially small fountains and waterfalls. Because they are in constant motion, algae will not build up, and mosquitoes stay away.

Apart from annual maintenance, once you set up a recirculating water feature, you can sit back and enjoy it all season long.

It will even work in a small yard. Don't let a compact green space or even no green space discourage you from enjoying the benefits of water. From tabletop fountains to small backyard bubblers, the sky is the limit when it comes to choosing a water feature that best suits your space.

It can stimulate creativity. There are so many different and innovative ways to bring water to your home garden. If you're artistic, you can let your creative juices flow and put your own signature on your work.

Just remember to have fun while you're doing it. Then, when you're finished designing and installing your water feature, you can sit back and enjoy the results of your work.

How to choose the best water feature for your needs

Now that you are ready to install an aquatic feature, it is crucial to do some homework to figure out which one is just right. Here are some helpful hints to get you rolling.

Let your space determine your device. Your first step is to take a walk around your home and garden and identify possible locations for a water feature. Some devices are prefabricated and require a certain amount of space.

Choose the area where you would like to add water. Keep in mind that installing a water feature under a tree can create some issues with falling leaves and lack of sunlight.

Consider your budget. Like any home project, it is important to set a budget. Think about the initial cost to either make or purchase a water feature along with any costs associated with maintenance.

The good news is that even if you are on a minimal budget, you'll find plenty of devices that won't break your bank.

Take a look at your yard. Is your landscape formal or more informal? Knowing this will help you decide what type of water feature works best.

Water features that blend well with more formal landscapes include symmetrical ponds or classical water fountains. An asymmetrical, free-form pond with a naturalistic feel is more appropriate for an informal landscape.

Don't forget about safety. If you have children or pets that hang out in your yard, consider the type of water feature that would best keep everyone safe.

Depending on the option you select, you may need a low-view fence or another way to keep children and pets safe while still allowing you to enjoy your water feature.

Rub-a-dub-dub, make a pond from a tub

A pond is an excellent addition to a backyard garden, but building one takes a lot of effort. And, yes, it can also be a hugely expensive undertaking. It requires careful planning and measuring, not to mention a lot of digging.

An easier and cheaper way to enjoy a pond is to create one out of an upcycled waterproof container, like an old bathtub.

First, you need to find a tub. Maybe you have one destined for the dump. If not, check your local thrift stores, junk yards, or online. Perhaps you can find an old claw-foot tub in need of restoration and rescue it. Look at architectural salvage companies.

Choose a location for the pond. Keep in mind how heavy it will be. The spot should be stable and include a little shade for water plants.

Clean the tub and fill it with water. You may want to install a pump to keep the water fresh, but you will need to locate the tub close to a power source. Another option is to use plants to keep the water clear and free of algae.

Add plants in containers to the tub. Elevate them as necessary by setting them on bricks, rocks, or concrete blocks. For plants that need soil, place gravel on top of the submerged soil to keep it in place.

- Floating plants, like water hyacinth and water lettuce, do an excellent job of filtering the water and keeping it clean and clear. They are heavy feeders, leaving little to nothing for algae to grow.

- Other plants to try include water iris, watercress, pickerel plant, and of course, water lilies, which come in varieties with a range of hardiness zones.

- Keep in mind that if you are in a colder climate, you may need to bring pond plants indoors to overwinter. For hardy plants, install a filter to keep the water aerated and prevent it from freezing during the cold months.

Build a potted bubbler fountain in 5 easy steps

A water feature complements any garden, and it doesn't have to be expensive or difficult to make. This bubbler fountain takes just five steps to complete.

The bubbling sound is softer and more soothing than fountains or waterfall features, adding a subtle relaxing element to your outside space.

What you need:

- 2 plastic pots, one big, one smaller

- submerged pond pump with plastic tubing

- decorative rocks and pea gravel

- caulk or sealant

- drill, drill bits

How to make it:

1. Drill a hole to thread the tubing through each pot. The holes should be on the side of the pots, toward the bottom.

2. Assemble the pots. Put rocks in the larger pot so that the small pot can sit inside it, elevated to the desired height. Add stones or gravel to the top, smaller pot.

3. Set up the pump and tubing. The pump goes in the top pot. Thread the cord through the plastic tubing, so it goes through the hole in the smaller pot, into the larger pot, and through the bottom hole. From there, you can plug it into the power source. Rearrange rocks as needed to make the pots and pump stable.

4. Seal the holes. Use caulking or another type of waterproof sealant to plug up the gaps around the tubing on the side of each pot.

5. Add water to each pot and turn on the pump. The pump should sit just below the surface of the water. You can adjust the water level to get the right kind of bubbling.

This plan is for a simple bubbler fountain, but you can always use your imagination and add more decorative elements.

If your fountain seems barren once you stop the water flow, use it to display seasonal greenery, pine cones, or other items that are easy to remove once warmer weather returns.

Create a koi sanctuary for your fish friends

If you're wondering what your backyard sanctuary is missing, it might be a relaxing water feature. A koi pond is a great way to add another level of Zen to any garden space. It will take some work and a little investment, but the peaceful benefits of a fish pond are well worth it.

Koi are colored versions of Amur carp. They are so beautiful that creating a pond for these stunning fish is a popular hobby for many people. Here's how to go about it.

Make a plan. A pond is a significant undertaking, so don't begin without a plan. Start with a budget, which will help govern your decisions.

- Choose a spot in the garden where you can enjoy the pond. It should have some sunlight and some shade. Keep in mind that an overhanging tree looks nice, but it will add to later maintenance.

- Decide on a size and shape, and map it out on the ground with stakes and string to get it right.

Dig a hole and add a filter. A pond is essentially a hole in the ground, so you'll have some tough physical work to do. With an outline for your pond, dig down at least 3 to 4 feet.

You can tier the bottom, but the fish need this much depth in at least part of the pond to overwinter. Add the filter according to its instructions.

Line the pond. A pond needs a liner or the water will seep into the soil of your garden. Look for a pond liner at a garden center, and use just one piece to avoid leaks. It should overlap the pond by a few feet. Secure the edges with large stones.

Add water, fish, and plants. With the hard work behind you, it is time for the last steps.

> Don't feed your koi fish more than once a day. Uneaten food can decay in the water, making it murky. Over-feeding can also lead to unhealthy fish and bacterial growth. Koi eat lots of different things, from small bugs and insects to plants and algae and store-bought koi food.

- Add water to fill the pond, and let it sit for a week or so to eliminate chlorine. Keep in mind that the ideal size for a koi pond is 1,000 gallons and at least 3 feet deep.

- You may want to add pond starter bacteria to make the water more accommodating to fish and plants.

- Next, add the pond plants, and finally, when the pond is stable, add your koi.

Perfect goldfish pond for a patio

If you don't have a lot of space but you have a small patio or balcony, this water garden is a perfect addition to your outdoor room.

With a few supplies and a sunny afternoon, you can create a soothing and beautiful patio goldfish pond.

What you need:

- half wine or whiskey barrel
- preformed liner

- water plants • bricks • goldfish

How to make it:

1. Position the half whiskey barrel in a location where it is level and receives at least six hours of sunlight daily.

2. Drop the preformed liner into the barrel. This will keep any dangerous chemicals from leaching into your patio pond.

3. Fill the barrel almost full and let the water sit, if chlorinated, for at least 48 hours before adding plants.

4. Use bricks on the bottom of the barrel to raise aquatic plant containers to various heights.

5. Add plants. A pond this size will fit about five plants. Good choices include dwarf papyrus, parrot feather, and yellow fig. Use heavy soil and a layer of gravel for potting larger water plants. Lighter soil may break loose and float on the surface of the pond.

6. Allow about a month to pass before adding any fish or snails to your pond. Add no more than three goldfish and five snails to this size pond.

7. If you want circulating water, you can add a submersible pond pump with an automatic shut off and a fountain.

Simple solutions for common pond problems

Once you have a pond, you will always want it to look its best. Overcoming some of the most common pond problems will give you a better understanding of what is necessary to create and maintain this beautiful focal point in your landscape.

Here are six things to be on the lookout for.

Algae overload. A layer of green algae over your pond is unattractive and also damaging to fish and plants. To fix it, add plants that compete with algae for nutrients and shade the water to prevent its growth.

You can also find beneficial bacteria at a garden center that will help combat the nasty green stuff.

Murky water. Everyone wants a crystal clear pond, so murky water is disappointing. This most likely results from issues with the pump and filter. Clean the filter regularly to keep the water clear and ensure the pump is working and is the right size for your pond.

Dying fish. If your fish seem unhealthy or are dying at unusual rates, they may need more oxygen. Add plants like eelgrass or duckweed to oxygenate the water.

If that doesn't help, get a test kit for the water to determine if chlorine or other chemicals are harming the fish.

> Barley straw is a natural algae destroyer. As the straw rots, it slowly releases small amounts of hydrogen peroxide that kills any algae growing. Throw a small bale of barley straw into your pond as soon as you spot algae, and be patient. Once the straw goes to work, you will be amazed at what it can do.

Low water. Keeping your pond topped off shouldn't be difficult. In the hot, dry days of summer, you can expect some evaporation. Add more water as needed. If the loss is significant, check your pond liner for tears, and repair them.

Leaf overload. Like a pool, you may need to take a skimmer to your pond — especially if you have overhanging trees. Plant debris also may mean that your pond plants are losing leaves. Check on plants and remove any dead or dying foliage regularly.

Sick water plants. If your water lilies have grown more leaves than flowers or look unhealthy, remove the containers and divide. These plants must be separated regularly to prevent crowding and to keep them healthy.

How can I protect my pond fish from predators?

Whether you stock your backyard pond with koi or native fish, turtles, and frogs, predators can ruin the peaceful bliss. Typical pond predators include large birds like herons and egrets and mammals like raccoons, opossums, and feral or neighborhood cats.

Protecting your pond critters requires that you make your pond a place predators don't want to be. Here's how.

Set up a decoy. A faux animal can be enough to keep many pests away from the pond. Depending on where you live, a plastic alligator may do the trick, but an owl is pretty scary nearly everywhere.

Animals are clever, so move the decoy from time to time and change out the animal type to keep them guessing.

Let your dog loose. Have a dog? Let it run after predators, chasing them away. The environment will become hostile enough that they likely won't return.

Install a motion sensor. It's tough to deal with nocturnal predators, but a motion sensor can scare off a predator at any time of night or day. One type, called a scarecrow, sprays water when it detects motion. The predator isn't hurt but is startled enough to get lost.

Place obstacles on the edge. Use tomato stakes or bamboo sticks around the pond's edge to make it an uncomfortable place for predators to hunt or fish. You can use clear plastic sticks for a less obstructed view of your pond.

Give your fish places to hide. When you build the pond, dig out fish caves for them to conceal themselves from predators. Include a lot of plants, such as floating lily pads, that will give them shelter if a heron approaches.

You may see suggestions for using fishing lines to protect your pond. A grid over and around the pond will protect your fish, but it can also damage wildlife. Animals can get caught in it and be injured, so only use this strategy as a last resort, if at all.

Unique rain chain is powered by nature

If you are looking for a unique water feature, consider a rain chain. This unusual structure guides rainwater down from a roof or downspout. It's an attractive, decorative alternative to the typical gutter downspout.

You can put one anywhere along a roofline, but it works best when placed over spots where you want the water to collect, such as a water-loving plant or a rain barrel.

Rain chains are available online or in garden centers, but why not get crafty and make your own? Old spoons strung together create a perfect chain for directing water downward.

You can assemble this rain chain so the spoon bowls all face up or down, or you can alternate them. Hang the completed chain in a location where water will flow over it, such as a gutter.

What you need:

- spoons
- pliers
- wire
- vise or clamp
- drill, drill bits

How to make it:

1. Use a vise or clamp with pliers to bend several spoons so the bowl is at a right angle to the handle. For every two that you bend, break the bowl off of a third spoon.

2. Drill a hole at the end of the broken spoon handles.

3. Place the handles of two bent spoons back to back so the bowls face away from each other. Put a handle with a hole in it between them so the hole extends above the handles. Wrap wire around the handles to hold it all together. Leave a small length of wire extended.

4. Use that length of wire to attach one bundle of spoons to another through the drilled holes. String a number of them together to make a chain of the size you need.

How to winterize your water feature — and why you should

If you live in an area where temperatures dip below freezing, you need to take some steps to winterize your water feature if you want to enjoy it next season.

Remove debris. The first step in preparing your water feature for winter weather is to clean it out. Remove leaves, dead plants, and other debris from ponds, fountains, and other water elements.

Drain out water. Drain out the water so it doesn't freeze and crack your fountain, bubbler, or other device.

Clean the pump. Remove the pump and wash it in a solution of vinegar and water. Pump clean water through the system until it runs clear. Store the pump in a warm location until spring.

Wash the water feature. Scrub any algae or other debris from your water feature using half water and half white vinegar solution and a scrub brush.

Keep it from freezing. If you have a pond with water plants and fish, they require air to survive. Check the table below to see if your pump will work all winter in your pond without freezing. It depends on the depth of your pond and the temperature.

If your pond is not deep enough to keep from freezing in your area, remove the pump, clean it, and store it for the winter. Remove t ender plants and pot them inside, and move your fish to an indoor aquarium.

Water depth	Cold hardiness
20 inches	14 degrees F
24 inches	-4 degrees F
30 inches	-22 degrees F
36 inches	-40 degrees F

Add vertical interest with stacked stone fountain

Nothing is quite as impressive in a garden space as a feature that promotes vertical interest. You can accomplish it using upward climbing plants on a trellis, a garden sculpture, or trees and shrubs.

If you'd prefer a water feature, how about a unique stacked stone fountain? As long as you are confident using a drill, or have someone to help you, you can easily create a stacked stone and slate fountain. This unique masterpiece deserves a special place in your landscape.

What you need:

- shovel
- large plastic bucket
- hand shovel
- pond pump
- river rocks
- flat stones
- drill
- scrap 2x4-foot lumber, 4 pieces cut to a little bigger than the bucket diameter

- gravel
- tin snips
- PVC pipe
- metal mesh
- handsaw
- flat pieces of slate
- masonry bit
- 3-foot metal pond pipe

How to make it:

1. Locate a special spot for your stacked stone fountain. It will need to be close to an outdoor electrical outlet.

2. Dig a hole that is just a bit bigger than the width and depth of the plastic bucket. Add 3 inches of gravel to the bottom of the hole, and set the bucket inside the hole.

3. Use tin snips to cut a notch in the bucket side that is a little bigger than the diameter of the electric cord on the pump.

4. Measure the distance between the electrical outlet and the fountain. Cut a piece of PVC pipe, measure this distance, and put the cord through the pipe.

5. Put the pond pump in the center of the bucket.

6. Dig a shallow trench for the PVC pipe. Place the pipe in the trench and cover it with dirt.

7. Cut a piece of metal mesh that is a bit bigger than the diameter of the top of the plastic bucket. Cut a 2-inch hole in the middle of the mesh piece.

8. Thread the pond pipe through the hole in the mesh and attach it to the pump's water delivery tube.

9. Place two of the 2x4-foot boards across the bucket on either side of the pipe. Place the other two in the other direction to make a box structure to support the stones.

10. Select and stack the stone and slate pieces in the order you want them for the fountain. Number each piece as you unstack.

11. Drill a hole through the stones and slate pieces using a drill and a masonry bit. The holes need to be slightly larger than the pipe diameter.

12. Thread the stones and slate pieces in the right order onto the pipe. Make sure that the stack is resting on the lumber frame.

13. Scatter the river rock over the fountain base. This will hide the plastic bucket.

14. Put water in the bucket and turn on the pump.

15. Water will pump up and flow down over the stack and into the bucket below.

Xeriscape and other low-maintenance gardens

The plain and simple guide to xeriscaping

Xeriscaping has been gaining popularity worldwide as more and more people discover the benefits of this low-maintenance landscaping method.

It started in the 1980s as a response to prolonged droughts in the Western United States because it reduces or eliminates the need for water from irrigation. But this technique is not limited to dry and arid regions. You can use it anywhere you want a minimal and low-maintenance area.

If you think your yard would benefit from xeriscaping, here are six principles that will help you create the perfect out-door space.

Design zones. Any good landscape plan begins with a great design. Xeriscapes have different zones, each with a different water requirement.

- An "oasis" zone has the highest water use and is generally an outdoor living area like a patio. This area has the highest maintenance and will usually be the most colorful of all areas.

- A transition zone has moderate water use and contains plants that demand less attention.

- A low water zone requires only natural rainfall or very infrequent watering.

Irrigation. Irrigation is necessary, at least while root systems establish. Both the oasis and the moderate water use areas have the greatest need for irrigation. But it is wise to install some kind of irrigation for the low water use area in a severe and prolonged drought. Water rules for xeriscape include deep and infrequent watering that encourages healthy root growth.

Mulch. Mulch plays an integral role in a xeriscaped landscape because of its ability to suppress weeds and retain moisture. Choose the best mulch for your garden type and climate zone.

Plants. You can have the best-looking yard in town, without all the watering and chemicals. Plus, attract gorgeous birds and butterflies. How? With naturally drought-resistant and pest-resistant plants. They're closer, and cheaper, than you think.

> The word xeriscape comes from the Latin xero, meaning dry, and scape, meaning landscape or view. This landscaping method uses drought-resistant plants and special techniques to conserve water.

Many of these plants have long blooming seasons and very attractive leaves. Choose plants that also have winter and fall interest for a beautiful landscape all year long.

Turf. Contrary to what you might think, turfgrass does have a place in a low-maintenance landscape. A small area of turf gives you a play space for children and pets and helps reduce erosion and decrease the glare from the sun. Determine the grass that best suits your needs and will tolerate prolonged periods of drought.

Upkeep. Occasional weeding, pruning, and fine-tuning of the irrigation system are necessary to keep your xeriscaped landscape looking its best. Pay special attention to new plantings until they're established.

6 tips for the perfect minimalist landscape

A minimalist landscape can mean a lot of different things. The key is to define what kind of landscape you desire and work towards your goal with simplicity and low maintenance being the top two goals.

Minimalist landscape design is about embracing the natural elements to create a beautiful space that requires little upkeep. Here are some tips to keep in mind when designing the perfect minimalist space.

- Native plants are best because they are at home in their growing zone and resistant to pests and disease. Native plants require less attention than alien plants.

- Simple furniture that is functional and attractive is a must. Select comfortable pieces that blend well with the natural surroundings and don't overpower the space. Hammocks and furniture made from teak are great choices.

- Add lawn ornaments that double as tools such as a rain barrel to collect and store valuable rainwater.

- If you'd like to grow some food or herbs, create a simple box garden or two that provides ample space to cultivate a delicious harvest without overrunning your space. Try vertical growing to add some height interest as well.

- Plant climate-specific grasses only that require less water and care than nonnative types. Break up small areas of native turf with rocks for a modern and streamlined look.

- Create no-mow spaces loaded with native wildflowers that offer color and interest. There is truly nothing more beautiful than a wildflower wonderland.

3 drought-tolerant plants at home in arid climates

If you live in an arid climate, it's essential to pay close attention to the type of plants you choose for your yard and garden. Plants must be able to thrive despite high temperatures and little rain.

The good news is, numerous attractive shrubs, vines, and flowers adapt well to heat and low water conditions, and many even thrive in poor soil, which is a bonus. Here are some top choices.

Group plants together in your landscape according to water needs. Doing this allows you to water only certain parts of your terrain, which reduces water use and waste.

Artemisia (Zones 4 to 8). You'll find hundreds of species of artemisia, including shrubs and hardy herbs such as California sagebrush, white mugwort, and tarragon. Plants in this group have beautiful silvery-gray foliage that is highly fragrant.

When combined with ornamental grasses, succulents, and other drought-tolerant species, artemisia looks fantastic. Artemisia does well in full sun but prefers protection from strong winds. Once established, these plants thrive with little water.

Aloe (Zones 10 to 12). Aloe includes hundreds of species of flowering succulents that do best in a hot and dry climate. In addition to the aloe vera species, jewel aloe, coral aloe, tiger aloe, and soap aloe do well as anchor landscape plants.

These attractive and hardy plants have bright green to gray leaves, and some even have a striped or molted appearance, bringing additional interest to the landscape.

For healthy aloe plants, provide water every other week in the summer, and allow natural rainfall and cooler temperatures to nurture plants in the winter. Do not let potted aloe sit in water, or it will rot.

Geranium (Zones 10 to 11). These flowering plants are as hardy as they are attractive. Most start showing their colors in late spring, and some will even keep blooming right up until the first fall frost.

Geraniums are mostly low growing and have a mounding habit that takes on the shape of a smallish shrub. Once geraniums establish, they will go a long time without water.

Pinching off spent flowers promotes profuse blooming on this long-lasting plant. Adding more of these lovelies to your landscape is as easy as propagating with cuttings.

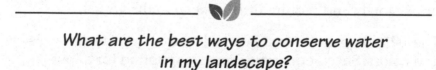

What are the best ways to conserve water in my landscape?

Water restrictions, limited access to water, or high water bills can push water conservation to your "to-do" list pretty quickly. Fortunately, you have many ways to reduce the amount of water you use in your gardens and yard, and many of these conservation techniques require minimal time and effort.

Use an adjustable sprinkler. Adjustable sprinklers allow you to water just what you need when you need to. These sprinklers can do small areas up to larger spaces with a wide range of settings without a ton of wasted overspray.

Install a rain shutoff device on your irrigation system. This device is relatively inexpensive and tells the system controller to shut off when a certain amount of rain has fallen. At about $200 to install, including labor, it can save enough water to pay for itself in one season.

Mulch wisely. Mulching keeps the root zone of plants cool and moisture locked into the soil. You can save a tremendous amount of water when you mulch correctly.

Choose drought-tolerant plants. Choosing your plants wisely makes a huge difference in the amount of water used. Plants such as white fir, yarrow, and yucca are safe and adapted to low water conditions.

Don't overwater. Even though it may seem simplistic, overwatering is just as catastrophic as underwatering. Too much water puts stress on soil and causes root rot and fungal and bacterial disease.

Drought and poor soil are no match for this garden

Succulents are a group of plants that have a natural ability to store water in their stems, roots, leaves, or petals. Succulents grow slowly and require little upkeep to thrive.

These hardy plants come in a wide variety of shapes, sizes, and colors. Succulents are an excellent option for a low-maintenance landscape because of their tolerance for hot sun, drought, and mediocre or poor soil.

Pairing rocks with succulents creates an interesting landscape feature that capitalizes on low-maintenance and hardy plants. The sky is the limit when it comes to designing a rock and succulent garden. You can keep it simple with rocks of various sizes paired with a few pretty plants or take it to the next level with large boulders, water features, and pathways.

Here are some design principles to keep in mind when creating a rock and succulent garden.

- Design your garden on paper and gather your supplies before planting.

- The ideal place for a succulent rock garden is on a hillside or slope. Creating the garden on a slope maximizes drainage and allows the soil to dry out quickly.

- Pick a location where plants will receive full sun most of the day. The hot sun keeps the soil dry and minimizes the risk of fungus and disease.

- Choose a site away from sprinklers, downspouts, and trees that create shade, absorb water, and have roots that can disrupt the garden.

- Use gravel to transition from turf to the succulent garden.

Top desert dwellers for shade and beauty

Shade trees and shrubs provide much-needed relief in hot and sunny climates. They not only give you a beautiful canopy to relax under, they also cool the ground and protect the beneficial insects, birds, and other pollinators that share your yard.

Here are some top shrubs and trees to consider for shade and beauty.

Castor bean. This perennial flowering bush is at home in small to medium-size spaces and is well known for its rapid growth rate. Reaching up to 10 feet in one season, castor bean plants die back in the winter if not protected.

Chaste tree. The chaste tree is a drought-tolerant, hardy shrub or small tree that is also a pollinator magnet. This tree grows fast, reaches up to 10 to 20 feet, and has an attractive spreading habit. Masses of purple flowers appear in spring, drawing pollinators. Good pruning techniques keep this tree looking its best all year long.

Desert willow. The beautiful desert willow is a fast-growing deciduous tree that is both heat and cold hardy. These beautiful trees bloom in a wide range of colors from white and pink to burgundy. The gorgeous blooms attract hummingbirds, bees, and butterflies.

Fig tree. Fig trees add great interest to any dry landscape and produce an abundance of delicious figs at your fingertips. Most backyard varieties are self fruiting. If you have a large area, choose fast-growing larger types such as Brown Turkey or Black Jack. Pick slower growers, including Tiger Panache, for smaller spaces.

How to create a relaxing outdoor garden

One low-maintenance garden idea has its roots in Japan. Zen gardens, also known as Japanese rock gardens, are places of peace and tranquility. These gardens promote a sense of serenity using simple natural materials.

> For a touch of green, install some artificial turf around the perimeter of your Zen garden. Or create a turf and stepping stone walkway leading to a sitting area. This touch of green is refreshing and relaxing without adding any maintenance.

Traditionally, these landscape features include rocks and boulders representing mountains and gravel or colored glass representing water. Think of this space as a relaxing retreat where you can pray, journal, or simply unwind.

What you need:

- rocks or boulders

- gravel, colored glass mulch, or a water feature

- river rock, small pebbles

- bench or seating area for a focal element

- plants — hardy ones such as cacti or succulents

- rake

- edging

How to make it:

1. Sketch your garden design on paper. It can be as small or large as you'd like.

2. Locate and clear a space for the garden away from other plants, grass, or weeds. Rake the soil flat and level it out.

3. Edge the area for your garden with rock or another decorative edging.

4. Place all of your larger elements such as a statue, bench, or boulders.

5. Place your gravel, colored glass, or water feature.

6. Add plants, either in the ground or in pots, or a combination of both.

7. Cover soil with smaller stones, river rock, or pebbles.

Yard and kitchen scraps: turn garbage into black gold

Composting: A+ way to perk up your plot

You've probably heard a lot about composting and its many benefits, but do you know why you should go through the effort to save your yard and kitchen scraps? If you've been on the fence about starting a compost pile, these five reasons are sure to convince you.

It is easy. Although certain resources make composting seem like a challenge, the process is incredibly simple, and you are guaranteed to succeed if you follow a few basic rules and guidelines.

It is free. Not only does composting help cut down on the amount of trash you send to the landfill, it creates nutrient-rich dirt without you having to spend a dime.

Unless you want to buy a compost bin or bucket — which isn't required — you can pile your materials and reap the rewards with minimal work and zero cost.

It is organic. Unlike other dirt that might contain unknown additives, compost is natural, safe, and organic since you know precisely what is in it.

It is good for plants. Compost enriches the soil, making it one of the best amendments you can add to your garden to help ensure a bountiful harvest and a full, vibrant flower garden.

It reduces the need for chemical fertilizers, promotes water retention, lightens clay soil, and helps prevent pests, disease, and weeds.

> Many urban areas have community compost clubs or centers where you can bring your compost, contribute to the piles' upkeep, and share in the wealth of black gold. This is a great way to meet fellow plant enthusiasts and others looking to reduce their environmental footprint.

It is clean. Many people have the wrong impression when it comes to compost, thinking it is smelly, dirty, and only suitable for attracting flies and other unsavory insects.

The truth is, when you do it right, compost is virtually odorless and doesn't take away from your enjoyment of your backyard in the slightest.

Hot or cold? Expert's guide to the right choice for you

Composting is incredibly simple once you understand the basic concept. But learning the "language" of composting when you first start may be a bit overwhelming. Here is a quick explanation of the two different types of compost and methods to achieve each one.

Hot composting. Hot compost piles are labor-intensive, but they are fast, making them a favorite choice for many backyard gardeners, as they can compost your scraps in just under two months.

This compost pile is created all at once, adding materials to a bin or pile to form a mound that is at least 3'x3'x3'. These dimensions are the minimum size required for the pile to heat up to the necessary 113 to 160 degrees F. Avoid adding new materials as that will slow decomposition.

The best container option for hot compost is an open bin or container without a lid. You can create a simple bin using wire and stakes or go for a more elaborate option, depending on your budget. Although it is less attractive, piling is a free method that creates a hot compost pile.

Cold composting. If watering, turning, and maintaining a hot compost pile's heat levels sounds like too much work, then cold composting is the method for you.

With this compost pile staying around 90 degrees F, it is much more low-key, meaning that it also takes a lot longer (about six months to a year) to fully break down into usable dirt.

You can choose to turn and water occasionally or avoid maintenance altogether, simply throwing your materials onto the pile and letting nature run its course.

> If you are new to composting, it can be helpful to invest in a compost thermometer. For around $20, you'll get the peace of mind of knowing whether your pile is hot enough to compost effectively or if you need to add different organic matter. It's an easy, stress-free solution to your problem.

You can use a closed or open bin method for cold composting. If you have a particular area you want to enrich with compost, you may want to try pit or trench composting, where you add the materials directly to a pit in your garden.

Do I need to add soil, fertilizer, or limestone to my compost?

Consider soil as just another brown material you can add to help even out the addition of food scraps and other green materials. Soil is rich in microbial activity, so it can help break down the pile faster and give it a kick-start into becoming black gold.

Soil can also help keep the insects at bay that are often attracted when you add fresh material. Sprinkle a little soil over your kitchen scraps in your bin or when you notice flies hanging around your pile.

But don't add too much or you'll turn your pile into nothing but slightly more nutrient-dense soil instead of compost.

Fertilizer shouldn't be necessary for your compost pile. Most fertilizer is rich in nitrogen, which you shouldn't need if you add enough green materials. Save the fertilizer for using directly on your plants during the growing season.

Although old-school composters may insist on adding limestone to their compost piles, it simply isn't necessary or helpful. It can create odor problems and also increase the pH levels of the pile, which limits the benefits for your plants once it turns to soil.

In short, basic is always best. Once you start complicating the process or thinking too much about the materials you add, you'll second-guess yourself and fail to let nature do its amazing work.

5 steps to perfect compost every time

With a little patience, effort, and practice, you can have a thriving compost pile in no time. Follow these helpful steps to ensure success and turn your scraps into black gold.

Choose your location. Once you start your compost pile or bin, you won't want to go through the effort of moving it. Carefully think through where you want to put it before starting.

Be sure to place it in an area that receives a fair amount of sunlight and isn't too far from your garden, as you'll be hauling the dirt there once it is ready.

Lay the foundation. Before you start piling materials willy-nilly into your compost bin, lay down a foundation of sticks and twigs to help encourage drainage and allow air to circulate under the pile.

Add green and brown materials. "Green" and "brown" are colors thrown around a lot in composting lingo. But they mean more than just green and brown materials.

- Green items include grass clippings, kitchen scraps, farm animal manure, and other "wet" materials that add nitrogen to the pile.

- Brown materials like leaves, cardboard, sticks, and wood shavings help balance out the pile with carbon and kick-start the decomposition process while preventing an odor.

Mix three parts brown material with one part green material, and add more of either if needed. If you notice the pile getting slimy or smelly, add more brown material. If it is incredibly dry and powdery, add green material and water to help restore moisture.

Water your pile. Keep your compost pile about as wet as a wrung-out sponge. If you live in a dry environment or added a few too many piles of leaves, you may need to water it down occasionally to restore it to the proper moisture level.

Don't forget about air. Air is an essential component of compost. Be sure to mix your pile at least once a week to create air pockets and encourage decomposition. A pitchfork works great for this purpose.

You may skip this step if you use lots of dried leaves or straw in your pile as these materials naturally hold air.

Worm composting — ideal for tiny spaces

If you don't have space in your yard for a compost pile but still want to create usable compost for your houseplants or patio plants, worm composting might just be the answer.

Vermicomposting uses worms in a plastic container system to digest and convert organic materials into nutrient-filled soil. It won't smell if it's properly cared for and can be kept in a laundry room, garage, or kitchen cabinet.

What you need:

- 3 plastic 5-gallon buckets and at least 1 lid

- drill with a 3/16-inch and a 1/8-inch drill bit

- shredded newspaper

- red wiggler composting worms. You'll need around 250 to 500 worms, which you can buy online.

How to make it:

1. Drill 3/16-inch holes on the bottom of two of the buckets, about an inch apart.

2. Drill a line of 1/8-inch holes near the lip of the two buckets towards the top, and use the same drill bit to puncture holes throughout the lid.

3. The bucket without holes will catch any liquid. Place it on the bottom.

4. Stack a bin with holes inside this bucket, and add about 4 inches of moistened, shredded newspaper. It doesn't need to be sopping wet.

5. Add your worms and a few handfuls of dirt, securing the lid on top.

6. Whenever you add your scraps, cover them with a layer of dirt and moist, shredded paper.

7. Once this layer starts to break down and look like dirt, stack the next bucket inside the existing one, and add more bedding and food scraps.

8. Place the lid on top, and add scraps as you usually would, waiting for the worms to migrate up to this new bucket.

9. After a couple of weeks, harvest the compost from the bottom bucket, and continue repeating the process.

> Collect your kitchen scraps in an attractive container with a lid. Let the scraps sit for about a week before adding to your vermicomposter or regular compost. That will save you from making so many trips. You also won't have to add as much bedding to your worm composter.

10. Drain the liquid from the bottom bucket every few weeks, and use it to water your houseplants to give them a little nutrient boost.

Surprising things you really can add to your pile

When you think about what goes into a compost heap, you probably picture fruit and vegetable peels, leaves, cardboard, and perhaps horse and rabbit manure. But there are so many other materials you can choose from.

Check out these unusual compost-safe substances that will enrich your pile and, as a bonus, cut down on what you send to the landfill.

Coffee grounds and filters. Coffee grounds and unbleached coffee filters can be sent straight to the compost bin. Remember, coffee grounds are acidic, so don't overload your pile with them.

Although they are brown, coffee grounds act as a "green" material and should be balanced with brown matter such as cardboard or sticks.

Freezer burned fruits and veggies. Believe it or not, that freezer-burned, half-used bag of frozen veggies that has been hiding in the back of your freezer for a year is a perfect compost pile additive.

Pet and human hair. When you brush your dog, cat, or your own hair, save it and add it to your compost pile. Although many believe hair isn't compostable, it is a great source of slow-releasing nitrogen.

Paper towel and toilet paper rolls. Since most come from cardboard, the endless paper towel rolls and toilet paper rolls you use up are safe to compost. Cut them into smaller pieces to help them disintegrate more quickly.

Dryer and vacuum lint. If you wear primarily cotton clothing or clothes made from other natural fibers, you can compost your dryer lint. When you empty your vacuum of dust, hair, and dirt, add it directly to your compost pile.

12 things to never put in the compost

While most organic material will decompose beautifully into rich soil, these 12 materials should never make their way into your compost pile.

Don't compost	Why not
meat and fish	can attract pests and rodents
dairy products	encourage harmful bacteria, pests, and rodents
treated sawdust	varnish, paint, or stain will introduce harmful chemicals to compost
acidic food scraps	take a long time to decompose, and kill off essential microorganisms
oil	slows down decomposition, attracts animals, and alters moisture content
diseased plants	transfer harmful diseases to soil
glossy paper	toxins that create gloss interfere with quality of compost and keep the paper from decomposing
rice	attracts bacteria and pests
bread and baked goods	will grow mold and start to stink
walnuts	contain juglone, which is a natural aromatic compound toxic to some plants
weeds	will likely grow in your compost, contaminating it and preventing you from using it in your garden
pet and human waste	contains bacteria and parasites

Best yard materials to toss on the heap

The kitchen is an excellent source of compostable materials, but you will likely find the bulk of your compost ingredients while caring for your yard and garden. Here are some of the best yard compostables, what type they are, and tips for each.

- Leaves (brown). Although whole leaves will break down, they will decompose faster when shredded or mulched.

- Dead plants (green). Avoid diseased or pest-infested plants as these can interfere with compost.

- Manure (green). Rabbit, cow, and horse manure are excellent sources of nitrogen. Although chicken excrement is too strong to use directly on plants, it can be composted effectively.

- Straw and hay (brown). Chop it up to speed composting. Straw is great for improving airflow in your compost pile. Keep in mind, hay may have seeds that could start to sprout in your compost.

- Grass clippings (green). Don't add a lot of grass clippings at once as they will form a mat and hinder decomposition. Mix grass into the pile in small batches, and turn the compost frequently in the summer when you're adding more grass.

- Pine needles (brown). They are highly acidic, so only add pine needles in moderate amounts.

- Bush or plant trimmings (green). Cut up large pieces so they fit in your pile and don't slow the composting process.

- Sticks and twigs (brown). Avoid large branches as it's too tricky to make them small enough for the compost. Break twigs and sticks into small pieces (no longer than 4 inches) before adding or they may look exactly the same when you go to use your compost.

Create the just-right, small-space bin

Apartment or condo living doesn't exactly give you room for a steaming compost pile. But don't despair — you can produce your very own black gold with nothing but a small patio or balcony. Create this perfect small-space composter today in just seven easy steps.

- Buy a sturdy tote with a lid. A large, plastic tote is your best option for small space gardening. You don't have to go through multiple steps to start composting, and it will still hold a lot of scraps.

- Drill about 10 small holes in the bottom to help keep the compost from getting soggy and improve aeration. You should also drill around 10 holes in the lid.

- Line the bottom of the container with brown materials like leaves and twigs to help jump-start the composting process.

- Add dirt. When composting in such a small container, adding a layer of soil can help speed up the process, prevent your bin from becoming unbalanced, and keep it from smelling up your patio.

- Mix in any kitchen scraps you have collected. Use a stick or shovel to stir them in. A yardstick is a great tool to keep around for this purpose.

- Add a little water. Spray your compost with water from a hose or watering can until it is slightly damp.

- Secure the lid and continue to add organic materials as you collect them.

You will likely need to wait around a year for your compost to become usable, but you can keep adding scraps as the materials break down, so there should be plenty of room in the bin.

If you have a large family or eat many fruits and vegetables, consider setting up multiple containers if you have space.

"

Troubleshooting tips from a longtime composter

While composting is a breeze most of the time, occasionally you can run into a snag that interferes with decomposition or hampers the quality of your soil.

Tom has been composting for years, and he's seen his share of problems. Here are a few of the most common stumbling blocks he's run across, along with advice on how to fix them.

Compost has an odor. If your compost smells like rotting food or bad eggs, it is likely due to an airflow problem, Tom says. To remedy it, you need to get "up close and personal" with your stinking pile.

"Turn it with a pitchfork to restore those air pockets and improve airflow," he says. "You may also want to mix in some brown materials, especially if your pile gives off an ammonia-like stench."

The pile is soggy. "Many people get overzealous when watering their compost pile and think they should drench it with water every time they give their plants a drink," Tom says. If you accidentally over-watered your pile and it starts to stink and become soggy, he recommends adding dry materials to soak up the moisture and aerate it.

Compost isn't breaking down. One of the biggest reasons your compost isn't breaking down is likely because the temperature is too low. "This is an incredibly common issue for those who are new to the idea of hot composting and aren't well-suited to the idea of balancing green and brown materials," he says.

If your compost isn't putting off heat, it could be too small. Remember, it needs to be at least 3'x3'x3' to heat up. Tom advises turning the pile, adding a little moisture if it's dry, and adding green materials to "activate" it again.

"

Zones and subzones: your guide to regional planting

How to make climate and conditions work for you

One of the best ways to make sure your plants thrive is to pick ones that do well in your particular growing zone.

The U.S. Department of Agriculture (USDA) produces a useful Plant Hardiness Zone Map *(see page 359)* to help gardeners determine which plants will do best in their given area based on minimum average winter temperatures.

Gardeners who live in the western United States can also refer to the Sunset climate zone map, which provides more detailed information, including the length of the growing season, summer temperatures, wind, humidity, and rainfall.

Every few years, the USDA updates its hardiness zone map to account for shifting climate patterns. For more details, you can go to the USDA's website at ars.usda.gov and search on hardiness zone map.

Here is some basic information that will help you make decisions based on your particular climate and conditions.

- Each zone has a 10-degree difference, with a 5-degree difference between subzones. Plants that fall into the lower-numbered zones can withstand cold weather, while those in the higher number categories prefer warmer regions.

- Although it may seem like the further north you go, the lower the zone gets, that is not always the case. Seattle is pretty far north but is in hardiness zone 8, and Baltimore is farther south but falls into zone 6.

- Because of this, it is important not to guess which plants will do well in your area. It is best to understand your zone before buying and planting.

- Although the USDA map is incredibly useful when selecting plants, it does not account for other important factors like precipitation, freeze dates, elevation, and other factors.

Keep in mind that no growing or hardiness zone map is perfect. Microclimates make it essential to study your growing area even beyond the zone and planting maps. For more on these mini zones, see *Manage microclimates like a pro* later in this chapter.

Heat zones — another helpful way to choose plants

You may have seen a plant tag with another number or range of numbers, along with the hardiness zone, and wondered what it was. It's most likely a heat zone.

The American Horticultural Society created a plant Heat Zone Map that divides the country into 12 zones based on the average number of "heat days" per year when the temperature is above 86 degrees F.

Locations with the fewest heat days — less than one — are in zone 1. Those with the most — more than 210 — are in heat zone 12.

Many garden centers are beginning to assign plants heat zones along with hardiness zones. For example, you may see 5-8, 11-12 on the label. If both zones are listed, the first number or range of numbers is always the hardiness zone, and the second is the heat zone.

These zones provide a gold mine of information to work with when selecting the best plants for your garden. They allow you to choose plants that will tolerate your coldest winter temperatures and your hottest summer temperatures.

Best perennials for extreme temperature zones

Extreme temperatures pose a challenge when choosing plants for your yard and garden. Whether it's freezing cold or excruciatingly hot, your plants will fare best if their hardiness is appropriate for those conditions.

Don't let the fact that you live in one of the colder planting zones discourage you from enjoying beautiful perennials. Some will withstand even the most severe winters and pop up strong in the spring.

On the other hand, if extreme heat is the norm where you live, you will be happy to know that many stunning perennial plants not only survive but thrive in extreme temperatures — even those that may drive you inside to the air conditioner.

Here are some of the top cold-hardy and heat-tolerant perennials to consider.

Cold hardy		Heat tolerant	
Plant	**Zones**	**Plant**	**Zones**
sedum	4-8	bulbine	8-11
coneflower	3-8	cosmos	9-10
peony	3-8	lantana	3-11
wild columbine	3-8	pavonia	8-11
Siberian iris	3-8	salvia	3-11
hosta	3-8	trumpet vine	4-9
catmint	4-8	verbena	7-11
bee balm	4-9	yarrow	3-9
baptisia	3-9		
lily of the valley	3-8		
New England aster	4-8		

Manage microclimates like a pro

Microclimates are areas within larger hardiness zones that create unique growing conditions. Cities, with their tall buildings, are large microclimates because of their "heat island" effect. Gardening in a city is different than gardening on the outskirts even if it is only a few miles away.

Microclimates exist within individual landscapes as well. Some areas may be warmer than others, while some might be wetter, sunnier, shadier, or drier. Get to know your microclimates, and your plants will thank you.

Along with plant hardiness zones and heat tolerant zones, be aware of these microclimates that may exist right in your backyard. Make a list and map of your microclimates. This information will help you plan, plant, and protect your garden plants.

- Elevation. Lower areas are usually colder and wetter, while higher spots are warmer and drier.

- Slopes. Those facing the south receive more sun and are warmer and drier than slopes facing the north that tend to be shadier, colder, and wetter.

- Orientation. Eastern-facing gardens receive morning sun while gardens on the west side are subject to the hotter afternoon sun.

- Trees. They create a unique microclimate by shading the ground below them. The soil tends to be drier here as well.

- Open areas. Unprotected and open spaces in the land-scape are subject to the wind, which may damage plants. Consider windbreaks if you plant in these areas.

- Hardscape. Large rocks, concrete, retaining and rock walls, and the south and west sides of buildings take up daytime heat and give it off at night. Plants that would normally be too cold in your landscape may do just fine when planted beside these heat absorbers.

> Once you know your cold hardiness zone, your heat zone, any Sunset zone information (for those in the West), and your microclimates, record this information in your garden journal. It will help you to make the best plant choices for your garden.

How can I make sure I get the right plants for my growing zone?

One of the best ways to ensure success in your garden for your particular zone is to grow native plants. They not only benefit the local wildlife and environment, but they can make your job as a gardener easy. Here's why.

- Native varieties have already adapted to your local growing zone. You may have to make slight tweaks if you have some harsh microclimates, but other than that, native plants are hugely forgiving and hardy.

- Native plants require far less maintenance and extra water than nonnative plants because they have evolved with their environment.

- They are efficient at using soil nutrients and other natural resources.

- They have a higher resistance to native insects, which means pest control is less critical.

You can find great resources online about native plants. The American Horticulture Society at *ahsgardening.org* and the North American Native Plant Society at *nanps.org* offer listings of state and regional native plants. They will also help you find the best expert advice for your area.

The U.S. Department of Agriculture Forest Service at *fs.usda.gov* also keeps an extensive list of native plant societies, botanical gardens, and arboretums you can visit to learn more about native plants.

As you start collecting your native plants, remember to stick with reputable growers in your area, and never gather plants from the wild without specific permission.

Map the sunshine to keep your plants happy

The type and amount of sun your landscape receives is another driving factor in making good plant choices. Trying to grow a plant that loves shade in a hot and sunny spot spells disaster. On the flip side, when the light is just right, the result is happy and healthy plants.

Sunshine mapping is a great way to identify the various levels of light in your landscape. To create a sunshine map, do the following.

- Draw your home on a piece of blank paper approximately where it sits on your property. Include hardscape elements like paths, driveways, and patios on your map. Also include trees and shrubbery.

- Watch the way the sunlight falls on your landscape closely. Note that the amount of light that your property receives will change with the season.

- Use three colored pencils to shade areas on your map that receive more than six hours of direct sunlight, between four and six hours of sunlight, and places that receive less than four hours of sunlight per day.

Use this map to place plants where they will be happiest.

> Do you live at a high elevation? If so, beware that six hours of sunlight per day can scald plants — even those well-suited for part-sun to full-sun. A good idea is to set up some shade cloths or plant trees that offer dappled sun in areas that get exceedingly hot.

Full sun. Areas considered full-sun get six hours of direct sun on most days. Most flowering perennials and annuals are happy basking in this unobstructed light.

Partial sun to partial shade. Plants that require partial sun need several hours of daily sun to set flowers and fruit but don't need a full day of sunshine to be happy.

Plants labeled as part shade need relief from the hot afternoon sun. Good places for these plants are near a tree that casts some afternoon shade or on the east side of a building.

Dappled sun. These areas are similar to partial shade areas. The sunlight trickles through a canopy of deciduous trees to the ground below. Woodland plants and understory trees and shrubs prefer this kind of light.

Keep in mind that these locations are sunnier in the spring before the trees get their leaves. This makes these areas perfect for spring bulbs.

Full shade. This is not the same as no sun. Plants with a light requirement of full shade thrive on less than three hours per day of direct sunlight. Examples include hostas and astilbes.

Many plants fall into more than one category, like partial shade to full shade. How can you tell if a plant is happy with the amount of light it's getting? The best test is by how well it's growing.

Protect against the cold with a DIY mini greenhouse

Make a mini greenhouse from a plastic bottle to protect newly planted seeds in early spring when the weather is still too unpredictable for direct outdoor sowing.

Winter-hardy salad greens like endive, lamb's lettuce, and winter lettuce do particularly well when grown this way.

What you need:

- plastic bottle, 20 ounces or bigger
- knife
- drill and drill bits
- permanent marker
- ruler
- seed-starting mix
- seeds
- tape

How to make it:

1. Wash the empty bottle thoroughly and let it dry.
2. Drill drainage holes in the bottom of the bottle.
3. Measure and mark two-thirds up from the bottle.
4. Cut the bottle open at this mark all the way around, leaving a small uncut piece at the back to form a flap.
5. Fill the bottle with seed-starting mix, and sow seeds.
6. Water the seeds.
7. Close the lid and seal it with a bit of heavy-duty tape.
8. Place the mini greenhouse in a sunny and protected spot.
9. Keep the soil moist.
10. When the seedlings begin to push against the lid, open it up.

Smart ways to prepare plants for heat and drought

With an increase in temperatures across the country, many areas are experiencing prolonged drought and excessive heat. Although the weather is unchangeable, you can take steps to prepare plants for these harsh conditions.

- Water plants deeply but less frequently. Deep watering encourages strong roots and flushes salt buildup in the soil. Install a drip irrigation system or tree water bags to conserve water but keep plants happy.

- Provide shade. It is pretty easy to erect shade cloths to protect plants from the hot sun. A couple of poles and a rectangular or triangular shade does the trick.

- Don't skimp on mulch. Apply a 3-inch layer of bark mulch, shredded leaves, or even pine straw to help keep the soil cool and conserve water.

- Don't feed. Feeding encourages new growth with greater water needs.

- Avoid heavy pruning of trees and shrubs. Just like feeding, pruning stimulates new growth, and new growth requires lots of water. Take a break from any heavy pruning during extreme heat and drought.

5 outstanding options to extend a short growing season

For gardeners in areas with a very short growing season, getting the most time out of the garden is a must. The good news is that there are several easy things you can do to stretch the growing season and increase your harvest.

Use a cold frame. Cold frames are small greenhouses that can be mobile or stationary. A square base, low to the ground, and a transparent top that opens make up a cold frame.

As the weather begins to cool, place a cold frame over your garden beds. With heat from the sun trapped inside, the soil will take longer to freeze, and you can keep on harvesting for longer.

Build a hoop house. If you have an extra-large veggie patch, try a hoop house. Hoop houses consist of plastic, metal, or wood hoops covered in a layer of greenhouse plastic. They work similarly to cold frames by trapping the sun's heat and protecting plants while keeping the soil warm.

Do you have some old windows lying around? If so, transforming these into the tops of cold frames is super easy. Make a sturdy wooden box frame, and attach a window to the frame using hinges. If you are lucky enough to have some scrap wood handy, this project could cost under $20 to make.

Take advantage of raised beds. Gardening in raised beds means that the soil sits above ground level, where it dries quickly and warms faster than garden beds directly on the ground.

Add row covers. For raised bed gardens, adding row covers protects plants from chilly nights. Row covers are similar to hoop houses, only smaller. A series of hoops keeps garden fabric — made from polyester or polypropylene — taut and allows rain to pass through.

Spread mulch. Not only does mulching keep weeds down, prevent erosion, build up the soil, and maintain moisture, it is especially good as a plant insulator.

Add a thick layer of straw or hay material when temperatures start to drop, and you will squeeze a little more time out of your favorite garden goodies.

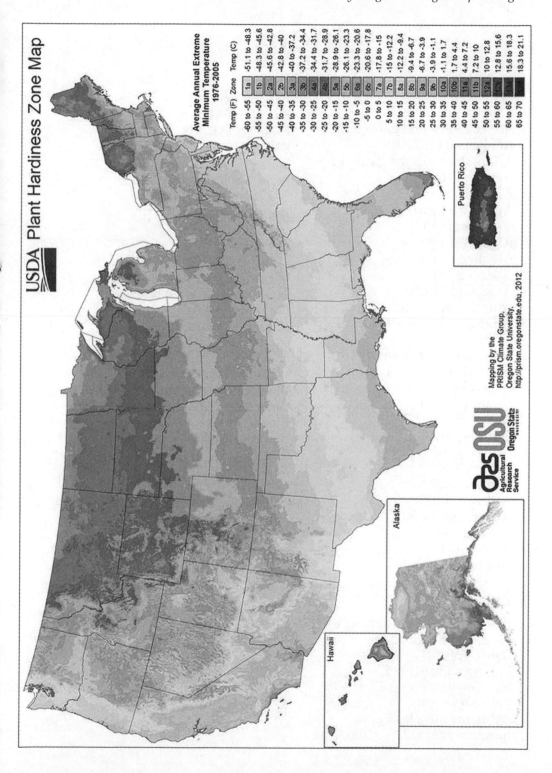

USDA Plant Hardiness Zone Map

Average Annual Extreme Minimum Temperature 1976–2005

Temp (F)	Zone	Temp (C)
-60 to -55	1a	-51.1 to -48.3
-55 to -50	1b	-48.3 to -45.6
-50 to -45	2a	-45.6 to -42.8
-45 to -40	2b	-42.8 to -40
-40 to -35	3a	-40 to -37.2
-35 to -30	3b	-37.2 to -34.4
-30 to -25	4a	-34.4 to -31.7
-25 to -20	4b	-31.7 to -28.9
-20 to -15	5a	-28.9 to -26.1
-15 to -10	5b	-26.1 to -23.3
-10 to -5	6a	-23.3 to -20.6
-5 to 0	6b	-20.6 to -17.8
0 to 5	7a	-17.8 to -15
5 to 10	7b	-15 to -12.2
10 to 15	8a	-12.2 to -9.4
15 to 20	8b	-9.4 to -6.7
20 to 25	9a	-6.7 to -3.9
25 to 30	9b	-3.9 to -1.1
30 to 35	10a	-1.1 to 1.7
35 to 40	10b	1.7 to 4.4
40 to 45	11a	4.4 to 7.2
45 to 50	11b	7.2 to 10
50 to 55	12a	10 to 12.8
55 to 60	12b	12.8 to 15.6
60 to 65	13a	15.6 to 18.3
65 to 70	13b	18.3 to 21.1

Puerto Rico

Alaska

Hawaii

OSU
Oregon State University
Agricultural Research Service

Mapping by the
PRISM Climate Group,
Oregon State University,
http://prism.oregonstate.edu, 2012

359

Index

C

Grounds, coffee 51, 96, 239, 343
Grubs 113

H

Hair, as fertilizer 52, 101
Hardwood 190
Hay 88
Headache, herbs for 132, 135
Health, herbs for 125, 134, 135, 136
Heat zones 349
Hellebore 210
Herb garden
  hanging 7
  spiral 128
Herbs
  companion planting with 20
  drying 140
  feeding 126
  for foot soak 124
  for repelling pests 161
  harvesting 138
  reasons to grow 124
  storing 127
  watering 127, 142
Holy basil 139
Honey, for plants 101
Honeysuckle 310
Hoop house 358
Horseradish 90
Hose
  soaker 14, 249
  unique uses for 249-250
Hosiery
  to aerate soil 240
  to protect fruit 239, 311
Hosta 174, 204
Hot compost 337
Houseplants. *See Also* Plants
  allergies and 158-160
  buying 143
  cuttings from 144
  diseases 152
  feeding 162

gas leaks and 157
pests and 160-162
watering 149-151, 250
Hummingbirds 21, 24
Hybrids 264, 269
Hydrangea 174
Hypertufa planter 38
Hyssop 131

I

Inflammation 5
Insects. *See* Pest control; Pests
Internet 283
Iris 217
Irrigation 328
  system 3, 118, 175

J

Jade plant 160
Japanese beetles 113
Japanese forest grass 112
Japanese maple 180
Jars 241, 253
Jeans, repurposing 284
Jerusalem artichoke 90
Journal. *See* Notebook, for gardening
June bugs 113

K

Kale 82, 90
Kentucky bluegrass 117
Koi 318

L

Ladder, repurposing 43
Ladybugs 221
Landscape fabric 187
Landscaping
  cheap projects 166
  colors and 203
  conserving water 331